HANDS-ON NETWARE®

A GUIDE TO
NOVELL® NETWARE 3.11/3.12
with Projects

Ted L. Simpson
Wisconsin Indianhead Technical College

Course Technology, Inc. One Main Street, Cambridge, MA 02142

Hands-On NetWare: A Guide to Novell NetWare 3.11/3.12 with Projects is published by Course Technology, Inc.

Editorial Director	Joseph B. Dougherty
Managing Editor	Marjorie Schlaikjer
Product Manager	Darlene Bordwell
Production Director	Myrna D'Addario
Production Editor	Darlene Bordwell
Production Specialist	Erin Bridgeford
Desktop Publishing Supervisor	Debbie Masi
Desktop Publishers	Thomas Atwood
	Erin Bridgeford
Copyeditor	Nancy Kruse Hannigan
Proofreader	Jane Kilgore
Indexer	Sherrie Dietrich
Technical Review Specialist	Jeff Goding
Academic Technical Review Supervisors	Michael Harris
	Andrew Townsend
Student Reviewer	Barbara Jaffari
Word Processor	Sean Barrett
Manufacturing Manager	Elizabeth Martinez
Print Buyer/Planner	Charlie Patsios
Text Designer	Will Winslow
Cover Designer	John Gamache

At Course Technology, Inc., we believe that technology will transform the way that people teach and learn. We are very excited about bringing you, college professors and students, the most practical and affordable technology-related products available.

The Course Technology Development Process

Our development process is unparalleled in the higher education publishing industry. Every product we create goes through an exacting process of design, development, review, and testing.

Reviewers give us direction and insight that shape our manuscripts and bring them up to the latest standards. Every manuscript is quality tested. Students whose backgrounds match the intended audience work through every keystroke, carefully checking for clarity and pointing out errors in logic and sequence. Together with our own technical reviewers, these testers help us ensure that everything that carries our name is error-free and easy to use.

Course Technology Products

We show both *how* and *why* technology is critical to solving problems in college and in whatever field you choose to teach or pursue. Our time-tested, step-by-step instructions provide unparalleled clarity. Examples and applications are chosen and crafted to motivate students.

The Course Technology Team

This book will suit your needs because it was delivered quickly, efficiently, and affordably. In every aspect of business, we rely on a commitment to quality and the use of technology. Every employee contributes to this process. The names of all our employees are listed below:

Tim Ashe, Thomas Atwood, David Backer, Stephen M. Bayle, Josh Bernoff, Erin Bridgeford, Ann Marie Buconjic, Jody Buttafoco, Jim Chrysikos, Susan Collins, John M. Connolly, David Crocco, Myrna D'Addario, Lisa D'Alessandro, Howard S. Diamond, Kathryn Dinovo, Katie Donovan, Joseph B. Dougherty, MaryJane Dwyer, Chris Elkhill, Don Fabricant, Kate Gallagher, Laura Ganson, Jeffrey Goding, Laurie Gomes, Eileen Gorham, Andrea Greitzer, Tim Hale, Roslyn Hooley, Tom Howes, Nicole Jones, Matt Kenslea, Wendy Kincaid, Suzanne Licht, Elizabeth Martinez, Debbie Masi, Dan Mayo, Kathleen McCann, Mac Mendelsohn, Laurie Michelangelo, Kim Munsell, Amy Oliver, Kristine Otto, Debbie Parlee, Kristin Patrick, Charlie Patsios, Jodi Paulus, Darren Perl, Kevin Phaneuf, Suzanne Phaneuf, George J. Pilla, Cathy Prindle, Nancy Ray, Marjorie Schlaikjer, Christine Spillett, Susie Stroud, Michelle Tucker, David Upton, Mark Valentine, Renee Walkup, Lisa Yameen.

CTI is proud to present the first textbook in its Networking series. *Hands-On NetWare: A Guide to Novell NetWare 3.11/3.12 with Projects* offers a unique project-oriented approach to teaching the NetWare 3.11/3.12 system environment and is specifically designed to prepare students to become Novell Certified Network Administrators (CNAs). This book is structured for either a data communications or networking course that has a lab component.

FEATURES AND APPROACH

Hands-On Netware sets itself apart from other networking books through its unique hands-on approach and its orientation to real-world situations and problem solving. To ensure that students comprehend how Novell NetWare concepts and techniques are applied in real business organizations, this text incorporates the following features:

Chapter Cases. In every chapter, network topics are explained in the context of a case in which students follow a CNA as she sets up a Novell NetWare network at the fictional PC Solutions. The sequence of topics presented in each case scenario follows the steps performed by real networking professionals who set up and maintain networks. Each case situation provides a motivational context and conceptual foundation for students before they embark on the hands-on Projects.

Hands-On Projects, Assignments, and Answer Sheets. At the end of each chapter, students have the opportunity to apply the concepts and techniques to their own network installation projects. Taking on the role of network administrator for the hypothetical institution Superior Technical College, each student performs the same steps that a professional CNA would in setting up a network. Because the Projects are modeled after the PC Solutions Case, students can use the Case as a template. The Projects build on each other from chapter to chapter so that by end of the book, each student will have set up a functional network environment complete with users, software menus, shared files, and printers. The Assignments that accompany each Project provide students with the chance to be creative in designing and developing a network system to support the processing needs of Superior Technical College. Perforated Answer Sheets at the end of each chapter can be submitted to the instructor, providing a simplified, useful way of tracking students' progress and understanding.

Command Summary and Review Questions. Each chapter concludes with meaningful Review Questions that test students' understanding of the concepts and commands presented in the chapter. A Command Summary provides a valuable reference to help students review the material covered in the chapter.

NetWare Version Information. This text emphasizes concepts and commands available in NetWare 3.11. However, throughout the text, areas in which 3.11 differs from NetWare 2.x or 3.12 are pointed out. The Appendix contains more detailed chapter-by-chapter information on NetWare 3.12. The Instructor's Manual that accompanies this text describes other versions of NetWare and explains how to adapt this text to your course if you are using a version other than 3.11 or 3.12.

THE SUPPLEMENTS

Instructor's Manual. The Instructor's Manual is written by the author and is quality-assurance tested. It includes:

- Answers and solutions to all Review Questions and Projects
- A disk containing solutions to all Review Questions
- Transparency Masters of key concepts
- Teaching notes containing tips from the author about the instructional progression of each chapter
- Technical notes, which include troubleshooting tips as well as information on computer hardware configuration and file server installation.

Student Work Disk. The Student Work Disk contains sample software, files for use in the Superior Technical College Project, and Review Questions. Adopters of this text are granted the right to distribute these files to any student who purchases a copy of this text.

File Server Setup Disk. The setup program can copy the contents of the Student Work Disk to the file server. One of the students' first assignments could be to copy the contents of the Student Work Disk onto a blank disk for use in the projects.

Test Bank. The Test Bank contains 50 questions per chapter in true/false, multiple choice, and fill-in-the-blank formats. The questions were tested by students to achieve clarity and accuracy.

ACKNOWLEDGMENTS

I would like to thank my wife Mary, without whose understanding, support, and patience this book would not have come to print. I also want to acknowledge the contributions of my parents, William and Rosemarie, who made many sacrifices to allow my family to have a stable, motivating environment in which to learn and grow.

The credit for making this book presentable goes to the CTI staff, especially Darlene Bordwell for her editorial wonders and divine patience. Thanks to reviewers David Cooper (Santa Rosa Junior College) and Michael Harris (Del Mar College) for their valuable input; to Joe Dougherty for his vision and commitment to this project, and to Matt Kenslea for contacting me about doing this book; Thomas Atwood for his technical help; and all the desktop publishing staff who transformed my scribbles into an attractive book.

A special acknowledgment is due Dave Thiele, University of Wisconsin, for his excellent work on the file server setup and Student Work Disk. I also want to acknowledge Phil Soltis, Lois Eichman, Mary Ellen Filkens, and Bert Richard at Wisconsin Indianhead Technical College, who had the foresight and perseverance to make our campus the first Novell Education Academic Partner. I would also like to thank K.C. Sue, Gary Clark, and Wayne Larson of Novell Education for their support of our partnership between college and industry. Finally, I would like to dedicate this book to the students at WITC and other colleges who are undertaking the challenge of becoming networking professionals. I hope the project orientation of this book will help you achieve this goal.

Ted L. Simpson
Certified NetWare Instructor/Engineer
Wisconsin Indianhead Technical College

HANDS-ON NETWARE

OVERVIEW

In this chapter you will:

- Be introduced to the cases and projects in this manual

- Be given information on your file server setup

- Compare Token Ring, ARCNET, 10BASET, and Ethernet topologies

- Obtain price information on network adapters

- Document the topology for your network

This project manual will guide you in applying the concepts and commands you are learning in your Novell NetWare course toward the goal of developing your own network system.

The manual will help you do this in three ways:

1. In the first part of each chapter, step-by-step cases walk you through the tasks required to achieve a particular network goal. You'll follow the fictitious employees of PC Solutions, a technology company, as they install, use, and maintain their own network.

2. The Command Summary and Review Questions following each chapter's case will help you review the NetWare concepts and commands presented in the chapter.

3. In the second part of each chapter, you will carry out the tasks discussed in the PC Solutions case to complete your own network project, in which you are a staff member of Superior Technical College. As you work on your project, refer back to the corresponding case steps, which you should use as a guide to completing the project.

The projects build on each other so that by the time you complete the last project in Chapter 12, you will have created an operational system. Each project consists of descriptive information and processing steps, followed by a Student Answer Sheet. As you go through the processing steps, you will be requested to create certain printouts and to record information on your Student Answer Sheet. Upon completion of a project, your instructor may request that you turn in your Student Answer Sheet and any printouts you've created.

Your instructor will provide you with a student work diskette that contains files you will need as you complete your network project. The diskette also contains a self-study system to help you test your Novell NetWare knowledge and aid you in preparing for exams, including the Novell Certified NetWare Administrator (CNA) test.

So that you can do the projects, your instructor has assigned you to a file server and given you a username, password, student reference number, and home directory. The reference number separates the users, groups, and other objects you create on your assigned file server from those of other students. Your username has been granted Workgroup Manager privileges, which means you will be able to create and manage other users and groups. Your home directory is the work area on your assigned file server where you have been given all rights to create and manage files and directories for the case project. Record the information your instructor gives you for your file server environment on Student Answer Sheet 1 at the end of this chapter.

THE PC SOLUTIONS CASE

Leslie Stevens has just been hired as the network administrator for PC Solutions, a firm that sells specialized computer equipment, interfaces, and software directly to customers and dealers. An organizational chart for PC Solutions is shown in Figure 1-1.

During her interview with Ed Low, Leslie learned that PC Solutions is a relatively new company that has grown substantially in the last two years. The company was started by Ben Avery and Ed Low to market voice-activated interfaces to handicapped users. Since then they have branched out into selling computer-based security systems and robotics. Currently they are using standalone PCs to perform processing in each department.

Ed told Leslie in the interview that he has supported the users' computer needs, but the demands of a growing company now take up all his time. That is why PC Solutions decided to hire a full-time microcomputer specialist, one who knows about PC networks. Ed will propose soon that the company set up a local area network (LAN) so that users can share printers and have a common menu access system.

After examining several network operating systems, Ed selected NetWare because of its reliability, speed, expandability, security, and fault tolerance. **Fault tolerance** is the measurement of how well a system can recover from hardware failures.

FIGURE 1-1: PC Solutions organizational chart

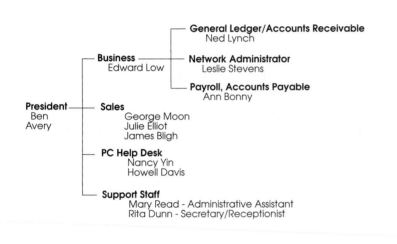

ASCERTAINING LAN BENEFITS

Ed has been given the green light by Ben Avery, president of PC Solutions, to investigate LAN options. Leslie's first assignment is to help Ed create a local area network proposal to present to Ben. Ed needs Leslie to develop a list of ways a LAN will benefit employees, along with the costs. He tells Leslie she has a budget of $9,000 to meet all the hardware and software requirements.

Currently, the Business Department has three 80386sx computers with 2MB RAM each. One, dedicated to payroll and accounting applications, has a 24-pin dot matrix printer attached. The other PCs, primarily used by Ned Lynch and Ed for budgets and word processing, have a 24-pin dot matrix printer attached as well. Ed also uses his computer for making graphics for his presentations.

The sales staff have one 80386sx, 2MB PC dedicated to the order entry system and printing of sales reports and invoices. The salespeople complain that they have to remove the invoice forms and mount standard paper before they can print their sales reports at the end of each day. The other PC in the Sales Department has a laser printer attached and is used for printing price quotations.

The company is planning to add another phone line for sales in the near future. This addition will allow two people to take orders at the same time, but it will also require another PC in the Sales Department that will allow access to the inventory and orders information.

The PC Help Desk staff have two PCs that they use for word processing, logging customer calls, and documenting problems. In addition, they need to notify the sales staff of any product problems as soon as possible. A switch box allows the two PCs to share a standard carriage 24-pin dot matrix printer, used to print reports and correspondence.

Mary Read, the administrative assistant for the company, has a powerful 80486DX computer with 6MB RAM that she uses for word processing and desktop publishing of the catalog and flyers. This computer is the envy of her co-workers because it has a PostScript-compatible laser printer attached. Ed often takes his graphics to Mary's computer for printing.

Rita Dunn is the company's secretary and receptionist. She has a PC at the reception desk that she uses for word processing. Final output is printed on Mary's laser printer. Rita also helps Mary enter product price and description data into the catalog files.

From the information Ed gave her, Leslie put together a list of the computers to be attached to the network, along with the benefits a LAN could provide. A copy of the LAN benefits list she produced is shown in Figure 1-2.

SELECTING A NETWORK SYSTEM

Leslie's next job is to recommend a network system. Ed told her that Ben is very cost conscious and that she should find a hardware system that will do the job and provide for expansion at the lowest price. If expansion continues, Ed believes the company will move to a larger facility within a year. Therefore, he wants to keep wiring installation costs at their current location to a minimum.

In her networking classes, Leslie learned that LANs are essentially high-speed communication systems that allow computers to share resources over distances ranging from several feet to a nearly a mile. The physical geometry or cable layout used to connect computers in a local area network is called the network's **physical topology**. She knows the major topologies are the star, bus, and ring.

FIGURE 1-2: Leslie's list of LAN benefits

Memorandum
To: Ed Low
From: Leslie Stevens
Subject: LAN Benefits

Date: 10/1

The following benefits can be achieved by installing a LAN at PC Solutions.

1.   Sharing Printers

a.   Eliminate the need for the mechanical switch used in the PC Help Desk. This will increase efficiency and reduce frustration.
b.   Give all users access to the PostScript laser printer when high-quality or graphics output is required. Currently users spend extra time saving documents on diskette and taking them to Mary's machine for printing.
c.   Allow Mary to use a dot matrix printer for internal memos and draft document printing. This will save money because the laser printer is several times more expensive to use than the dot matrix.
d.   Allow output to be directed to other printers in case of a printer failure. This will reduce downtime and increase productivity.

2.   Sharing Data

a.   Adding another phone line will require that at least two computers have access to the inventory and orders files. A network will allow one copy of these files to be shared by all users.
b.   All users can have access to common forms and documents.
c.   The PC Help Desk personnel will be able to cooperate and interact in documenting customer or equipment problems.

3.   Sharing Software

Currently a separate copy of the word processing and spreadsheet software needs to be maintained on each PC. A network will make it possible to share one copy of the software (we would need to use a network version and license all users, of course) and therefore make it easier to keep software updated and standardized for all users.

4.   Common Menu Access System

Using the menu system that comes with NetWare, we can have common menu functions for each user while providing individual users with options for their specific applications.

5.   Communication

An e-mail package will make it easier for the PC Help Desk personnel to keep Sales abreast of any new product information or problems. This same system can be used to improve communications and scheduling throughout the entire company by facilitating distribution of internal memos and providing maintenance of distribution lists and confirmation reports.

6.   Backup and Security

Centralizing data on the file server makes it easier to ensure regular backups and support a better recovery plan in case of data loss.

A file server can provide improved data security. For example, anyone with physical access to Ann's computer could open the payroll files. However, if the payroll files were stored on a file server, they could be protected by requiring the proper username, password, and access rights before granting access to the data.

FIGURE 1-3: A star topology

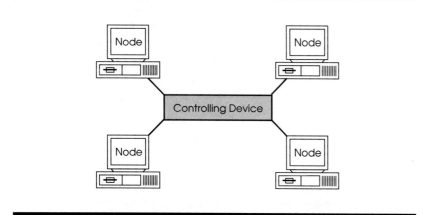

FIGURE 1-4: A linear bus topology

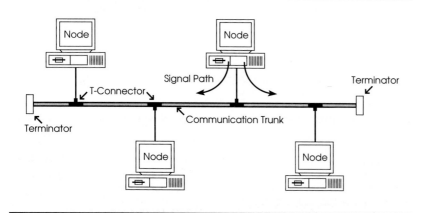

FIGURE 1-5: A ring topology

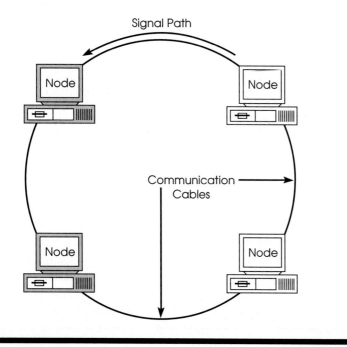

In a **star topology** (see Figure 1-3), a cable from each computer runs to a central device, which may be a mainframe computer or a passive signal splitter similar to the ones used on cable TV systems. In the past, the star topology was commonly used to connect terminals to a mainframe or microcomputers to a disk-sharing system. Twisted pair cable, similar to that used for phones, is commonly used with the star configuration. Today, the star topology is popular on many LANs. For example, IBM Token Ring, 10BASET, and ARCNET (short for Attached Resource Computer Network) all use star topologies.

A **bus topology** (see Figure 1-4) consists of cable segments in a linear format. Multiple computers are attached to the cable segment by means of T-connectors or media access units. Each end of the cable segment must be terminated. Signals put on the bus are instantly available to all attached nodes. Coaxial cable is often used with the linear bus topology. Thick and thin Ethernet are the most common products that use the linear bus topology.

In a **ring topology** (see Figure 1-5), the cable also runs from one computer to the next, but with no termination points. Each computer in the ring receives a message and then retransmits it to the next computer. The signal travels around the network until it returns to the sending device. In the real world, there are very few pure ring topologies, since a broken cable or a disabled machine could stop all communication in the ring.

To get more information on networking hardware options, Leslie contacted Jake, a Certified NetWare Engineer working for a local Novell Authorized Reseller. Jake was in Leslie's Advanced System Manager class and impressed her with his

FIGURE 1-6: A token ring topology

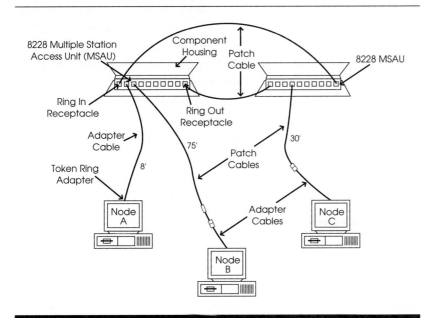

knowledge of and experience with computer network systems. Jake explained that current network systems — Ethernet, 10BASET, ARCNET, and Token Ring — are all based on the three physical topologies.

To determine the lowest hardware costs required to do the job, Leslie needs to compare the costs and capabilities of the current popular network systems. Jake explained that most popular network systems have been standardized by IEEE, the Institute of Electrical and Electronic Engineers, working through its 802.x committee.

According to Jake, the Token Ring system is the Cadillac of network systems. The IEEE standard for Token Ring, 802.5, is based on a combination of the star and ring topologies, as shown in Figure 1-6. In a Token Ring system, each station or node is connected to a Multiple Station Access Unit (MSAU). The physical topology of Token Ring is a star, but the signals actually travel in a ring. Standard Token Ring signals travel at 4Mbps (million bits per second), but with special cards can travel at 16Mbps.

Jake explained that a signal from node A is transmitted to the MSAU, then the MSAU relays the signal to node B. Node B repeats the signal and sends it back to the MSAU. The MSAU relays the signal to the wire running to node C, then node C transmits the signal back to the MSAU, where it is relayed back to the originating node A. If the wire running from the MSAU to node B is broken, or if node B is shut down, a relay in the MSAU will pass the signal on to the connection leading to node C. In this manner the ring is very fault tolerant, or resistant to breakdowns.

Leslie believes the advantages of Token Ring are speed, expandability, and fault tolerance. Its disadvantage is the higher cost per network card, plus the additional cost of the MSAUs. Because Leslie wants to minimize wiring installation, Token Ring also has the disadvantage of requiring more wiring; each machine must have two pairs of twisted wire leading back to an MSAU.

Jake said the 10BASET network system is becoming very popular. A combination of the bus and star configurations, it has been standardized by the IEEE 802.3 committee. A device called a **concentrator** acts as a hub to connect all machines to the network, as shown in Figure 1-7 on the following page. Twisted pair wire is used to connect each machine to the concentrator. In this respect the wiring for 10BASET requires a star, much the same as in Token Ring. However, the signals are not sent from one station to the next as in Token Ring; instead, they are broadcast on the cable bus and available to all stations, much like a CB radio. Jake explained to Leslie that when two or more stations attempt to

FIGURE 1-7: A 10BASET topology

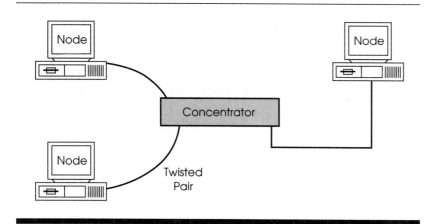

FIGURE 1-8: A thin Ethernet topology

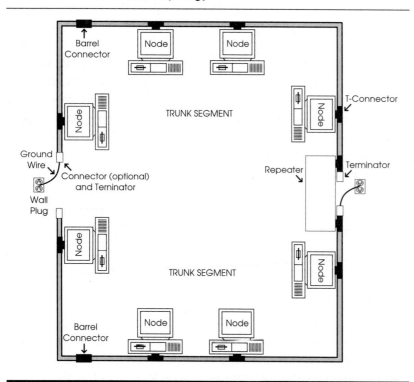

transmit at the same instant, a **collision** occurs and the stations must retransmit after waiting a random period of time. This system is referred to as **Carrier Sense Multiple Access/Collision Detection (CSMA/CD)**.

10BASET is a fast network system with transmission speeds of 10Mbps. Under light loads, 10BASET performance can be faster than Token Ring, but it might bog down with collisions when the number of stations and level of activity grow. Because the CSMA/CD system is simpler than the token-passing system, the card costs are lower. Its disadvantages for Leslie's system are the additional cost of a concentrator and the need to run cable from each workstation to the concentrator.

The popular Ethernet system, shown in Figure 1-8, is based on the bus topology. Like 10BASET, Ethernet is standardized under the IEEE 802.3 committee, but that version is known as 10BASE2. A thin coaxial cable, type RG58, is used along with T-connectors to allow as many as 30 machines to be attached to a single cable run, called a **segment**. A segment cannot exceed 607 feet in length. Up to five segments can be joined to form the entire network. No MSAUs or concentrators are necessary. Jake said many network people refer to this system as *Thinnet*.

10BASE2 or Thinnet cards use the same CSMA/CD system and 10Mbps speed that 10BASET uses. Jake said he has installed many Ethernet or 10BASE2 systems and that they provide excellent throughput under normal network loads. Wiring is also simplified, because one coaxial cable can be run from one machine to the next. Jake told Leslie that if PC Solutions decides to run its own cable above the ceilings, she should be sure to obtain cable that meets the building's fire codes.

Jake explained that the ARCNET system, shown in Figure 1-9, is a combination of the bus and star topologies. Even though ARCNET does not follow the IEEE 802.4 committee standards as closely as the other network systems follow their corresponding standards, it is still very popular. Jake has installed ARCNET on many smaller networks.

FIGURE 1-9: An ARCNET topology

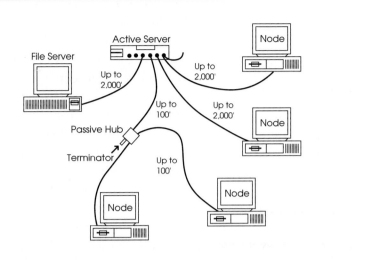

He explained that the active hub is used to connect as many as eight cable runs. The **active hub** acts as a signal repeater, allowing cable runs of up to 2,000 feet between an active hub and a node. **Passive hubs** are simple signal splitters that can be used at the end of a run to split the cable and allow up to three workstations to be attached to one cable run. When a passive hub is used, wire length must be limited to 100 feet. Either twisted pair or coaxial cable, type RG68, can be used.

The advantages of ARCNET are low card cost and flexible wiring options. The disadvantages are speed (standard ARCNET is only 2Mbps), higher cabling costs than 10BASE2, and lack of standardization.

"Novell NetWare is compatible with all the major network systems," said Jake. Leslie's concern is choosing a system that will meet her current needs, be economical, and provide expansion options in the future. To help her make her decision, Jake provided Leslie with a list of the prices of the components for each network type. Jake's list is shown in Figure 1-10.

FIGURE 1-10: Jake's price list

ITEM	COST
Token Ring card	450.00
10BASET card	325.00
Ethernet (10BASE2) card	185.00
16-bit ARCNET card	115.00
10BASET 12-port concentrator	700.00
Token Ring 8-port MSAU	500.00
8-port ARCNET active hub	200.00
ARCNET passive hub	55.00
Terminators (grounded)	12.00
Ethernet-type RG58 cable	10.00 + .25/ft
ARCNET-type RG62 cable	10.00 + .30/ft
4 pair twisted wire	.40/ft

From this information, Leslie decided to install Novell NetWare using an Ethernet 10BASE2 network system. Although ARCNET comes in at a lower price than 10BASE2, it will involve more wiring, give slower response times, and be less expandable. Leslie feels that Token Ring is too expensive for her system, and, like 10BASET, involves too many wiring costs. PC Solutions can wire the Ethernet 10BASE2 system itself, perhaps with the help of a wiring expert, and it will give them equal or better performance.

FIGURE 1-11: PC Solutions floor plan

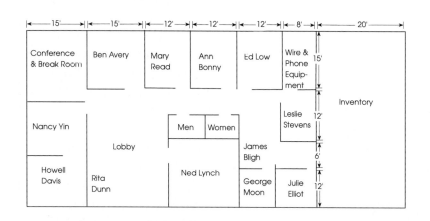

FIGURE 1-12: Leslie's wiring diagram

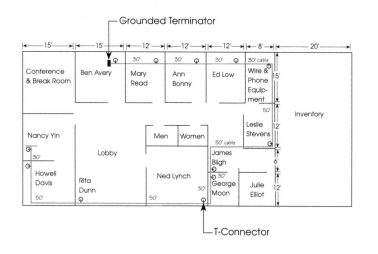

DIAGRAMMING THE NETWORK LAYOUT

Ed told Leslie that the equipment closet next to his office can be cleaned out to provide a home for the file server. Currently Leslie occupies the sales cubical across from the equipment room. Given the current floor plan of the PC Solutions building (see Figure 1-11), Leslie next documents the layout of the network, showing each workstation and the file server. Each workstation and the file server will need an Ethernet card and T-connector to attach it to the cable. Jake said T-connectors usually come with the Ethernet cards, but that his company can supply them along with cable assemblies with connectors on each end for the prices shown in the price list.

Once the location of each computer has been identified, Leslie draws the cable runs and calculates the amount of cable, along with the number of network cards and connectors she will need. Her drawing is shown in Figure 1-12.

CALCULATING NETWORK COSTS

Using the price information supplied by Jake and her cable wiring diagram, Leslie assembled a price list detailing the required network hardware and software. She has included the cost of NetWare (to be installed by the seller), Ethernet cards, and cables. The cost of the file server has been estimated because actual specifications will require more time to develop. A copy of the detailed cost analysis that Leslie prepared is shown with her LAN proposal in Figure 1-13.

FIGURE 1-13: Leslie's LAN proposal

Memorandum
To: Ed Low   Date: 10/12
From: Leslie Stevens
Subject: LAN Proposal

After analyzing our current system, I have found that a Novell NetWare LAN system could greatly benefit our company (see my memo dated 10/1). I am recommending Novell NetWare because of its reliability, security, speed, and expandability. Excellent technical support is available in our area, and as a Certified NetWare Administrator, I feel I can install and maintain the system without additional training.

LAN Hardware Recommendation

After researching costs and capabilities of the most popular network hardware systems, I recommend the Ethernet 10BASE2 system for our network. Comparative costs of the most popular network systems are provided in the table below.

Item	Token Ring	10BASET	Ethernet (10BASE2)	ARCNET
Cards (10)	$4,500.00	$3,250.00	$1,850.00	$1,150.00
Hub/MSAU	1,000.00	700.00	n/a	400.00
Cabling installation requirements (high, medium, low)	High	High	Low	Medium
Total Cost	**$5,500.00**	**$3,950.00**	**$1,850.00**	**$1,550.00**

As can be seen, the costs of Token Ring and 10BASET are considerably more than the costs of Ethernet or ARCNET. In addition, these systems would require considerable wiring to be installed in our building. ARCNET would meet our current needs, but it does not have the speed or expandability to connect other devices that we may need in the future.

LAN Costs

The cost to install a Novell NetWare 3.11 Ethernet system for our existing 10 workstations is shown in the table below. The file server cost has been estimated and could vary within $1,000, depending on additional disk storage needs.

Item	Quantity	Cost Each	Total
Ethernet cards	10	$195.00	$1950.00
30-ft. cables	7	17.50	122.50
50-ft. cables	4	22.50	90.00
Terminators	2	15.00	30.00
File server (approximate cost)	1	2,900.00	2,900.00
Novell NetWare 3.11 (50 users) and installation	1	3,500.00	3,500.00
Leslie's 80486sx 4MB	1	1,500.00	1,500.00
Total Cost			**$10,092.50**

If you have any questions or if I can provide more information, please let me know. I will be very happy to assist you in any way I can.

TAKING A NETWARE TEST DRIVE

Jake mentioned that he was going to visit Ron, a network administrator for Automated Diagnostic Instruments (ADI). Ron has been a network administrator for some time, and Jake recently upgraded one of his file servers from NetWare 2.15 to NetWare 3.11. Jake said he needed to replace a faulty network card and asked Leslie if she would like to come along to see a demonstration of the network.

At ADI the next day, Ron explained that he has 95 users on two file servers. Both file servers are attached to a Token Ring network. One of the file servers also has an Ethernet card that connects to 25 users in the R&D department. He explained that these users needed the Ethernet cards to communicate with a minicomputer system attached to the Thin Ethernet system.

While Jake replaced the defective card, Ron showed Leslie the file server room and emphasized the importance of keeping the server in a secure location. The new **uninterruptible power source (UPS)** attached to the file server was equipped with a sensor to detect noise on the power line. The UPS protects the system from brownouts and is an important part of any file server setup.

Ron next took Leslie to a workstation attached to the Ethernet network. While booting the workstation, Ron explained that the AUTOEXEC.BAT file would automatically load the software necessary to attach to the network. When the workstation finished booting, Ron changed to the first network drive, F:, and used the SLIST command, as shown in Figure 1-14, to obtain a list of servers on his network.

Ron then proceeded to log in to the server HOST2 by entering the LOGIN command, shown in Figure 1-15. He explained that he needed to type the server name followed by a slash because the workstation had been attached to server HOST1. Typing the server name ahead of the LOGIN name forces the workstation to send the LOGIN request to the desired file server.

To show Leslie the contents of the SYS volume on file server HOST2, Ron used the LISTDIR command shown in Figure 1-16. The /S option will display the names of all subdirectories. Using the LIST-DIR command, Ron was able to show Leslie how he stored general-purpose software packages under the directory SOFTWARE. Ron also explained how DOS command files are stored in subdirectories within the PUBLIC directory. This allows him to store and maintain DOS versions on the file server rather than on each individual PC's hard disk.

FIGURE 1-14: The SLIST command

```
F:\LOGIN>SLIST
Known NetWare File Servers           Network   Node Address Status
----------------------------         -------   ------------ ------
HOST2                                [    311][            1]Default

Total of 1 file servers found

F:\LOGIN>
```

FIGURE 1-15: The LOGIN command

```
F:\LOGIN>LOGIN HOST2\RON
Enter your password:
Device LPT1: re-routed to queue CLASSROOM on server HOST2.
Good morning, RON.

Drive  A:   maps to a local disk.
Drive  B:   maps to a local disk.
Drive  C:   maps to a local disk.
Drive  D:   maps to a local disk.
Drive  E:   maps to a local disk.
Drive  F: = HOST2\SYS:  \
            ------
SEARCH1:   = Z:. [HOST2\SYS:   \PUBLIC]
SEARCH2:   = Y:. [HOST2\SYS:   \PUBLIC\IBM_PC\MSDOS\V5.00]

F:\>
```

FIGURE 1-16: The LISTDIR command

```
F:\>LISTDIR /S

The sub-directory structure of HOST2/SYS:
Directory
-----------------------------------------------------------------
->LOGIN
->PUBLIC
->   IBM_PC
->     MSDOS
->       V4.01
->       V3.30
->       V5.00
->MAIL
->   19000001
->SOFTWARE
->   WP
->   DB
->   SP
->   WP51
->   GLXFONTS
->   DBASE
->   UTILITY
17 sub-directories found

F:\>
```

FIGURE 1-17: Using LISTDIR to view effective rights

```
The sub-directory structure of HOST2/SYS:
Effective    Directory
-----------------------------------------------------------------
[ R    F ]  ->LOGIN
[ R    F ]  ->PUBLIC
[ R    F ]  ->   IBM_PC
[ RWCEMF ]  ->     MSDOS
[ RWCEMF ]  ->       V4.01
[ RWCEMF ]  ->       V3.30
[ RWCEMF ]  ->       V5.00
[   C    ]  ->MAIL
[ RWCEMF ]  ->   19000001
[ RWCEMFA]  ->SOFTWARE
[ RWCEMFA]  ->   WP
[ RWCEMFA]  ->   DB
[ RWCEMFA]  ->   SP
[ RWCEMFA]  ->   WP51
[ RWCEMFA]  ->   GLXFONTS
[ RWCEMFA]  ->   DBASE
[ RWCEMFA]  ->   UTILITY
17 sub-directories found

F:\>
```

FIGURE 1-18: The TLIST command

```
F:\>TLIST SOFTWARE

HOST2\SYS:SOFTWARE
User trustees:
  RON                               [ RWCEMFA]
  -----
Group trustees:
  EVERYONE                          [ R    F ]

F:\>
```

Ron explained that the LISTDIR command can be used to view the effective rights in each directory. Ron typed

LISTDIR SYS: /E /S

with the results shown in Figure 1-17. The letters indicate the access rights allowed. *R* is the Read right; *F*, for File Scan, provides the right to see file-names in a directory. *W* grants the ability to write and change information in a file. *C* allows the user to create new files. *E* allows the user to delete files. *M* lets the user modify the file-name and change file attributes. *A*, for Access Control, allows a user to grant rights to other users or groups.

Ron added that he uses the LIST-DIR /E command when he creates new users. After he creates the new users and assigns them their rights, he then logs in with the new usernames and runs the LISTDIR /E command. It lets him see if the new users will have the rights they need to perform their work.

To show Leslie who has rights to use the general-purpose software, Ron entered the command TLIST SOFTWARE, as shown in Figure 1-18.

The TLIST command displays trustee assignments for the specified directory or file name. A **trustee** is a user or group who has been assigned rights to a specific directory or file. The TLIST *.* command can be used to list trustee rights of all files and directories in the current path. When rights are assigned to a directory, those rights automatically flow down to its subdirectories, unless the rights are reassigned or blocked at a lower level. To see how much disk space the DOS versions take up, Ron used the CHKDIR command (see Figure 1-19 on the following page) to show how much space is used in the directory and all its subdirectories.

FIGURE 1-19: The CHKDIR command

```
Directory Space Limitation Information For:
HOST2\SYS:PUBLIC\IBM_PC\MSDOS

    Maximum      In Use    Available
    25,200 K    17,816 K     7,384 K   Volume Size
                   144 K     7,384 K   \PUBLIC\IBM_PC\MSDOS

F:\>
```

FIGURE 1-20: The USERLIST command

```
User Information for Server HOST2
Connection  User Name      Network    Node Address   Login Time
----------  ---------      -------    ------------   ----------
     1    * RON          [   DAD] [    E8FFA42E]   1-02-1980 10:59 am
     2      GUEST        [   DAD] [    C0AC9D56]   1-02-1980 10:23 am

F:\>
```

FIGURE 1-21: The SEND command

```
F:\>SEND "How's it going Jake?" TO Guest
Message sent to HOST2/GUEST (station 2).

F:\>
```

To see who was using the file server, Ron entered the USERLIST command, with the results shown in Figure 1-20. Ron explained that the /E option also provides the login times of each user, along with the address assigned to each card. The card addresses are used by the network to route data packets to the correct workstation. Ron's USERLIST command shows that GUEST is logged in to workstation address C0AC9D56. Ron remarked that Jake was probably logged on as GUEST to test the LAN card.

To send a message to the user GUEST, Ron used the SEND command, as shown in Figure 1-21. The SEND command includes the message in quotation marks followed by the word *TO* and the name of the currently logged-in user. Ron explained that the SEND command can only be used to send messages to users who are currently logged in. Within a few seconds, a message is returned from Jake: "FROM GUEST: All is well. Meet you in the lobby. (CTRL-ENTER to clear)." Ron holds down the Ctrl key and presses [Enter] to clear the message.

Ron mentioned that a message can be sent to a group of users by entering the name of the group after the word *TO*. To "broadcast" a message to all users, enter the group name EVERYONE. Because Ron's menu options use the CASTOFF command to prevent messages from interrupting most applications, sending the message will not affect other users. When the application ends, the menu system uses the CASTON command to allow the workstation to again receive messages while the menu options are displayed.

Leslie then entered the command *SEND "Ron says it's break time!" TO Everyone*. In a few seconds the message "FROM SUPERVISOR: Ron says it's break time! (CTRL-ENTER to clear)" appeared on the bottom of their workstation screens. Ron entered the command LOGOUT and pressed the Enter key. Leslie noticed that the LOGOUT command displayed the date and time they logged in and the date and time they logged out.

When Leslie returned to PC Solutions, Ed told her that her proposal had been accepted. As he congratulated her on a job well done, he told her that he and Ben want her to move on her proposal immediately. Leslie will need to examine the processing needs of the organization and develop specifications for the file server environment. We will follow Leslie as she goes about this task in Chapter 2.

In this chapter the following NetWare commands were used to perform the functions described below.

SLIST This command displays the name and address information for all file servers on your network. Your default file server is identified by the word *default* following the file server information.

LOGIN
server-name\user-name The LOGIN command provides the file server with your username. The file server specified will look up the username in its bindery files. If the username has a password associated with it, or if the username is not defined on the server, the server will ask you for the password. The server-name parameter is optional if the server you want to log in to is your default file server. See the SLIST command.

LISTDIR
[path] [option] The LISTDIR command will list all directories in the path you specify. If you do not specify a path, the LISTDIR command will list all subdirectories within your current directory. Possible options include:

- **/Rights**: Displays the inherited rights mask for each subdirectory

- **/Date or /Time**: Displays the creation date of each subdirectory

- **/Effective**: Displays the user's effective rights in each subdirectory

- **/All**: Combines all the above options

- **/Subdirectories**: Displays the subdirectories of a directory and all subsequent subdirectories

TLIST *[path]* The TLIST command is used to view the trustee list of the directory or file specified in the path. The trustee list consists of all users or groups who have been granted rights to that directory or file. If no path is specified, the trustee list of the current directory is displayed. TLIST *.* will display a trustee list for each subdirectory of the current directory.
The trustee rights that can be granted to a user or group:

- Read: Read from a file

- Write: Write data into a file

- File Scan: Scan directory information

- Create: Create new files

- Erase: Erase or delete files

- Modify: Change filenames and attributes

- Supervisory: All rights; cannot be blocked

CHKDIR *[path]*   This command will provide you with information about directory and volume specified, including maximum space available, space in use, and the amount of storage space available for use. The space in use includes the current directory and all its subdirectories. If no path is specified, information is given on the current directory. This command will not work on DOS local drives such as A: or C:.

USERLIST *[file-server] [/E]*   The USERLIST command will provide you with a list of all users who are currently logged in to the specified file server. If no file server is specified, users logged into your default file server are listed. Lists address information about the user's workstation

SEND *"message"* *[to] user-name*   The SEND command can be used to send a brief message to a user who is currently logged in to the file server. The message must be enclosed in quotes.

CASTOFF [ALL]   Prevents your workstation from receiving messages from other users. The ALL option also prevents receipt of messages from the file server console.

CASTON   Allows your workstation to again receive messages from other network users and the file server console.

1. List four LAN benefits.

2. In the _____ network topology, a cable runs from each computer to a central device.
   a. Ring
   b. Star
   c. Bus
   d. Backbone

3. The _____ network system is based on a combination of the ring and star topologies.
   a. Ethernet (10BASE2)
   b. 10BASET
   c. IBM Token Ring
   d. ARCNET

4. The _____ network system is based on the bus topology.
   a. Ethernet (10BASE2)
   b. 10BASET
   c. IBM Token Ring
   d. ARCNET

5. The _____ network system is based on the star and bus topologies.
   a. Ethernet (10BASE2)
   b. 10BASET
   c. IBM Token Ring
   d. LocalTalk

6. The _____ network system would require the least amount of wire when computers are close together.
   a. Ethernet (10BASE2)
   b. 10BASET
   c. IBM Token Ring
   d. ARCNET

7. An MSAU is used with the _____ network system.
   a. Ethernet (10BASE2)
   b. 10BASET
   c. IBM Token Ring
   d. ARCNET

8. The _____ network system allows up to 2,000-foot cable runs.

    a. Ethernet (10BASE2)
    b. 10BASET
    c. IBM Token Ring
    d. ARCNET

9. Thinnet is another name for the _____ network system.

    a. Ethernet (10BASE2)
    b. 10BASET
    c. IBM Token Ring
    d. ARCNET

10. The 10BASET network system requires the use of a/an _____.

    a. Active hub
    b. Passive hub
    c. Concentrator
    d. MSAU

11. The _____ command will display your effective rights in all directories.
    a. TLIST /E /S
    b. TLIST *.*
    c. LISTDIR /S
    d. LISTDIR /E /S

12. The _____ command can be used to determine how much space is being used by a directory and all its subdirectories.
    a. CHKDIR
    b. LISTDIR /S
    c. DIR
    d. TLIST

13. The _____ command will show all the file servers attached to your network and identify your default file server.
    a. TLIST
    b. SLIST
    c. USERLIST /E
    d. SESSION

14. Before you can log in to the file server you must first _____.

    a. Use the SLIST command
    b. Use the USERLIST command
    c. Change to the network drive (F:)
    d. See your psychologist

15. The _____ command will prevent messages from being displayed at your station.
    a. STOPIT
    b. OFF
    c. CAST OFF
    d. CASTOFF

16. The _____ command allows you to see the node address of other workstations that are logged in to the file server.
    a. TLIST
    b. SLIST
    c. USERLIST /E
    d. USERLIST

17. Which command would you use to send a message to Engineer Scott?
    a. SEND TO Scott "Beam me up Scotty!".
    b. SEND Beam me up Scotty TO Scott
    c. SEND "Beam me up Scotty" TO "Scott"
    d. SEND "Beam me up Scotty" TO Scott

18. How do you clear a message from your screen?

19. If messages are not being displayed on your screen, you should _____.
    a. Call Novell and report the problem
    b. Reboot your computer
    c. Type the command HELP, I'M NOT GETTING MESSAGES
    d. Try using the CASTON command

SUPERIOR TECHNICAL COLLEGE PROJECT 1

You have just been hired by Superior Technical College as its network system manager. This is a new position within the Data Processing department; you have been hired because of your knowledge of microcomputer hardware, software, and local area networks.

Superior Technical College has an enrollment of 3,000 students. The college offers two-year technical degrees in accounting, computer information systems, marketing, and secretarial programs.

Your job will be to set up and manage the personal computer network for the college administrative office. Your supervisor, Dave Johnson, has given you an organizational chart for the administrative office, shown in Figure 1-22, along with a layout of the building, shown in Figure 1-23. (The figures appear on the following page.) Looking at the organizational chart, you will see that the Superior Technical College administrative office has four departments: Business, Data Processing, Instructional Services, and Student Services.

FIGURE 1-22: Superior Technical College organizational chart

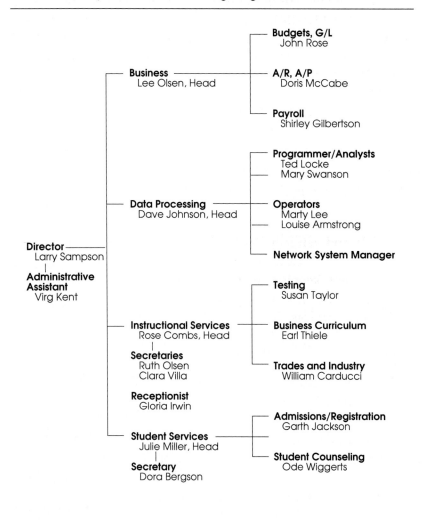

FIGURE 1-23: Superior Technical College office layout

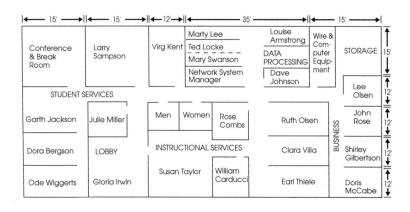

Most of the data processing applications for Superior Technical College are currently being done on the school's mid-sized computer. The system is wired to the terminals using twisted pair cable. The building has been wired so that each office has eight twisted pairs coming to an outlet. Two pairs are for the phone system, another two pairs are for the main computer, and the remaining four pairs are not used at this time.

For the last several years, the administrative office staff has used standalone PCs to perform most secretarial tasks. In the Business office, both John Rose and Lee Olsen have 80386SX PCs with 2MB of RAM on their desks, and use spreadsheet programs to work with budget data. In addition to the spreadsheet software, Lee also has a word processing program that he uses to type correspondence. Lee has a 24-pin dot matrix printer that is capable of producing correspondence-quality output. As part of managing the Business Department, Lee needs to present the budget to the school board. Recently he has been using Lotus 1-2-3 graphs in his presentations. To print final copies of his presentations, Lee frequently uses Virg Kent's computer, which is connected to a laser printer. John has a little 9-pin dot matrix that adequately prints basic spreadsheets.

Virg Kent is the administrative assistant for the four departments and, in addition to helping keep Larry and Lee organized, she is responsible for maintaining program flyers and the school catalog. Virg has an 80486DX computer with 6MB RAM and a PostScript-compatible laser printer. She uses this computer for word processing and desktop publishing.

The secretaries, Ruth Olsen and Clara Villa, often work with Virg Kent. They both have 80386SX computers with 2MB of RAM and use the word processing program to work on correspondence and course outlines. They currently use a switch box to share a laser printer. Ruth helps Virg maintain the school catalog files. She now does this by using Virg's computer while Virg is working on other tasks.

Susan Taylor has an 80386sx computer that has 2MB RAM in her office that is often used for student testing. Since Susan took a word processing class, she has wanted another computer in her area that she can use for either word processing or testing when the current computer is in use. She has a laser printer attached to the testing computer because the testing software requires an HP LaserJet II compatible printer for its output. The printer is used only when the computer is used for testing.

Earl Thiele and William Carducci both use PCs to access course outline and schedule files. Because course outlines are also maintained by Ruth and Clara, keeping the files current on their computers has become a problem. Currently they both use older dot matrix printers.

The Student Services Department has two computers. One computer, used mostly by Garth Jackson for graduate admissions tasks, tracks student placement after graduation. Reports are printed on 11×14" paper using a wide-carriage dot matrix printer. When Garth uses the computer for word processing, he has to change to standard $8\frac{1}{2} \times 11$" paper. Ode Wiggerts and Dora Bergson share the other computer for word processing. This computer has a laser printer attached that provides high-quality correspondence printing.

The Data Processing Department consists of your supervisor, Dave Johnson; two programmer/analysts; two operators; and yourself. You will be the only member of the DP staff to use the PC network at this time.

Dave said you should order your computer as soon as possible. In the meantime, there is a 80286 1MB RAM computer in the wire closet that you can use until your new computer arrives. After that, he would like to place the older PC at the receptionist's desk and connect it to the network. This will allow Gloria to help the clerical staff work on their word processing projects.

Dave said the school has budgeted a maximum of $10,000 for the network and your new system. Budgets are tight this year, so he would appreciate it if you could stay under that figure as much as possible without sacrificing the reliability and functionality of the network.

Assignment 1-1: **Ascertain LAN Benefits**

Dave Johnson would like to draft a recommendation to install a network system to support PC users and applications throughout the office. The network will allow all office staff to access the necessary printers, run the common application software through a menu system, and have access to needed documents and data.

One of your first jobs is to recommend a network system and supply Dave with a list of benefits and costs. Because of your background and training, Dave said he is going to rely on you to design and install the network system to support the processing needs of Superior Technical College.

❶ Given the above information about Superior Technical College's processing needs, as well as the procedures you learned about in the case at the beginning of this chapter, document the benefits the college would gain by implementing a Novell Netware LAN. Record your list of benefits under Assignment 1-1 of Student Answer Sheet 1, appears at the end of ths chapter.

Assignment 1-2: **Select a Network System**

❶ Determine the number and locations of all computers in the Data Processing Department. Record the number of machines to be attached to the network on Student Answer Sheet 1.

❷ Fill in the price comparison cost table on Student Answer Sheet 1. Your instructor will provide you with sources for network hardware costs, or you can use the costs that Jake provided in Figure 1-10.

❸ At this time your instructor will either ask you to select a network system for Superior Technical College or will assign a network system to you. On Student Answer Sheet 1, justify implementing your network system at Superior Technical College.

Assignment 1-3: **Diagram the Network Layout**

❶ Using the floor plan for Superior Technical College provided in Assignment 1-3 of Student Answer Sheet 1, diagram the cable runs necessary to connect all computers and the file server to the network. Indicate the length of each cable run and the location and number of any extra network hardware devices, such as MSAUs, concentrators, hubs, or terminators.

Assignment 1-4: **Calculate Network Costs**

❶ Using the cable information from Assignment 1-3 along with the hardware costs from Assignment 1-2, fill out the detailed price list table under Assignment 1-4 in Student Answer Sheet 1. Your instructor might provide you with a source for cable costs or might ask you to use Jake's price information, found in Figure 1-10.

The cost of the file server computer can be estimated by checking the current price of an 80486sx or 80386dx computer with at least 8MB RAM and 500MB fixed disk. (More detailed file server specifications will be developed in Chapter 2.) Try to keep total costs, including that of your new computer, under the $10,000 budget.

Assignment 1-5: **Develop a LAN Proposal**

❶ Following Leslie's example, create your own LAN proposal to be presented to Dave Johnson. The proposal should include the benefits to Superior Technical College of using a LAN, the justification for your network hardware selection, and estimated cost of the network hardware plus NetWare. Your instructor will provide you with additional information regarding pricing, along with the contents and layout of your proposal.

Assignment 1-6:   **Take a NetWare Test Drive**

❶ Boot a workstation attached to the network, change to the first network drive (usually F:), and use the SLIST command to fill in the table under Assignment 1-6 of Student Answer Sheet 1.

❷ Use the LOGIN command to log in to your assigned file server using the username provided by your instructor. (You should have recorded the file server name and username provided by your instructor at the top of Student Answer Sheet 1.) Record the LOGIN command you used on Student Answer Sheet 1.

❸ Use the appropriate options of the LISTDIR command to list all directories on the SYS volume, along with your effective rights. Record this information on Student Answer Sheet 1. Also record the LISTDIR command you use.

❹ Use the TLIST command to document the trustee assignments given to each subdirectory of the SAMPLE directory. Record the directory path and trustee assignments on Student Answer Sheet 1.

❺ Use the CHKDIR command to determine the amount of space used by the SAMPLE directory and all its subdirectories. Record the CHKDIR command you used along with the results on Student Answer Sheet 1.

❻ Use the USERLIST /E command to determine the number of users currently accessing your file server and the node address of your workstation. Record the number of users along with the node address and username of your workstation and at least one other user on Student Answer Sheet 1.

❼ Use the SEND command to send a message to the user you recorded under step 6 above. Record the SEND command you used on Student Answer Sheet 1.

❽ Use the CASTOFF command to prevent messages from being displayed on your workstation. What message do you get when you enter the CASTOFF command? Have another student try to send you a message, or send a message to yourself. Record the results of using CASTOFF on Student Answer Sheet 1.

❾ Use the CASTON command to continue receiving messages. Have another student send you a message, or try sending a message to yourself. Record the results on Student Answer Sheet 1.

❿ Use the LOGOUT command to log off from the server. Record your login and logout times on Student Answer Sheet 1.

Turn in Materials   If instructed to turn in materials, make sure you have completed Student Answer Sheet 1 and turn it in to your instructor on or before the due date.

Student Name: _____

Assigned File Server Name: _____

Username: _____ Student Reference No.: _____

Work Directory: _____ Volume: _____

Assignment 1-1:   LAN Benefits

❶   List potential benefits of a LAN for Superior Technical College in the space below.

Assignment 1-2:   Select a Network System

❶   Identify each computer on the proposed network in the chart below.

Computer	Location (user)	Computer	Location (user)

❷   Complete the price comparison chart below.

Item	Token Ring	10BASET	Ethernet (10BASE2)	ARCNET
Cabling requirements				
Total cost				

❸ Network system selected: _____

Justification for network system:

Assignment 1-3: **Diagram the Network Layout**

    ❶ Diagram your cable runs, as Leslie did in Figure 1-12.

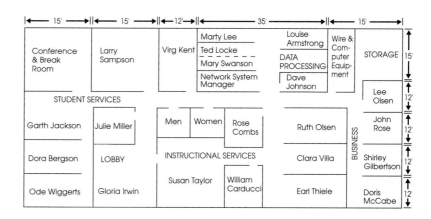

Assignment 1-4: **Calculate Network Costs**

    ❶ Record estimated prices and calculate totals below.

Item	Quantity	Cost	Total

Assignment 1-5: **Develop a LAN Proposal**

Create your LAN proposal on a separate sheet of paper. (Use more than one sheet of paper if necessary.)

Assignment 1-6: **Take a NetWare Test Drive**

    ❶ Record SLIST command information on the following page.

File Server Name	Network Address	Node Address	Status

❷ LOGIN command used: _____

❸ LISTDIR command used: _____

Directory Name	Effective Rights

❹ Record TLIST command information below.

Directory Path	Username	Trustee Assignment
SYS: SAMPLE		
SYS: SAMPLE/SALES		
SYS: SAMPLE/ACCTS		
SYS: SAMPLE/WORK		

❺ CHKDIR command used:_____
Results:

❻ Record USERLIST command information below.
Number of users: _____

Username	Node Address

❼ SEND command used: _____

❽ Record CASTOFF command results: _____

❾ Record CASTON command results: _____

❿ Login time: _____
Logout time: _____

In this chapter you will:

- Identify the components of a directory structure

- Apply directory design concepts

- Determine the volume to be used for your directory structure

- Allow for NetWare-created directories

- Design directories for shared software and data

- Locate user home directories

- Document your directory structure design

DESIGNING A DIRECTORY STRUCTURE

A **directory structure** is used to organize information stored on a network. Therefore, a properly designed directory structure is very important because it will facilitate the setup, use, and growth of your network system. A typical directory structure consists of four parts, as shown in Figure 2-1. The highest level in the structure is the file server. The file server's disk storage is divided into one or more volumes. You can think of a **volume** as being equivalent to the root of a disk drive in the DOS system. In NetWare 3.11 and 3.12, volumes can consist of up to 32 disk drives and occupy up to 32 terabytes (trillion bytes) of capacity. For functional as well as organizational needs, volumes are divided into **directories**. Depending on the directory structure design, the directories can be further subdivided into one or more layers of **subdirectories**.

FIGURE 2-1: Skeletal directory structure

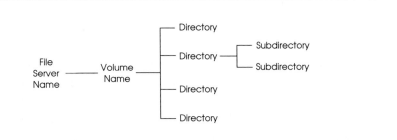

In this chapter you will learn how to design a workable directory structure that supports the processing needs of an organization. By following the network activities at PC Solutions, you will learn about directory design concepts and techniques. The Superior Technical College project at the end of the chapter will give you an opportunity to apply these concepts and techniques in designing your own directory structure.

THE PC SOLUTIONS CASE

Leslie found that talking with Ron reinforced what she had learned in her Novell NetWare class regarding the importance of a good directory structure design. Ron had compared designing a directory structure to creating a blueprint. Just as the blueprint allows the builder to determine materials needed as well as construction details, the directory structure allows the network administrator to determine storage requirements and provides a plan for the network's implementation. Ron said designing a workable directory structure first requires the network administrator to have a good understanding of the processing needs for each user.

DEFINING PROCESSING NEEDS

For the last week Leslie has worked to develop a good understanding of the processing that PC Solutions' network system must support. To help her understand each user's processing needs, Leslie will develop a table that will help her to:

1. Identify each network user

2. Determine the software applications the user accesses

3. Identify the data storage requirements of the user

4. Document printer needs

5. Identify users who work together on projects

From this information Leslie will be able to define file server storage requirements, as well as the composition and makeup of workgroups. A **workgroup** consists of two or more users who need to work together and who share files or printers. Defining workgroups can help organize the directory structure and simplify implementation of security and user setups.

One of Leslie's first tasks was to identify the network users. Using the organizational chart shown in Chapter 1 (see Figure 1-1) along with the information Ed Low gave her, Leslie identified each user and made an appointment to discuss his or her current and future network processing needs. Leslie noticed that getting the users involved in planning the network made them more enthusiastic about the new system.

Ann Bonny's main computer applications involve company payroll and accounts payable. The accounting package, which includes general ledger, accounts receivable, accounts payable, and payroll, is currently installed on her computer and requires about 25MB of disk space. These applications require a dot-matrix printer with a tractor feed for forms. Ned Lynch shares the general ledger package on Ann's computer, but only Ann is responsible for the payroll and accounts payable data. She trusts Ned, but she is concerned about security once her applications are on a file server.

In addition to accounts receivable and general ledger, Ned Lynch works with Ed Low and Ben Avery to develop the company's budgets. Leslie estimated storage requirements for the budgets to be about 10MB. Ned currently has to use Ann's computer to do his accounting work but would rather do this work from his own computer. Ned needs to enter into his customer file new customer data that the sales staff gives him. Keeping current both customer files, one on the sales computer and one on Ann's computer, is a problem. Ned uses the latest version of Lotus 1-2-3 to work with budget data. Ed and Ben also review and make changes to the budget reports. A wide-carriage dot-matrix printer is used to print reports from the general ledger system.

Ed Low works closely with Ben Avery to define the company's direction. In addition to using a spreadsheet program to work with Ned and Ben on budget forecasts, Ed often makes presentations to investors and new customers; he currently uses a graphics presentation program along with Lotus 1-2-3 graphs to develop his presentations. The presentation files are kept on his directory and require about 15MB of storage space. The dot-matrix printer works fine for budget printouts, but Ed uses Mary's laser printer for certain documents and graphics output for his presentations.

As president of the company, Ben Avery spends most of his time managing and planning. Currently he reviews and makes changes to Ed's budget printouts, but he would like to use a networked computer to work directly with the budget data. Ben would like to network PC Solutions' computers so that his staff can use electronic mail for messaging and memos, and so they can schedule meetings electronically. He would also like to prepare initial drafts on his computer, then forward them to Mary for final processing.

The Sales staff all seemed to have the same needs. They currently use one computer to enter orders, record new customer data, and print invoices. They send a copy of the invoice to Ned Lynch for accounts receivable use; they also send Ned information on new customers, which he then enters into the customer file on Ann's computer. Sometimes the Sales staff forgets to send Ned the information on new customers.

Leslie checked the customer file and found it currently requires 13MB of disk space. The order entry system, including the orders file, requires about 20MB of disk space.

James Bligh also uses the Sales computer to keep the inventory file up to date by entering items when they are received. He sends the invoices he receives from vendors to Ann Bonny for accounts payable processing. The inventory file currently occupies 15MB of disk space. A standard dot-matrix printer attached to this computer is used to print both invoice forms and reports. For most of each work day, invoice forms are loaded in the printer. At the end of the day, standard paper is put in the printer and reports are then printed. Everyone agrees that this method is less than ideal. The Sales staff has a second computer that is used to prepare price quotations; this application requires approximately 10MB of disk space. This computer, which has a laser printer attached, is often idle while James Bligh waits to enter inventory data on the order entry computer.

The PC Help Desk staff, Nancy Yin and Howell Davis, each have computers. They use a word processing program to record information on what they refer to as a **problem log** form. The problem log form contains the date, customer data, product data, a description of the problem, and the eventual solution. Each problem log is stored by customer number in a regional directory. Current regions are Northeast, South, Midwest, West, and Canada. For example, problem logs for customers in Boston would be stored in the NE directory. The combined disk capacity of both problem logs is currently 10MB. Nancy and Howell use a switch box to share a 24-pin dot-matrix printer. Product problems are reported to Julie Elliot in the Sales Department by sending her a printout of the problem log. They agreed that an electronic mail system could make this process a lot more efficient. A network would also provide easy access to the printer and allow Nancy and Howell to share access to one set of regional directories rather than having to maintain them on two separate computers.

As the administrative assistant, Mary Read prepares correspondence for Ben and Ed. She agreed that it would save her time if Ben and Ed created their own draft documents for her to edit. She often works with the secretary, Rita Dunn, on common projects. They use diskettes to pass files between them. In addition, Mary is responsible for the company catalog. She has a desktop publishing program on her computer that she uses to maintain the catalog files. Leslie did a directory listing of Mary's disk and found that the catalog files require about 40MB of disk space. Rita Dunn also helps Mary enter price and product description data into the catalog. She has a high-speed PostScript laser printer that she says Ed is always interrupting her to use.

Rita Dunn also acts as receptionist. In addition to transferring phone calls and filing, Rita helps Mary with data entry and word processing. She has a computer at the reception desk that she uses for word processing. Rita transfers files to Mary's computer on diskette. She is anxious to use the network to give her easy access to the documents she is working on for Mary. In addition. she also needs access to a printer and recognizes the possible uses for an electronic mail messaging system.

To help her analyze users' needs, Leslie created the table shown in Figure 2-2 on the following page. In the Files Updated column she identified the files or directories each user is responsible for maintaining. In the Files Accessed column, she identified files or directories from which the user needs to access information, but which the user is not responsible for maintaining. The Printers Needed column will help Leslie determine printer placement and sharing.

FIGURE 2-2: Leslie's user table

Username	Applications Used	Files Updated	Files Accessed	Printers Needed	Works With	Size
Ann Bonny	Payroll	Payroll		Dot matrix		5MB
	Accounts payable	Accounting		Dot matrix		20MB
Ned Lynch	Accounts receivable	Accounting	Customers	Dot matrix (wide)		
	Spreadsheet	Budgets		Dot matrix	Ed, Ben	10MB
	General ledger	Accounting		Dot matrix	Ned, Ann	
Ed Low	Spreadsheet	Budgets		Dot matrix	Ben	
	Graphics		Budgets	Laser		
	Word processor	Personal files	Forms	Laser		25MB
Ben Avery	Spreadsheet		Budgets	Dot matrix	Ed	
	Word processor	Personal files	Forms	Laser		5MB
George Moon	Order entry	Orders, Customers, Inventory	Inventory	2 Dot matrix (invoices, reports)	Julie, James	48 MB
	Word processor	Price quotations	Forms	Laser	Julie, James	10 MB
James Bligh	Order entry	Orders, Customers, Inventory		2 Dot matrix	Julie, George	
	Word processor	Price quotations	Forms	Laser	Julie, George	
Nancy Yin	Word processor	Problem log	Forms	Dot matrix	Howell, James	10MB
Howell Davis	Word processor	Problem log	Forms	Dot matrix	Nancy, James	
Mary Read	Word processor	Ben & Ed's personal files	Forms	Laser, dot matrix		
		Personal files				30MB
		Forms				5MB
		Shared			Rita	10MB
	Desktop publisher	Catalogs		Laser	Rita	40MB
Rita Dunn	Word processor	Personal files	Forms	Laser, dot matrix		30MB
		Shared			Mary	
	Desktop publisher	Catalogs		Laser	Mary	
Leslie Stevens						

Using this information, Leslie created a workgroup table, shown in Figure 2-3, to help her identify users by common job function or department. Leslie will also use this table to identify who will manage each of the directories. Keeping workgroup names to eight characters or fewer will allow Leslie to use them as directory names in the future. The Users column includes only the names of staff who will be accessing the network in the near future.

FIGURE 2-3: Leslie's workgroup table

FIGURE 2-3: Leslie's workgroup table

Workgroup Name	Users
Business	Ben Avery, Edward Low, Ned Lynch, Ann Bonny, Leslie Stevens, Mary Read
Sales	Mary Read, Julie Elliot, James Bligh
Support	Mary Read, Rita Dunn
HelpDesk	Nancy Yin, Howell Davis

Total current users = 12

DETERMINING STORAGE REQUIREMENTS

Before designing the directory structure, Leslie needs to determine what storage areas or directories are needed, how much space the directories will require, and which users will need access to these directories. To determine this information and calculate the total amount of space required for all PC Solutions' data, Leslie developed the storage requirements table shown in Figure 2-4.

FIGURE 2-4: PC Solutions' storage requirements table

Directory	Files	Controlling Users	Other Users	Disk Space Required
Home directories		The User		(20MB/User) 240MB
Accounting system	General ledger, receivables, payables	Ned Lynch, Ann Bonny	Business	20MB
Payroll system	Payroll	Ann Bonny		5MB
Budgets	Worksheet files	Ned Lynch, Edward Low	Ben Avery	10MB
Price quotations	WP files	Sales		10MB
Order entry	Orders	Sales	Business	20MB
Inventory	Inventory	James Bligh	Sales, Business	20MB
Customers	Customer	Sales	Business	20MB
Forms	WP forms	Mary Read	All	5MB
Catalog	Desktop publishing files	Mary Read, Rita Dunn		40MB
WP pool	WP files	Mary Read, Rita Dunn		10MB
Problem log	WP log files	Nancy Yin, Howell Davis		10MB
Menus		Leslie Stevens	All	1MB
Software: WP, SP, and DB		Leslie Stevens	All	9MB

Total disk space = 420MB

Leslie knows that she should try to separate software and data directories whenever possible. This approach allows software to be shared by multiple users while still storing the files in separate directories for security and organizational purposes. However, certain applications such as general ledger or the order entry system might require that the data files be stored within the application software directory.

By referring to the installation instructions, Leslie determined the required location of the data files for each of the applications. The documentation for the order entry package states that the orders, invoice, inventory, and customer files can reside in any accessible directory. The path to the directory containing each of these files must be specified during installation. The installation instructions for the general ledger package require that the accounts payable and receivable files be stored in the general ledger system directory. The payroll system also requires that the data files be stored in the payroll system directory.

In the storage requirements table (Figure 2-4), Leslie documented each directory area she will need to meet the user processing requirements she documented in her user table (Figure 2-2). By using the current requirements along with the projected growth for the next two years, Leslie estimated the amount of disk storage for each of the directory storage areas, as shown in the Disk Space Required column in Figure 2-4.

Leslie determined the entries in the Controlling Users column of Figure 2-4 from the Files Updated information given in Figure 2-2. Leslie used this column to document the user or workgroup that is to be given rights to maintain the information and files in that particular directory. The Other Users column of Figure 2-4 indicates other users or workgroups that will be able to access the data but will not be given rights to update the information. Knowing which users maintain and access the data will help Leslie determine where to place the directories when she designs the directory structure. Directories that contain files accessed by many users normally should be close to the top of the structure.

In addition to the shared data and software, all users will need their own home directories to store their work and any temporary files. Based on budget and disk space limitations, Leslie has assigned an average of 20MB per user.

Next Leslie must determine the total disk capacity needed on the file server. She knows that she should normally plan to reserve at least 5MB for a DOS partition and at least 70MB for the NetWare system to use. This allocation will provide room for the operating system, utilities, print queues, and audit files. A breakdown of the disk space required on the file server is given in Figure 2-5.

FIGURE 2-5: File server disk usage table

Purpose	Disk Capacity
DOS partition	5MB
NetWare system files	75MB
PC Solutions data	420MB
Total	500MB

DETERMINING THE VOLUMES

Leslie learned in her NetWare training that a file server can be compared to a filing cabinet. In this analogy, the **root** of the volume can be compared to a drawer in the file cabinet. Creating directories in the root of the volume is analogous to hanging folders in a drawer of a file cabinet. Just as manila envelopes can be used to subdivide a hanging folder, subdirectories can be used to further partition directories. There are about as many ways to design and implement a directory structure as there are network administrators.

The SYS volume, which contains at least four volumes created during installation, is the only required volume on the file server. The LOGIN directory contains files and programs that can be accessed prior to logging in. The MAIL directory contains a subdirectory for each user created. User profile information such as the LOGIN script command are kept in each user's MAIL subdirectory. The PUBLIC directory contains NetWare commands and utilities available to all users after they log in. Novell recommends making subdirectories within PUBLIC for each DOS version. The SYSTEM directory contains operating system files and commands. The Supervisor (in this case, Leslie) is the only user who should have access to this directory.

In her NetWare class, Leslie also found out that many network administrators prefer to use at least two volumes in their directory structures. When using multiple volumes, the SYS volume is reserved for the operating system and certain general-purpose software. One or more DATA volumes are then created to store the organization's files. Placing files on separate volumes allows the administrator to ensure that free space is always available on the SYS volume for NetWare's use. In NetWare 3.11, up to 32 disk drives can be combined to form one volume.

After analyzing her users' processing needs and storage requirements, Leslie decided to create a file server specification requiring a 120MB drive for the SYS volume and a 500MB drive for the PC Solutions' DATA volume. Once she knew the disk capacity requirements, Leslie proceeded to document the file server specifications, shown in Figure 2-6. (Your instructor can provide you with an explanation of each file server specification.)

FIGURE 2-6: File server specifications

Network Component	Specification
Microprocessor	33Mhz 80486
Bus	32bit EISA
RAM	12MB
Video	Color VGA
Keyboard	101 Enhanced
Disk controller	SCSI
Disk drives	120MB, 500MB
Diskette drive	3½ inch, 2.88MB
Uninterruptible power source (UPS)	NetWare compatible, with 15 minutes of backup power, including surge protector and power conditioner
Backup tape drive	720MB to 1GB capacity

In the future, if it becomes necessary to expand the capacity of either volume, Leslie will be able to install another disk drive and include its space in an existing volume. One of the reasons Leslie decided to use a Small Computer System Interface (SCSI) controller card and drives is their capability to connect up to six drives or other SCSI-compatible devices, such as CD-ROMs or tape drives, to a single controller card.

While Leslie waited for price quotes, she planned the layout for each volume in the file server's directory structure.

DESIGNING THE DIRECTORY STRUCTURES

Leslie has decided to keep the SYS volume structure as simple as possible. Currently her SYS volume will contain only the NetWare required directories, along with the DOS versions and the general-purpose software shared by all users. A copy of the volume worksheet for the SYS volume is shown in Figure 2-7.

After analyzing various options, Leslie decided to use a departmental structure to organize the directories within her DATA volume, shown in Figure 2-8. In a **departmental structure**, the user home directories and applications are located within the workgroups or departments that control them. General-purpose directories that are available to all users, such as FORMS and MENUS, are located near the root of the DATA volume.

An **application-oriented structure** for the DATA volume was an alternative that Leslie considered. Ron used this type of structure on his HOST2 file server, which had only a SYS volume, as shown in Figure 2-9.

Ron explained that in this type of structure, user home directories are normally placed under a common directory called USERS, and the shared data directories are arranged by application rather than by workgroup or department. Ron said that application-oriented structures are usually more "shallow" and have fewer subdirectories than workgroup-oriented structures. This structure makes it easier to specify the path to a particular file, but in a more complex structure, it requires the network administrator to make more trustee

FIGURE 2-7: PC Solutions' volume worksheet for the SYS volume

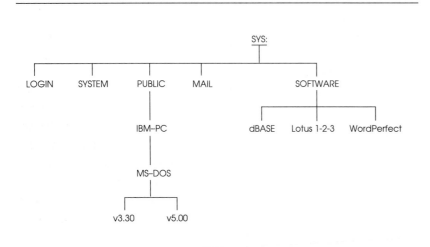

FIGURE 2-8: PC Solutions' volume worksheet for the DATA volume

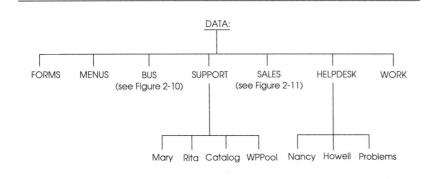

FIGURE 2-9: Ron's SYS volume worksheet for the HOST2 file server

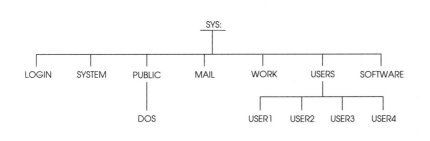

FIGURE 2-10: PC Solutions' directory worksheet for the BUS directory

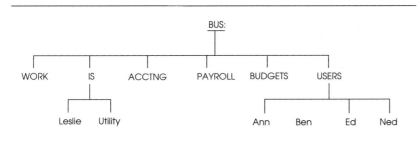

FIGURE 2-11: PC Solutions' directory worksheet for the SALES directory

assignments. Leslie felt that an application-oriented structure would meet the needs of her organization, but she decided that the departmental structure would provide a better foundation for implementing her system.

Because it is often difficult to draw all the directory structure detail on one sheet of paper, Leslie used volume and directory worksheets to diagram the structure. Ron described to Leslie how he uses a separate volume worksheet to show each directory on the root of the volume. If a directory has a simple structure consisting of one or two subdirectories, the entire structure fits on the volume worksheet.

Ron said he uses the directory worksheets to detail the subdirectory structure of a directory shown on the volume worksheet. He used one of these whenever the subdirectory structure would not fit nicely on the volume worksheet. Leslie's BUSINESS and SALES directory worksheets are shown in Figures 2-10 and 2-11, respectively.

Ron suggested to Leslie that she define a WORK directory within each level of the directory structure. The WORK directory allows users to exchange files and work on joint projects by placing shared files in the appropriate WORK directory, which is accessible only to the other users who need them. For example, if Mary Read wanted Julie Elliot to add information to a sales flyer, Mary would place the sales flyer file in the WORK directory of the DATA volume (see Figure 2-8). If Julie Elliot wanted James Bligh to review a document, she would place the document in the WORK subdirectory of the SALES directory (see Figure 2-11).

Now that Leslie has designed her directory structure, she begins to think about how she will go about creating it. In Chapter 3 you'll follow Leslie as she creates the PC Solutions directory structure.

1. _____ is the name of a required NetWare volume.

    a. SYS
    b. DATA
    c. SYSTEM
    d. PUBLIC

2. The _____ directory contains NetWare utilities that can be accessed by all users after they have logged in.

    a. SYS
    b. SYSTEM
    c. PUBLIC
    d. LOGIN

3. The _____ directory contains files and programs available only to the SUPERVISOR.

    a. SYS
    b. SYSTEM
    c. PUBLIC
    d. LOGIN

4. When a file cabinet is compared to a file server, the drawer on the file cabinet is analogous to a _____.

    a. Hard disk
    b. Volume
    c. Directory
    d. Subdirectory

5. A _____ consists of two or more users who work together and need to share files or printers.

    a. DATA volume
    b. PUBLIC directory
    c. Workgroup
    d. Distributed processing system

6. The _____ type of directory structure generally contains fewer levels of subdirectories.

    a. Application-oriented
    b. Departmental
    c. Workgroup
    d. Distributed

7. In a/an _____ directory structure, the user home directories are located under a common directory generally called USERS.

    a. Application-oriented
    b. Departmental
    c. Workgroup
    d. Distributed

8. In NetWare 3.11 and 3.12, a volume can contain storage areas on more than one disk drive.
   a. True
   b. False

9. Files and programs available for users to access prior to logging in are stored in the _____ directory.
   a. MAIL
   b. PUBLIC
   c. SYSTEM
   d. LOGIN

10. When designing a directory structure, which of the following is true regarding software and data?
    a. Data should be kept in the directory that contains the software that accesses it.
    b. Whenever possible, data and software should be kept in separate directories.
    c. Software should be kept on the SYS volume and data kept on a separate volume.
    d. Software should be kept on the SYS volume and data kept in each user's home directory.

11. List the five items Leslie used to help her understand the users' processing needs.

12. Identify and describe the components of a directory structure.

In Chapter 1 you were introduced to the organizational chart for Superior Technical College, which is repeated in Figure 2-12. Now it's time to outline a directory structure for your network.

Personal computers have been installed at most user locations, and the staff has received basic word processing instruction. All users will share the word processing and database software. In addition, users need access to standard forms and a menu system to provide easy access to the system functions and application software.

The accounting functions (payroll, accounts receivable, and accounts payable) are all currently performed on the minicomputer; therefore, Doris McCabe and Shirley Gilbertson have dedicated terminals and will use the network at this time.

John Rose and Lee Olsen use a spreadsheet program to work with budgets and to print reports and charts for board meetings. Current usage shows that 10MB will be sufficient for the budget and report files. Lee uses the word processing program to create initial drafts. He stores these documents on a diskette and then gives them to Virg Kent for final editing and printing.

FIGURE 2-12: Superior Technical College organizational chart

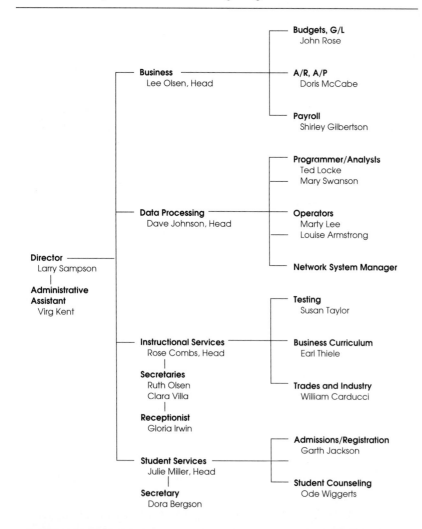

Larry Sampson is too involved in directing the organization to be a computer user, and Virg Kent performs word processing for him. In the future, Larry would like to do some of his own document entry, as Lee does. He also wants to use the network for electronic mail and scheduling.

All Instructional Services staff except Rose Combs currently have PCs that will be attached to the network. In addition to correspondence and reports, the Instructional Services Department uses a word processing program to create and maintain schedules and outlines for each of the college's academic departments. These departments are divided into the Business Division and the Trades Division. The network directory structure will require an area that contains subdirectories for each of the academic programs offered by Superior Technical College. Now an average of 3MB is used to store outlines and schedules for each program.

Current majors in the Business Division are accounting, computer information systems, marketing, and secretarial studies. Earl Thiele is responsible for maintaining these outlines, but Ruth Olsen actually does a lot of the editing and entry for him.

The majors in the Trades Division include telecommunications, mechanical design, construction, and machine tool programs. William Carducci is responsible for maintaining these outlines; Clara Villa helps with the editing and document entry. Approximately 5MB should be reserved for outlines and schedules for each major.

Susan Taylor maintains a testing application that is used to help students select majors and determine if they need any remedial work before entering a specific program. Currently, this package requires about 15MB on an existing standalone computer.

The Student Services Department uses an application package that allows it to keep track of graduates and their employment status. The staff use this data to send out mailings to graduates notifying them of job openings and to print reports showing placement statistics. This application, along with the data files, currently requires 20MB on an existing standalone system. Some additional space for expansion should be included in the planning. Garth Jackson is responsible for maintaining the graduate database. Dora Bergson assists him in data entry and report printing.

Dora uses her computer to do word processing for Julie and Garth. Ode Wiggerts uses Dora's PC for word processing. Ode often creates files that Dora will then edit and print. Ode needs about 10MB for her personal files. Dora will need close to 30MB for her own work plus the documents for Julie.

Although the programmers in the Data Processing Department will not be network users at this time, Dave wants you to provide a directory for their future use. You decide to place your home directory and a directory for software utilities within the Data Processing storage area.

Assignment 2-1: **Define Processing Needs**

❶ Using the Superior Technical College processing information provided in Project 1, plus the additional information provided, fill in the user table on Student Answer Sheet 2.

❷ From the user table you created, define workgroups for Superior Technical College. Record your workgroups and members on the workgroup table on Student Answer Sheet 2.

Assignment 2-2: **Determine Storage Requirements**

❶ Using the processing information provided, determine the directories needed to support the processing needs, who will control the directories, and the amount of storage space required. Record your information on Student Answer Sheet 2.

❷ At this time your instructor will provide you with information regarding the physical environment of the file server on which you will implement your system. Based on this information, record the specifications of the file server to be used in the appropriate tables on Student Answer Sheet 2.

Assignment 2-3: **Determine the Volumes**

❶ The file server to which you have been assigned already has the volumes you will use for your Superior Technical College project. Your instructor will give you information regarding the structure of your assigned file server. Record your file server's volume information on Student Answer Sheet 2.

Assignment 2-4: **Design the Directory Structure**

❶ Design a directory structure that will meet the processing needs of Superior Technical College's administrative office. When you design the structure, include a programs directory that contains subdirectories for the academic programs divided by the Business and Trades divisions, as shown in Figure 2-13.

FIGURE 2-13: Subdirectories for the Business and Trades Divisions

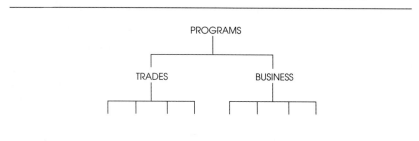

Record your structure using the volume and directory worksheets provided on Student Answer Sheet 2. Grading will be based on the neatness and readability of your directory structure as well as the design. Use valid DOS (eight-character) names for your directories and subdirectories. At this time, use an employee's first or last name for home directories.

A volume worksheet records the basic structure of each volume. This worksheet should show only the primary directories of the volume. Use a directory worksheet to record the details of more complex directory structures. (*Note*: Because you are sharing your file server with other student organizations, in Chapter 3 you will create your structure in your home directory rather than on the root of a volume.) If a directory has a simple structure consisting of one or two subdirectories, you can include the entire structure on the volume worksheet.

The directory worksheet records detailed information about each directory structure not completely recorded on the volume worksheet. Use a separate subdirectory worksheet for each structure that needs to be more fully defined.

Turn In Materials If instructed to turn in materials, assemble Student Answer Sheet 2, the volume worksheets, and the directory worksheets and turn them in to your instructor on or before the specified due date. *Note:* Be sure you save a copy of your finished directory structure and volume and directory worksheets to refer to when you do the Chapter 3 project.

Student Name: _____ Date: _____

Assignment 2-1: **Define Processing Needs**

❶ Fill in your user processing requirements below.

Username	Applications Used	Files Accessed	Printers Needed	Works With

❷ Define your workgroups below.

Workgroup Name	Users

Assignment 2-2: **Determine Storage Requirements**

❶ Complete the storage requirements table below.

Directory Area	Files or Description of Data	Controlling Users	Other Users	Disk Space Required

Total disk space = _____

❷ Fill in file server specifications and disk usage below.

File Server	Disk Usage
DOS partition	
NetWare system files	
Superior Technical College data	
Total	

File Server	Hardware Specifications
Microprocessor	
Bus	
RAM	
Video	
Keyboard	
Disk controller	
Disk drives	
Diskette drive	

Assignment 2-3: **Determine the Volumes**

❶ Record your file server's volume information below.

Volume Name	Capacity

Assignment 2-4: **Design the Directory Structure**

❶ Design your directory structure and record it below. Complete your volume and directory worksheets on the following page. *Note:* Be sure to keep a copy of your completed directory structure and volume and directory worksheets. You'll need them as you complete projects in later chapters.

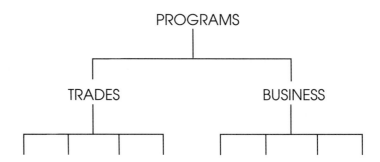

Directory Worksheet

Created by: _____   Date: _____

Directory name:

_____

Volume Worksheet

Created by: _____   Date: _____

Volume name:

_____

In this chapter you will:

- Load ODI driver software to attach a

  workstation to the network

- Use the NETX shell to access a file server

- Log in to your assigned file server

- Establish a password for your user

  account

- Use NetWare commands to see

  information about each volume

- Create the directory structure you

  designed in Chapter 2

- Transfer files within your directory

  structure

- Document your directory structure and

  files

CREATING THE DIRECTORY STRUCTURE

In this chapter you will continue to follow Leslie, the network administrator for PC Solutions, as she learns to use NetWare commands to attach her workstations to the network, log in to her file server, and create and work with the directory structure she designed in Chapter 2. The Superior Technical College project at the end of the chapter gives you the opportunity to apply these commands by creating and working with your own directory structure. (*Note*: So that the chapter case parallels the Superior Technical College project you will do at the end of the chapter, the PC Solutions structure will be created in a directory rather than on the actual root of the volume.)

THE PC SOLUTIONS CASE

On Saturday morning Leslie and Jake, a Certified NetWare Engineer from EDP, an equipment provider, installed the new file server and set up the workstations. Leslie was glad that Ben followed her recommendation to purchase the equipment from EDP; the company even installed the RG58 cable for PC Solutions and tested all the connections. Jake agreed with Leslie's decision to use the Ethernet topology because it is economical and can provide adequate speed and expansion capability for a network of the size that PC Solutions requires. During the installation process, Jake asked Leslie what volumes she wanted him to create on the server. Because she had spent some time designing the directory structure prior to getting the file server, she knew that she needed to create a SYS volume on the 120MB drive and a DATA volume on the 500MB drive. (Your instructor can provide you with a detailed description of the installation process.)

ATTACHING TO THE FILE SERVER

Once the file server was running and the RG58 cable connected to each of the workstations, Leslie was anxious to attach the workstations to the file server so that she could implement the directory structure. Jake explained that before a DOS workstation can use a network card to communicate to the file server it needs three software components. The first of these is the network card **driver**, a software component that controls the physical transmission of data packets over the wire.

The second software component is the **protocol stack**, which controls the formatting of the data within the physical packets. "By default NetWare uses the IPX protocol on DOS machines," said Jake, "but TCP/IP is another popular protocol stack that is used on many computers running the Unix operating system."

Jake explained that two methods are used to load the card driver and IPX protocol on the workstation. The first method is to create a customized IPX.COM program by running the WSGEN.EXE program from the WSGEN diskette supplied with the NetWare software. To customize an IPX.COM program, the user inserts the WSGEN diskette in a drive, changes the DOS prompt to that drive, and types the command "WSGEN." When WSGEN is run, the program first asks the user to select the type of network card. Then it allows the user to select the configuration for the card, including interrupt number and memory address. WSGEN then links the selected card driver to the IPX protocol, thus creating a customized IPX.COM program that can send packets over the network topology. Once the IPX.COM program has been created, the card driver and IPX protocol stack can be loaded by simply running the IPX.COM program.

The second method is to use ODI drivers. "I prefer to use ODI drivers because you don't need to run WSGEN to create a customized IPX.COM," said Jake. Jake showed Leslie how she could copy the ODI driver files (LSL.COM and IPXODI.COM) from the \DOSODI subdirectory of the WSGEN diskette to her workstation. "Novell ships several popular ODI-compatible card drivers with the WSGEN diskette," explained Jake. He told Leslie that if she were using IBM Token Ring cards she would also need to copy the program TOKEN.COM along with LSL.COM and IPXODI.COM.

Next Jake showed Leslie how to load the ODI drivers into a workstation. He told her to first load a program called LSL.COM, which allows the workstation to work with more than one protocol on the same network card. For example, LSL.COM lets you communicate to a Unix host using TCP/IP at the same time your workstation is attached to a NetWare file server using IPX.

FIGURE 3-1: Leslie's screen after drivers are loaded

```
C:\NETWARE>LSL
NetWare Link Support Layer  v2.01 (921105)
(C) Copyright 1990, 1992 Novell, Inc.  All Rights Reserved.

Max Boards 4, Max Stacks 4
Buffers 8, Buffer size 1500 bytes, Memory pool 4096 bytes

C:\NETWARE>PEMLID
Ethernet Pocket Adapter MLID  v1.02A (921117)


Int 7, Port 378, Node Address E8FFA42E
Max Frame 1514 bytes, Line Speed 10 Mbps
Board 1, Frame ETHERNET_II
Board 2, Frame ETHERNET_802.3

C:\NETWARE>IPXODI

NetWare IPX/SPX Protocol  v2.10 (930122)
(C) Copyright 1990-1993 Novell, Inc.  All Rights Reserved.

Bound to logical board 2 (PEMLID) : Protocol ID 0

C:\NETWARE>
```

After LSL was loaded, Leslie loaded the card driver program. The cards came with a driver program called SMCPLUS.COM. Jake elaborated on how the card driver will look for a file called NET.CFG. "The NET.CFG file contains options for the driver such as interrupt and memory addresses," he explained. "If there is no NET.CFG file, the card driver will use the default values documented in the card's manual."

After the card driver program initialized the network card, Leslie loaded the IPX protocol by running the ODI program IPXODI.COM. Figure 3-1 shows the results of loading ODI software to access the network.

"See if you can access the network drive F: yet," prompted Jake. Leslie typed "F:" and pressed the Enter key. She received the message "Invalid drive specification" because, as Jake explained, DOS is not designed to use the NetWare drivers. DOS needs more software to allow it to access the network.

The third software component necessary on DOS machines, the **shell** program, provides an interface between the DOS version on the workstation and the network software. Jake explained that the shell program acts as a traffic cop, directing requests to the file server, sending them through the IPX protocol, or sending them directly to the local DOS for processing at the workstation. "When you type a command," explained Jake, "the shell will examine it. If it is a NetWare command it will be sent to the file server; otherwise it is passed along to DOS."

FIGURE 3-2: The relationship between software and DOS

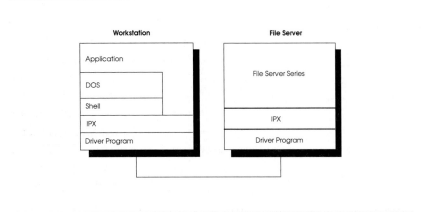

Jake drew the diagram shown in Figure 3-2 to illustrate the relationship between the three layers of software and DOS. Packets coming from the network card are received by the card driver program. The LSL program passes the packet to the proper protocol stack, which in this case is the IPXODI software. IPX makes the request contained in the packet available to the shell. The shell program interprets the request and passes it to the correct DOS routine. The DOS routine "thinks" it received a message from one of its devices and passes the message on to the application or user.

The shell program most commonly used on DOS-based computers is called NETX.COM. "The X represents the version of DOS," said Jake. "In the old days there were several shell programs: NET2, NET3, NET4, and NET5, one for each version of DOS." Jake told Leslie that Novell has created a version of the shell called NETX that automatically adapts to the DOS version on which it is running.

The latest version is NETX.EXE. Jake warned Leslie to erase the NETX.COM program before upgrading a workstation to NETX.EXE. "If you don't, the workstation will continue to use the old NETX.COM version because when two files have the same name, DOS will load the program with the COM extension before the program with the EXE extension," he cautioned.

Leslie typed the command "NETX" and pressed the Enter key. In a few seconds the NETX program displayed a message that it is running on DOS 5.0 and that it is attached to file server VOYAGER_311. Leslie knew this meant that NETX had found the file server. She next typed "F:" and pressed the Enter key to change the network drive letter to F:.

FIGURE 3-3: Leslie's screen after attempt to access NetWare drive F:

```
C:\NETWARE>NETX

NetWare Workstation Shell  v3.32 (930217)
(C) Copyright 1993 Novell, Inc.  All Rights Reserved.
Patent Pending.

Running on DOS V5.00

FILE HANDLES 60
Configuration File NET.CFG

Attached to server VOYAGER_311
06-20-93    1:40:10 pm

C:\NETWARE>F:

F:\LOGIN>
```

FIGURE 3-4: Leslie's screen after the DOS MEM/P | MORE command is used

Name	Size in Decimal		Size in Hex
MSDOS	17072	(16.7K)	42B0
STACKER	41792	(40.8K)	A340
HIMEM	1072	(1.0K)	430
ANSI	4192	(4.1K)	1060
COMMAND	3456	(3.4K)	D80
win386	3344	(3.3K)	D10
DOSKEY	4128	(4.0K)	1020
WIN	1584	(1.5K)	630
LSL	4992	(4.9K)	1380
SMCPLUS	4144	(4.0K)	1030
IPXODI	16288	(15.9K)	3FA0
NETX	49104	(48.0K)	BFD0
COMMAND	3616	(3.5K)	E20
FREE	500128	(488.4K)	7A1A0

```
Total  FREE :     500128    (488.4K)

Total bytes available to programs :
500128    (488.4K)
Largest executable program size :
499904    (488.2K)

F:\LOGIN>
```

The results of loading the NETX program and accessing drive F: are shown in Figure 3-3.

Leslie remembered that when the shell program loads, it sends out a request for a file server. Unless you specify otherwise, the shell program will attach to the first file server that responds. If the shell does not receive a response from a file server, possibly due to a bad cable connection or improperly installed software, it will display the message "File server not found." If there are multiple file servers on the network, NETX may attach to a file server other than the one normally used. In that situation, you can type the name of the preferred server following the NETX command, NETX *ps=server_name*. The *Preferred Server = server_name* statement could also be placed in the NET.CFG file to tell NETX to attach to a specific file server.

Leslie knew that the SLIST command can be used to check which file server her shell attached to. When a user cannot log in on a multiserver network, this is one of the first things to check.

"The NETX program takes up about 50K of the 640K DOS conventional memory," Jake stated. To check the contents of the workstation memory, Leslie entered the DOS command, MEM /P | MORE, with the results shown in Figure 3-4. "The combination of NETX, IPXODI, SMCPLUS, and LSL takes up over 72K," Leslie noted. Jake explained how the XMSNETX program could be used to load the shell into extended memory. However, Jake warned her that she cannot use this program if she specifies the DOS=HIGH statement in the CONFIG.SYS file. "If your workstation uses expanded memory, you can use the program EMSNETX to load the shell into the expanded memory area," Jake explained. "However, expanded memory is slower and you will lose some performance if you take that option." (Your instructor can provide you with an explanation of expanded and extended memory.)

FIGURE 3-5: Leslie's screen after the NETWARE.BAT file is created

```
C:\>COPY CON NETWARE.BAT
@ECHO OFF
CD \NETWARE
LSL
SMCPLUS
IPXODI
NETX PS=VOYAGER_311
F:
^Z
        1 file(s) copied

C:\>TYPE NETWARE.BAT
@ECHO OFF
CD \NETWARE
LSL
SMCPLUS
IPXODI
NETX PS=VOYAGER_311
F:

C:\>
```

Because typing all these commands takes time and it's easy to make mistakes, Leslie decided to create a DOS batch file called NETWARE.BAT to automate this process. She used the DOS COPY CON command to create the NETWARE.BAT file, as shown in Figure 3-5.

After all the commands were entered, Leslie pressed the F6 key, then the Enter key. The COPY command then saved the file to disk. Now whenever she types the command NETWARE from the C:\> DOS prompt, the ODI drivers and NETX shell program will be automatically loaded.

Jake and Leslie decided they had accomplished all the tasks needed to set up the file server. Leslie determined that she would build the directory structure on Monday.

FIGURE 3-6: Leslie's screen showing the file server welcome message

```
F:\LOGIN>LOGIN VOYAGER_311\SUPERVISOR
Device LPT1: re-routed to queue CLASSROOM on server VOYAGER_311.
Good morning, SUPERVISOR.

Drive  A:   maps to a local disk.
Drive  B:   maps to a local disk.
Drive  C:   maps to a local disk.
Drive  D:   maps to a local disk.
Drive  E:   maps to a local disk.
Drive  F: = VOYAGER_311\SYS:  \SYSTEM
    -----
SEARCH1:  = Z:. [VOYAGER_311\SYS:  \PUBLIC]
SEARCH2:  = Y:. [VOYAGER_311\SYS:  \PUBLIC\IBM_PC\MSDOS\V5.00]
SEARCH3:  = C:\WINWORD
SEARCH4:  = C:\WINDOWS
SEARCH5:  = C:\DOS
SEARCH6:  = C:\MOUSE
SEARCH7:  = C:\APM
SEARCH8:  = C:\SOFTWARE\WP51
SEARCH9:  = C:\SOFTWARE\DBASE

F:\SYSTEM>
```

LOGGING IN AND SETTING THE PASSWORD

On Monday morning, Leslie was anxious to begin building her directory structure. She turned on her workstation and typed "NETWARE" to run her DOS batch file. It attached to the file server and presented her with the F:\LOGIN> prompt. She next typed the command "LOGIN SUPERVISOR". The username SUPERVISOR gives Leslie all rights to the server, users, and file system. Jake suggested that she create a username called ADMIN and give it all rights to the software and data directories she normally works with. "You can use the ADMIN username to do most of your work, logging in as SUPERVISOR only when necessary," Jake said. After she logged in, Leslie's workstation displayed a welcome screen from the file server, as shown in Figure 3-6.

FIGURE 3-7: Leslie's screen after she entered her password

```
F:\>SETPASS
Enter new password for VOYAGER_311/SUPERVISOR:
Retype new password for VOYAGER_311/SUPERVISOR:
The password for VOYAGER_311/SUPERVISOR has been changed.


F:\>
```

FIGURE 3-8: Leslie's screen after she tested her password

```
F:\>LOGOUT
SUPERVISOR logged out from server VOYAGER_311 connection 1.
Login time:  Monday  June  21, 1993  8:00 am
Logout time: Monday  June  21, 1993  9:01 am


F:\LOGIN>LOGIN SUPERVISOR
Enter your password:
Device LPT1: re-routed to queue CLASSROOM on server VOYAGER_311.
Good morning, SUPERVISOR.

Drive  A:   maps to a local disk.
Drive  B:   maps to a local disk.
Drive  C:   maps to a local disk.
Drive  D:   maps to a local disk.
Drive  E:   maps to a local disk.
Drive  F: = VOYAGER_311\SYS:  \SYSTEM
         ----
SEARCH1:  = Z:. [VOYAGER_311\SYS:  \PUBLIC]
SEARCH2:  = Y:. [VOYAGER_311\SYS:  \PUBLIC\IBM_PC\MSDOS\V5.00]

F:\SYSTEM>
```

FIGURE 3-9: Leslie's screen after she used the VOLINFO command

Volume Information 3.54					Monday June 21, 1993 9:02 am		
User SUPERVISOR On File Server VOYAGER_311							

Page 1/1	Total	Free	Total	Free	Total	Free
Volume name	SYS		DATA			
KiloBytes	25,200	7,360	5,388	992		
Directories	3,424	2,405	2,208	1,676		
Volume name						
KiloBytes						
Directories						

```
            Available Options
            Change Servers
            Update Interval
```

Leslie's first action was to establish a password for her SUPERVISOR account. Using the SETPASS program she was able to enter a password, as shown in Figure 3-7. The SETPASS program does not display the password as the user enters it; the program also asks that the password be reentered for verification. To test her new password, Leslie performed a log out, then logged in again, as shown in Figure 3-8.

OBTAINING VOLUME INFORMATION

Next Leslie wanted to check the status of the volumes Jake created. She needed to determine what volumes were mounted and how much space was available. To do this she used the VOLINFO command, as shown in Figure 3-9. She decided to record the screen to save the information for future reference.

Next she used the CHKVOL command she learned in her NetWare class. The CHKVOL command obtains additional information about the space used in each volume, as shown in Figure 3-10 on the following page. One of the advantages of NetWare 3.11 and 3.12 is that you can salvage deleted files until they are purged or their space is needed by the operating system. The CHKVOL command shown in Figure 3-10 shows the amount of space available from deleted files.

FIGURE 3-10: Leslie's screen after she used the CHKVOL command

```
F:\SYSTEM>CHKVOL SYS:

Statistics for fixed volume VOYAGER_311/SYS:

Total volume space:                        25,200  K Bytes
Space used by files:                       17,840  K Bytes
Space in use by deleted files:              6,620  K Bytes
Space available from deleted files:         6,620  K Bytes
Space remaining on volume:                  7,360  K Bytes
Space available to SUPERVISOR:              7,360  K Bytes

F:\SYSTEM>
```

FIGURE 3-11: Leslie's screen after she executed the LISTDIR /E command

```
F:\>LISTDIR SYS: /S /E

The sub-directory structure of VOYAGER_311/SYS:
Effective    Directory
-------------------------------------------------------------------
[SRWCEMFA]  ->LOGIN
[SRWCEMFA]  ->SYSTEM
[SRWCEMFA]  ->PUBLIC
[SRWCEMFA]  ->  IBM_PC
[SRWCEMFA]  ->    MSDOS
[SRWCEMFA]  ->      V5.00
[SRWCEMFA]  ->      V4.01
[SRWCEMFA]  ->      V3.30
[SRWCEMFA]  ->MAIL
[SRWCEMFA]  ->  1
[SRWCEMFA]  ->  2000001
[SRWCEMFA]  ->DELETED.SAV
[SRWCEMFA]  ->SOFTWARE
[SRWCEMFA]  ->  SP
[SRWCEMFA]  ->  DB
[SRWCEMFA]  ->  WP
16 sub-directories found

F:\>
```

FIGURE 3-12: Leslie's screen after the first and second time she executed the CD DATA: command

```
F:\>CD DATA
Invalid directory

F:\>CD DATA:

F:\>LISTDIR

Sub-directories of VOYAGER_311/DATA:
Directory
-------------------------------------------------------------------
->DELETED.SAV
1 sub-directory found

F:\>
```

Over the weekend, Leslie and Jake installed the word processing, database, and spreadsheet programs on the SYS volume. On Monday, she decided to document these directories by using the LISTDIR /S /E command, as shown in Figure 3-11. The /E option shows that the SUPERVISOR has all rights in each of the directories.

A DELETED.SAV directory, also located on each volume, is used by the NetWare operating system to keep deleted files after their directories have been deleted. If Leslie were not logged in as SUPERVISOR, she would not be able to see this or the SYS:SYSTEM directories.

CREATING THE DIRECTORY STRUCTURE

To create the directory structure for the PC Solutions data, Leslie first needed to change to the DATA volume. She recalled from her NetWare class that the NETX shell provides the ability use the DOS CD command to change to a different NetWare volume. This can be done by using the CD DATA: command, as shown in Figure 3-12. The first time Leslie typed the command, however, she received an "Invalid drive" message because she forgot to include a colon after the volume name. After correcting this mistake, she used the LISTDIR command to view the directories on the DATA volume.

(*Note*: In the real world, Leslie would create her directories at the volume level. To make this case similar to the Superior Technical College project, the PC Solutions structure Leslie will create in a directory rather than on the actual root of the DATA volume.)

FIGURE 3-13: Leslie's screen after she built the directory structure from her volume worksheet

```
F:\>MD FORMS

F:\>MD MENUS

F:\>MD BUS

F:\>MD SUPPORT

F:\>MD SALES

F:\>MD HELPDESK

F:\>MD WORK

F:\>MD SUPPORT\CATALOG

F:\>MD SUPPORT\WPPOOL

F:\>MD HELPDESK\PROBLEMS

F:\>
```

FIGURE 3-14: Leslie's screen as she built the directory structure from her BUS directory worksheet

```
F:\>CD BUS

F:\BUS>MD IS

F:\BUS>MD IS\UTILITY

F:\BUS>MD GL

F:\BUS>MD PAYROLL

F:\BUS>MD BUDGETS

F:\BUS>MD USERS

F:\BUS>MD WORK

F:\BUS>
```

FIGURE 3-15: Leslie's screen after she typed "LISTDIR /S"

```
The sub-directory structure of VOYAGER_311/DATA:
Directory
---------------------------------------------------
->DELETED.SAV
->FORMS
->MENUS
->BUS
->   IS
->      UTILITY
->   GL
->   PAYROLL
->   BUDGETS
->   USERS
->   WORK
->SUPPORT
->   CATALOG
->   WPPOOL
->SALES
->HELPDESK
->   PROBLEMS
->WORK
18 sub-directories found

F:\>LISTDIR /S > PRN
```

In Leslie's NetWare class she learned that user home directories can be created by the SYSCON utility, along with the usernames. Therefore, she has decided not to make other user home directories at this time. It will be easier to let NetWare do this for her later, when she creates the user accounts. All Leslie needed to do is make the directories where the user's home subdirectories will be located. She then proceeded to use standard DOS commands to build the directory structure from her volume and directory worksheets, as shown in Figures 3-13 and 3-14.

Next Leslie typed the NetWare command LISTDIR /S to document the directory structure, as shown in Figure 3-15. In her NetWare class, Leslie learned that she can enter the LISTDIR /H command to see all possible LISTDIR options.

COPYING FILES

Mary Read gave Leslie a diskette containing some of the standard forms that PC Solutions uses. In addition to copying all files with the extension FRM, Leslie will need to copy certain specific files by filename into the forms directory she just created. In her NetWare class, Leslie learned that it is best to use the Novell NCOPY command whenever you copy files to or from NetWare directories. The DOS COPY or XCOPY commands will work, but NCOPY is more efficient because it goes directly to the network instead of being redirected by the shell. In addition to being more efficient, NCOPY also allows you to specify the complete NetWare path, as shown in Figure 3-16 on the following page. As with the DOS XCOPY command, the /V option can be used to verify that the files are copied correctly. The /S option will copy all subdirectories

FIGURE 3-16: Leslie's screen after she executed the NCOPY command

```
F:\>NCOPY A:*.FRM    DATA:FORMS /V
From A:
To   VOYAGER_311/DATA:\FORMS
     WORK.FRM       to WORK.FRM
     MEMO.FRM       to MEMO.FRM
     SIRS.FRM       to SIRS.FRM
     ORDER.FRM      to ORDER.FRM

     4 files copied.

F:\>NCOPY A:STAFF.DEV  DATA:FORMS /V
From A:
To   VOYAGER_311/DATA:\FORMS
     STAFF.DEV      to STAFF.DEV

     1 file copied.

F:\>
```

FIGURE 3-17: Leslie's screen after she used the RENDIR command

```
F:\>RENDIR DATA:BUS  BUSINESS
Directory renamed to BUSINESS.

F:\>LISTDIR

Sub-directories of VOYAGER_311/DATA:
Directory
-----------------------------------------------------------------------------
->DELETED.SAV
->FORMS
->MENUS
->BUSINESS
->SUPPORT
->SALES
->HELPDESK
->WORK
8 sub-directories found

F:\>
```

and associated files into the target directory. As with the LISTDIR command, you can use the /H option to display a list of all available NCOPY option flags.

RENAMING DIRECTORIES

After looking at her directory structure, Leslie decided she didn't like the name BUS for the business office directory; she wanted to change the directory name to BUSINESS. Because the DOS RENAME command cannot be used to rename directories, this can be a messy process when only DOS commands are used: Leslie would need to create the new directory, use XCOPY to copy all files into the new directory, and then use DOS commands to remove the old directory structure.

However, Leslie remembered that NetWare has a RENDIR command, which has the same syntax as the DOS RENAME command. To use RENDIR, Leslie specified the original path name, followed by the new path name, as shown in Figure 3-17. Leslie could have used the NetWare FILER utility to rename and create directories, but she felt it was faster to use the DOS commands rather than start FILER and go through all the menus. She will want to use the FILER utility later when she performs more complex tasks, such as assigning trustees to her directories.

DOCUMENTING DIRECTORIES AND FILES

Leslie wanted to document the work she's done before she stopped for lunch. After lunch, she planned to ask to Ed Low for his spreadsheet files for the budget directory.

To list all the directories, Leslie used the LISTDIR /S >PRN command, similar to the one she used earlier on the SYS volume. Next, Leslie wanted to get a directory of all files in the FORMS directory. She planned to give this list to Mary to verify that all the files she wanted have been copied. She could have used the DOS DIR command, but she recalled that NetWare versions 2.2 and above have a command called NDIR. This command will give her more information than the DOS DIR command about files stored on a NetWare drive. To get a list of all the files in the FORMS directory, Leslie decided to use the NDIR command, as shown in Figure 3-18.

FIGURE 3-18: Leslie's screen after the NDIR command is executed

```
F:\>NDIR DATA:FORMS
VOYAGER_311/DATA:FORMS

Files:               Size      Last Updated      Flags              Owner
---------------      --------  ------------      ------------------ --------
MEMO       FRM            143  8-30-92   3:17p [Rw----------------] SUPERVISO
ORDER      FRM          1,405  6-21-92   3:02p [Rw----------------] SUPERVISO
SIRS       FRM          7,146 10-06-90   8:29a [Rw----------------] SUPERVISO
STAFF      DEV          1,758 10-06-90   8:39a [Rw----------------] SUPERVISO
WORK       FRM          1,998  8-30-90   3:12p [Rw----------------] SUPERVISO

        12,450 bytes in   5 files
        24,576 bytes in   6 blocks

F:\>
```

The NDIR command has a large number of options and uses. The format of the NDIR command is

NDIR (*path*) (/*option*...)

The path can be any valid Net-Ware path specified as *volume:directory\subdirectory\filespec*. The *filespec* can contain the global file identifiers (* and ?) similar to the DOS DIR command. For example, to list all files in the FORMS directory that have the extension .WP, Leslie would enter

NDIR DATA:TUTORIAL\FORMS*.WP

Leslie could also have used the NDIR command to scan the current directory and all subdirectories by specifying the /SUB option. For example, to find the file named JAN93.WK1 anywhere in the TUTORIAL directory structure, Leslie would type

NDIR DATA:TUTORIAL\JAN93.WK1/SUB

The /FO option can be used to list only the files, while the /DO option lists only directories and subdirectories. The /OW EQ *user-name* option lists only files created by the username specified. The /SI GR # option lists all files with byte size greater than the value specified. To list all files smaller than a specified number of bytes, use the /SI LE # option. The /AC BEF *mm-dd-yy* option can be used to list all files that have not been accessed since the date specified.

FIGURE 3-19: Leslie's screen after the list of files is sorted

```
F:\>NDIR DATA:FORMS/*.*  /SI GR 1500  /SORT SI
VOYAGER_311/DATA:FORMS

Files:               Size      Last Updated      Flags              Owner
---------------      --------  ------------      ------------------ --------
STAFF      DEV          1,758 10-06-90   8:39a [Rw-A------------] SUPERVISO
WORK       FRM          1,998  8-30-90   3:12p [Rw-A------------] SUPERVISO
SIRS       FRM          7,146 10-06-90   8:29a [Rw-A------------] SUPERVISO

        10,902 bytes in   3 files
        16,384 bytes in   4 blocks

F:\>
```

You can use the /SORT option to sort the files by OWner, SIze, ACcessed, UPdate, or CReate dates. Multiple options can be combined on one NDIR command. Figure 3-19 shows Leslie's use of the /SI and /SORT options to list all files greater than 1,500 bytes in sequence from smallest to largest. The /SI GR 1500 is a restriction parameter that causes NDIR to include only files larger than 1,500 bytes. Other possible comparisons include /SI LE 1500 for files less than 1,500 bytes and /SI EQ 1500 to list files having a length equal to 1,500 bytes. The /SORT SI option tells NDIR to sort the files by size. Later you will follow Leslie as she uses these and other options of the NDIR command to obtain additional information.

In Chapter 4 you'll follow Leslie's steps as she sets up a way for PC Solutions users to access files on various devices and storage areas.

In this chapter the following NetWare commands were used to perform the functions described below.

WSGEN This program is found on the WSGEN diskette provided by Novell with NetWare. It allows the installer to create a customized version of the IPX.COM program that contains the correct driver software and configuration for the network card installed in a workstation.

IPX.COM This program is created by the WSGEN process and contains the card driver software and NetWare IPX protocol. It must be loaded first in order to attach the workstation to the server.

ODI Drivers Open Data Interface (ODI) drivers are a more flexible alternative to using the IPX.COM program because they provide the ability to use other protocols such as TCP/IP and do not need to be created using the WSGEN software each time a change is needed. The following ODI programs are provided on the WSGEN diskette in the DOSODI directory.

LSL.COM This is the link support layer when the ODI drivers are used. LSL allows multiple protocols such as IPX and TCP/IP to run on a workstation and access the network card to send packets on the network.

Network Card Drivers ODI-compatible driver software controls the network card. Examples in the text include TOKEN.COM and SMCPLUS.COM. Standard drivers such as TOKEN.COM are included on the WSGEN diskette in the DOSODI directory.

IPXODI.COM This is the IPX protocol software. It must be loaded after both LSL and the card driver software have been run.

NETX.COM or NETX.EXE This is the shell program that attaches DOS to the file server and provides the workstation with access to drive F:. It acts as a traffic cop, redirecting network functions to the file server and sending local workstation requests to DOS.

MEM /P This is a DOS 5.0 command that will display the contents of memory. In the text, Leslie used this command to see where DOS loaded the network driver software. (In DOS 6.0, the /P is replaced with a /D option.)

SETPASS   This command can be used to set or change the password of the currently logged-in user.

VOLINFO   This command displays the current status of all volumes on the file server. It includes the amount of disk space and number of directory entries that are used and available. It is a real-time command that is upadated while it is running on the workstation. Use the Esc key to exit the VOLINFO screen.

CHKVOL   This command displays the total volume space, space used by files, space in use by deleted files, space remaining on the volume, and space available to the user on the current volume.

RENDIR *old-directory-name*   This command allows you to rename a directory by specifying the old
new-directory-name   directory name followed by a space, then the new directory name.

NCOPY *source*   This command should be used to copy files to and from NetWare
destination **/S /V**   directories. The /S option will include the files in all subdirectories. The /V option will verify all files copied. The NCOPY command will work faster than the DOS COPY or XCOPY commands because more work is done at the file server.

NDIR   This is the NetWare version of the DOS DIR command. It allows the user to see more network information, such as Last Updated, Flags, and Owner. In addition, NDIR has many options to allow the user to select and sort directory information.

1. The _____ software controls the physical transmission of data packets over the network hardware.

2. Formatting the request inside the packet is controlled by the _____ software.

3. _____ is a program used to generate a customized IPX.COM program.

4. What are the names of the two ODI driver programs that are used with any network card?

5. The _____ acts as a traffic cop and redirects requests to either DOS or NetWare.

6. Given an IBM Token Ring network, which uses an ODI driver called TOKEN.COM, list software commands in the correct sequence necessary to load the ODI drivers and attach to the file server named HOST2.

7. Given a customized IPX.COM for the Token Ring network, list the software commands in the correct sequence necessary to attach the workstation to the file server named HOST2.

8. List at least one advantage of using ODI drivers compared to customizing an IPX.COM program for your workstation.

9. How much conventional memory does the NETX program use? _____K

10. In the space below, list two alternatives NetWare provides to save conventional memory space, along with a disadvantage of each.

Method	Disadvantage
_____	_____
_____	_____
_____	_____
_____	_____
_____	_____

11. Assuming file server HOST2 is your default file server, write a NetWare command to log in to file server HOST1 as SUPERVISOR.

12. What command is used to set or change the password for the username under which you are currently logged in?

13. What command will tell you how much space is currently being occupied by deleted files?

14. Assuming your default drive (F:) is currently pointing to the SYS volume, write a NetWare command to view all directories and subdirectories on the DATA volume, along with your effective rights.
F:\> _____

15. Briefly describe the purpose of the DELETED.SAV directory and its location.

16. Assuming your default driver (F:) is currently pointing to the root of the SYS volume, write an NCOPY command to copy all files from a diskette in drive A into the \BUSINESS\SPDATA directory of the DATA volume.
F:\> _____

17. Write a NetWare command to rename the SPDATA subdirectory in the previous question to \BUSINESS\BUDGETS.
F:\> _____

18. Write an NDIR command to list all files in the \BUSINESS\ BUDGETS in sequence from smallest to largest.
F:\> _____

19. Write an NDIR command to list only files larger than 5,000 bytes in the \BUSINESS\BUDGETS subdirectory.
F:\> _____

20. Write an NDIR command to search all directories and subdirectories of the DATA volume and list all files that have the extension WK1.
F:\> _____

SUPERIOR TECHNICAL COLLEGE PROJECT 3

To allow you to share the file server with other students and be able to complete your own projects, your instructor has assigned you to a file server and given you a username and directory, prefixed by your assigned student number. Depending on your file server installation, your directory may exist on either the DATA or SYS volumes. When you log in with your username, you will have all rights to your directory. In a sense, you are a "supervisor" of that portion of the file server. Other users will not have rights to access your work area.

In this project, you will work with DOS and NetWare commands to create the directory structure from the volume and directory worksheets you designed in Project 2 for Superior Technical College.

Assignment 3-1: **Attach to Your File Server**

Use either ODI drivers or a customized IPX.COM program to attach your workstation to the file server. If necessary, your instructor will supply you with a copy of the WSGEN diskette and instructions on using ODI drivers or run WSGEN to create a customized IPX.COM for your workstation.

❶ Load the driver program(s) and record the requested information about the network card on Student Answer Sheet 3. When you load the shell, type the command (replacing *server_name* with the name of your default file server) **NETX PS=server_name** and press **[Enter]**.

❷ Create and test a batch file that will automate the loading of the drivers and shell programs. Record the contents of the batch file on Student Answer Sheet 3.

Assignment 3-2: **Log In and Set a Password**

❶ Use the LOGIN program to log in to your assigned file server using the name assigned to you by your instructor. Type **LOGIN** and press **[Enter]**. Record the name in the appropriate location on Student Answer Sheet 3.

❷ Use the SETPASS command to set a password for your username. Record it on Student Answer Sheet 3.

❸ Use the LOGOUT command to log out of the server. Record the logout information on Student Answer Sheet 3.

❹ Replacing the variables with the correct server name and your name, type the command **LOGIN server_name\your_name** and press **[Enter]**. Record the command you enter on Student Answer Sheet 3.

Assignment 3-3: **Obtain Volume Information**

❶ Use the VOLINFO command to determine the name, kilobyte, and directory information for all volumes mounted. Record the information on Student Answer Sheet 3.

❷ Use the CHKVOL command to determine the amount of space available from deleted files on each volume. Record the information on Student Answer Sheet 3.

❸ Use the LISTDIR command to list the name of each directory on the SYS volume, along with your effective rights. Record the LISTDIR information on Student Answer Sheet 3. Use the information from the LISTDIR /S command to fill out a volume worksheet form for the SYS volume on a separate sheet of paper.

❹ If necessary, use the CD command to change to the volume which is to contain your Superior Technical College directory. Record the CD command you used on Student Answer Sheet 3.

Assignment 3-4: **Create Your Directory Structure**

❶ Within your directory, use DOS MD and CD commands to make all the directories and subdirectories you defined on your volume and directory worksheets. (Do not make the users' home directories at this time. It will be easier to do this later when you create the usernames.) Print your screen after creating the directories and subdirectories for each volume and directory worksheet. Attach the printouts to Student Answer Sheet 3.

Assignment 3-5: **Copy Files**

❶ Use the DOS CD command to change your default path to the beginning of your home directory. The DOS prompt should display the F:\ prompt followed by your directory name. Insert your student work diskette in drive A: or B: of your workstation. Use the NCOPY command to copy all files from the \FORMS directory of your diskette in the shared FORMS directory you created for Superior Technical College. Record the command you used on Student Answer Sheet 3.

Assignment 3-6: **Rename Directories**

❶ Use the LISTDIR command to obtain a hard copy of all the directories and subdirectories in your work area. Attach the printout to Student Answer Sheet 3.

❷ Use the RENDIR command to rename the shared forms directory to STCFORMS. Record the command you used on Student Answer Sheet 3.

Assignment 3-7: **Use the NDIR Command**

❶ Use the NDIR command along with DOS redirection to obtain a printout of a directory listing all the files you copied to the CTSFORMS directory. Attach the printout to Student Answer Sheet 3.

❷ Use the NDIR command to obtain a hard copy of a directory listing all the files in your CTSFORMS directory that are larger than 1K. Sequence the listing by file size. Record the command you used on Student Answer Sheet 3.

Turn in Materials Assemble Student Answer Sheet 3 and the printouts from Assignments 3-4, 3-6, and 3-7. If instructed, turn in the materials to your instructor on or before the scheduled due date.

Student Name: _____ Date: _____

Assignment 3-1: **Attach to Your File Server**

❶ Record your network card information below.
Type of card: _____
Name of ODI driver: _____
Interrupt: _____ Memory address: _____
I/O port: _____

❷ In the space below, record the contents of the batch file necessary to automate loading your workstation network drivers.

Assignment 3-2: **Log In and Set a Password**

❶ Record your assigned name here. _____

❷ Record your password here. _____

❸ Record your logout information below.
Connection number: _____
Login time: _____
Logout time: _____

❹ Command used: _____

Assignment 3-3: **Obtain Volume Information**

❶ Record VOLINFO command information below.

Volume Name	Kilobytes		Directories	
	Total: Free:		Total: Free:	
	Total: Free:		Total: Free:	
	Total: Free:		Total: Free:	

❷ Record CHKVOL command information below.

Space used by files		
Space in use by deleted files		
Space available from deleted files		
Space available to you		

❸ Record LISTDIR command information below.

Directory Name	Effective Rights

❹ Command used: _____

Assignment 3-4: **Create Your Directory Structure**

❶ Attach printouts of your screen, showing your directories and subdirectories.

Assignment 3-5: **Copy Files**

❶ Command used: _____

Assignment 3-6: **Rename Directories**

❶ Attach the printout showing the results of the LISTDIR command.

❷ Command used: _____

Assignment 3-7: **Use the NDIR Command**

❶ Attach the printout showing the results of the NDIR command.

❷ Command used: _____

In this chapter you will learn to:

- Plan drive pointer usage for an organization

- Use the MAP command to view drive mappings

- Use the MAP command to create and delete regular drive pointers

- Use the MAP command to create and delete search drive pointers

- Use the SESSION utility to maintain drive pointers

- Include drive-mapping commands in your personal LOGIN script

- Test your personal LOGIN script

WORKING WITH DRIVE POINTERS

In both DOS and NetWare environments, drive pointers play an important role in accessing files on different devices and storage areas. A **drive pointer** is a letter of the alphabet that is used to reference areas in which files can be stored. By default DOS reserves the first five drive pointers, A through E, for its use. In Novell NetWare the DOS pointers are referred to as the **local drive pointers** and usually reference physical disk drives. For example, letters A and B are reserved for the diskette drives, and C represents the first fixed drive. Drive letters D and E can be used for additional fixed disk drives or CD-ROMs, or they can be assigned by the SUBST command to point to a directory on one of the existing drives. By using a local drive pointer, you can use the CD command to move from directory to directory on that drive.

In NetWare, drive pointers are used to reference locations within the directory structure. The DOS shell, NETX, assigns the first drive letter not reserved for DOS, usually F, to the SYS:LOGIN directory of the file server to which it attaches. Thereafter, any reference to a NetWare drive pointer will be rerouted by the shell program to the file server. When a user logs in, the first NetWare drive pointer, F, is usually remapped to point at a designated area within the directory structure.

Drive pointers play an important role in the network environment. In Novell NetWare, drive pointers are defined as local, network, or search. Local drive pointers, A through E, are controlled by DOS. **Network drive pointers**, letters that are mapped to point at areas in the network directory structure where files are stored, can help users move around the directory structure more easily. Many application software packages also require network drive pointers to find files and overlays.

Network drive pointers can be of two types: regular or root. A **root drive pointer** appears to the user or an application as if the default path is at the root or beginning of the drive or volume. For example, if drive F: were mapped as a regular drive pointer to the DATA:\BUSINESS directory, the default prompt would appear as F:\BUSINESS. If it were mapped as a root drive pointer to the same DATA:\BUSINESS directory, the default prompt would appear as F:\>.

Search drive pointers allow a user located in a data directory to access software and commands located in other directories. Using search drives allows data to be placed in directories separate from the application software. In many ways search drives work much like the DOS PATH command. When a command file or program is not in the default directory, the DOS PATH command specifies a sequence of directories for DOS. If the command or program is not in any of the directories specified in the PATH statement, the message "Bad command or file name" is displayed.

Just as the DOS PATH command can be used to tell DOS where to look for command or program files, search drives can be used to specify software areas for the shell to look in when files are not located in the default directory. Search drives work for finding both program files (extension .COM, .EXE, or .BAT) and data files.

Each search drive is assigned the letter S followed by a sequential number, starting with S1. A maximum of 16 search drives, S1 through S16, can be assigned. Each search drive points to only one directory path. In addition to being assigned S1 through S16, search drives are assigned a drive pointer, starting with Z:. The S1 search drive would be assigned to drive pointer Z:, S2 assigned to drive pointer Y:, S3 to X:, and so forth.

When the shell looks for software on NetWare directories, search drives are more efficient than the DOS PATH statement because the shell can work directly with search drives and does not need to go through DOS. Search drives also make it easier to add, change, or remove directories from the search sequence rather than retyping the DOS PATH statement.

Because each workstation keeps track of its drive pointers in memory, each workstation can use the same drive letter to point to different directory paths. For example, Leslie's workstation can have drive F: mapped to the DATA:\BUSINESS\IS directory, while George Moon's workstation has its drive F: mapped to the DATA:\SALES directory.

Planning and implementing a proper set of network and search drive pointers are important steps in setting up a successful network environment. In this chapter's case, you will see how Leslie works with NetWare drive mapping commands to plan a proper drive mapping environment for PC Solutions. The Superior Technical College project at the end of the chapter will allow you to apply these commands and concepts to your own network.

THE PC SOLUTIONS CASE

Once Leslie established a working directory structure, she wanted to make it easier to use. To allow users to move around the structure and access data and applications easily, she knew she would need to establish some network and search drive pointers. However, she was aware that too many drive pointers can be confusing, inefficient, and difficult to maintain. Leslie wants to develop a universal set of drive pointers that will be available to all users.

PLANNING DRIVE POINTERS

She reasoned that if a user wanted some special drive pointers to meet specific needs, she could establish them later. She decides that, at a minimum, she now wants to establish the following network drive pointers for each user:

■ A drive pointer to the root of each volume:

F: to the SYS volume

G: to the DATA volume

These drive pointers will allow all users to change to another volume quickly without using the CD *volume-name:* command. They also provide a path for running applications. Certain application software installation programs require that a drive letter and path be assigned to reference file locations. This is one reason it is important to assign the same drive letter to each volume for all users.

■ A root drive pointer mapped to the user's home directory:

H: to the DATA:\path to user's home directory

This drive letter will be the starting point for users when they log in. Making this a root drive pointer is important because it prevents the user from accidentally changing the H: pointer to a different volume or directory. For example, a user can create subdirectories with the MD command and use the CD command to move around within these subdirectories, but the CD \ command will bring the user back to the beginning of the home directory rather than change to the root of the volume.

■ A root drive pointer mapped to the user's workgroup directory:

L: to the DATA:\path to user's department directory

Users can use this drive pointer to access files within their workgroup. For example, Leslie created a WORK subdirectory within each workgroup to allow those users to access common files. If a user wants to access a file in the WORK subdirectory, he or she could use the path L:\WORK*filename* instead of entering the complete path, DATA:\BUSINESS\WORK*filename*.

■ A regular drive pointer to the FORMS directory:

S: to the DATA:\FORMS directory

This drive pointer will provide access from the word processing program to the shared forms.

In addition to the network drives, Leslie wants to establish the following search drive pointers for each user:

■ Search drive S1: to the SYS:PUBLIC directory

■ Search drive S2: to the correct DOS version directory

■ Search drive S3: to the word processing software directory

■ Search drive S4: to the database software directory

■ Search drive S5: to the spreadsheet software directory

USING THE MAP COMMAND

To implement her drive pointers, Leslie decided first to set up the mappings for her SUPERVISOR account. To set up the network drive pointers, Leslie logged in as supervisor and then used MAP commands to create the drive pointers, as shown in Figure 4-1. The ROOT option used on the H: and L: drive mappings will make these drive pointers appear as though they were at the root of the drive or volume. After

FIGURE 4-1: Leslie's screen after she mapped her network drives

```
F:\>MAP G:=DATA:

Drive  G: = VOYAGER_311\DATA: \

F:\>MAP ROOT H:=SYS:SYSTEM

Drive  H: = VOYAGER_311\SYS:SYSTEM  \

F:\>MAP ROOT L:=DATA:BUSINESS\IS

Drive  L: = VOYAGER_311\DATA:BUSINESS\IS  \

F:\>MAP S:=DATA:FORMS

Drive  S: = VOYAGER_311\DATA:  \FORMS

F:\>
```

FIGURE 4-2: Leslie's screen after she checked her drive mappings

```
F:\>MAP

Drive  A:    maps to a local disk.
Drive  B:    maps to a local disk.
Drive  C:    maps to a local disk.
Drive  D:    maps to a local disk.
Drive  E:    maps to a local disk.
Drive  F: = VOYAGER_311\SYS:  \
Drive  G: = VOYAGER_311\DATA:  \
Drive  H: = VOYAGER_311\SYS:SYSTEM  \
Drive  L: = VOYAGER_311\DATA:BUSINESS\IS  \
Drive  S: = VOYAGER_311\DATA:  \FORMS
       _____
SEARCH1:   = Z:. [VOYAGER_311\SYS:  \PUBLIC]
SEARCH2:   = Y:. [VOYAGER_311\SYS:  \PUBLIC\IBM_PC\MSDOS\V5.00]

F:\>S:

S:\FORMS>H:

H:\>
```

FIGURE 4-3: Leslie's screen after the M: drive pointer was mapped and the S: drive pointer was deleted

```
H:\>MAP M:=S:

Drive  M: = VOYAGER_311\DATA:  \FORMS

H:\>MAP DEL S:

The mapping for drive S: has been deleted.

H:\>MAP

Drive  A:    maps to a local disk.
Drive  B:    maps to a local disk.
Drive  C:    maps to a local disk.
Drive  D:    maps to a local disk.
Drive  E:    maps to a local disk.
Drive  F: = VOYAGER_311\SYS:  \
Drive  G: = VOYAGER_311\DATA:  \
Drive  H: = VOYAGER_311\SYS:SYSTEM  \
Drive  L: = VOYAGER_311\DATA:BUSINESS\IS  \
Drive  M: = VOYAGER_311\DATA:  \FORMS
       _____
SEARCH1:   = Z:. [VOYAGER_311\SYS:  \PUBLIC]
SEARCH2:   = Y:. [VOYAGER_311\SYS:  \PUBLIC\IBM_PC\MSDOS\V5.00]

H:\>
```

entering the mappings, she viewed her drive pointer assignments by typing just the MAP command, as shown in Figure 4-2. In her NetWare class, Leslie learned that the backslash (\) at the end of a path indicates that a drive pointer is a root mapping drive pointer.

Next Leslie checked the drive mappings, shown in Figure 4-2. She first changed to the S: drive mapping and observed that the DOS default prompt changed to inform her that she is in the DATA:\FORMS directory. She then changed to her H: drive pointer. Because H: is a root mapping drive pointer, the DOS prompt does not show the default path to her home directory. As far as DOS is concerned, this is the beginning of the H: drive even though it is actually mapped to the SYS:SYSTEM directory.

Leslie next proceeded to create her search drive mappings. She remembered that search drive pointers start at Z: and work back through the alphabet to reduce the chance of a search drive pointer using the same letter as a network drive pointer. Because there can be as many as 16 search drive pointers, their letters could possibly range from Z to K. Leslie decided that using the letter S for the FORMS directory may interfere with assigning future search drives if she should ever need more than eight. She decided to remove the mapping of drive S: from the FORMS directory and assign drive letter M: to the FORMS directory instead. Leslie did this by first using the MAP command to map drive pointer M: to the same path as mapped for drive pointer S:. She next used the MAP DEL command to remove the S: drive pointer, as shown in Figure 4-3.

By looking at the output from the MAP command shown in Figure 4-3, Leslie saw that the S1: and S2: search

FIGURE 4-4: Leslie's screen after she established her search drive

```
F:\>PATH
PATH=Z:.;Y:.

F:\>MAP S3:=SYS:SOFTWARE\WP

SEARCH3:   = X:.  [VOYAGER_311\SYS:    \SOFTWARE\WP]

F:\>MAP S4:=SYS:SOFTWARE\SP

SEARCH4:   = W:.  [VOYAGER_311\SYS:    \SOFTWARE\SP]

F:\>MAP S16:=SYS:SOFTWARE\DB

SEARCH5:   = V:.  [VOYAGER_311\SYS:    \SOFTWARE\DB]

F:\>PATH
PATH=Z:.;Y:.;X:.;W:.;V:.

F:\>
```

FIGURE 4-5: Leslie's screen after the S: drive mapping was deleted

```
MAP DEL S3:
The search mapping for drive X: was deleted

F:\>MAP

Drive  A:   maps to a local disk.
Drive  B:   maps to a local disk.
Drive  C:   maps to a local disk.
Drive  D:   maps to a local disk.
Drive  E:   maps to a local disk.
Drive  F: = VOYAGER_311\SYS:   \
Drive  G: = VOYAGER_311\DATA:   \
Drive  H: = VOYAGER_311\SYS:SYSTEM  \
Drive  L: = VOYAGER_311\DATA:BUSINESS\IS   \
Drive  M: = VOYAGER_311\DATA:FORMS
          ———
SEARCH1:   = Z:.  [VOYAGER_311\SYS:    \PUBLIC]
SEARCH2:   = Y:.  [VOYAGER_311\SYS:    \PUBLIC\IBM_PC\MSDOS\V5.00]
SEARCH3:   = W:.  [VOYAGER_311\SYS:    \SOFTWARE\SP]
SEARCH4:   = V:.  [VOYAGER_311\SYS:    \SOFTWARE\DB]

F:\>PATH
PATH=Z:.;Y:.;W:.;V:.

F:\>
```

drives are already mapped to the SYS:PUBLIC and SYS:PUBLIC\IBM_PC\MSDOS\V5.00 directories, respectively. The default LOGIN script commands built into the NETX shell program made these mappings.

To map search drives to the SYS:SOFTWARE subdirectories, Leslie entered the MAP commands shown in Figure 4-4. In the last MAP command of Figure 4-4, Leslie used S16: as the search drive. She noticed that instead of skipping search drive numbers, NetWare used S5: because it is the next available search drive number. She recalled that NetWare will not skip search drive numbers, thus making the use of S16: a handy way to map the next search drive number instead of entering the next search drive number specifically.

The NetWare shell program uses the "path" area of the DOS environment space to store the search drive sequence. Whenever a search drive is added, NetWare includes the drive pointer associated with that search drive in the DOS path. The position of the drive pointer in the DOS path indicates its search drive number. Leslie knows that changing the DOS PATH statement will affect the NetWare search drives. To help her see how new search drive mappings affect the DOS PATH, Leslie typed the DOS PATH command before and after her MAP commands, as shown in Figure 4-4.

The MAP DEL command can also be used with search drives. Because Leslie had no software in the WP51 directory at this time, she decided to remove the search drive mapping from WP51. Figure 4-5 shows the results of removing a search drive mapping. Leslie noticed that after she deleted the search drive S3:, which she mapped to SYS:SOFTARE\WP in Figure 4-4, the search drive for SYS:SOFTWARE\SP became S3: and the search drive for SYS:SOFTWARE\DB became S4:. She also observed that the letters assigned to these directories did not change. Whenever a search drive is removed, all the higher numbered drives are resequenced to fill in any gaps. Typing the PATH command before and after deleting the drive mapping helped Leslie follow how deleting search drives changes the DOS path.

FIGURE 4-6: Leslie's screen after the S4: search drive was inserted

```
F:\>MAP INS S4:=SYS:SOFTWARE\WP
SEARCH4:  = X:. [VOYAGER_311\SYS:  \SOFTWARE\WP]

F:\>PATH
PATH=Z:.;Y:.;W:.;X:.;V:.

F:\>MAP
Drive  A:    maps to a local disk.
Drive  B:    maps to a local disk.
Drive  C:    maps to a local disk.
Drive  D:    maps to a local disk.
Drive  E:    maps to a local disk.
Drive  F: = VOYAGER_311\SYS:  \
Drive  G: = VOYAGER_311\DATA:  \
Drive  H: = VOYAGER_311\SYS:SYSTEM  \
Drive  L: = VOYAGER_311\DATA:BUSINESS\IS \
Drive  M: = VOYAGER_311\DATA:FORMS
        ─────
SEARCH1:  = Z:. [VOYAGER_311\SYS:  \PUBLIC]
SEARCH2:  = Y:. [VOYAGER_311\SYS:  \PUBLIC\IBM_PC\MSDOS\V5.00]
SEARCH3:  = W:. [VOYAGER_311\SYS:  \SOFTWARE\SP]
SEARCH4:  = X:. [VOYAGER_311\SYS:  \SOFTWARE\WP]
SEARCH5:  = V:. [VOYAGER_311\SYS:  \SOFTWARE\DB]

F:\>
```

FIGURE 4-7: Leslie's screen after she returned from break

```
F:\LOGIN>LOGIN SUPERVISOR
Enter your password:
Good morning, Supervisor

Drive  A:    maps to a local disk.
Drive  B:    maps to a local disk.
Drive  C:    maps to a local disk.
Drive  D:    maps to a local disk.
Drive  E:    maps to a local disk.
Drive  F: = VOYAGER_311\SYS:  \SYSTEM
        ─────
SEARCH1:  = Z:. [VOYAGER_311\SYS:  \PUBLIC]
SEARCH2:  = Y:. [VOYAGER_311\SYS:  \PUBLIC\IBM_PC\MSDOS\V5.00]

F:\SYSTEM>
```

New search drives can be inserted before existing search drives by using the MAP INS command as shown in Figure 4-6. Figure 4-6 also shows the use of the MAP INS command to reinsert the WP drive mapping within the existing list of search drives. After reinserting the search drive, Leslie notices that drive letter X was reassigned and existing search drives were resequenced; X was the first available drive letter NetWare found when it started from Z.

If Leslie had omitted the INS option and used the command MAP S4:=SYS:SOFTWARE\WP, the existing letter assigned to search drive 4, in this example V:, would become a regular drive pointer and the new drive mapping would be assigned to search drive 4. For that reason if she wanted to replace an existing search drive mapping, she would first use the MAP DEL command to delete the desired search drive, then use the MAP INS command to create another search drive with the same number.

INCLUDING DRIVE MAPPING IN THE LOGIN SCRIPT

Leslie decided to take a break, so she logged out of the file server. When she logged in again, she noticed that all her drive mappings were gone, as shown in Figure 4-7. Immediately she realized that she should have expected this to happen. In her NetWare class she learned that drive mappings are maintained only for the current session. When a user logs out, NetWare removes all drive mappings; they have to be remapped the next time the user logs in.

The drive mappings to SYS:PUBLIC and DOS were established by the default LOGIN script built into the NETX shell program. In Leslie's NetWare class, the instructor explained that a **LOGIN script** is a set of NetWare commands that are performed every time a user logs in. There are three types of LOGIN scripts: the system LOGIN script, the personal LOGIN script, and the default LOGIN script. The **system LOGIN script** is stored in the SYS:PUBLIC directory and is executed by all users. The **personal LOGIN script** is optional and is stored in a user's subdirectory of the SYS:MAIL directory. If a personal LOGIN script does not exist for a user, the shell program will execute the **default LOGIN script**, which contains the following commands:

```
WRITE "Good %GREETING_TIME, %LOGIN_NAME."
MAP DISPLAY OFF
MAP ERRORS OFF
MAP *1:=SYS:
MAP INS S1:=SYS:PUBLIC
MAP INS S2:=S1:IBM_PC\MSDOS\%OS_VERSION
MAP DISPLAY ON
MAP
```

To prevent losing her drive mappings in the future, Leslie decided to write her own personal LOGIN script for the SUPERVISOR account consisting of the above commands and the drive mappings she wants to use. In addition to the greeting and drive mappings, Leslie would like the system to remind her of the weekly Business Department meeting, held Mondays at 10:00 a.m. Eventually she plans to create a system LOGIN script containing necessary commands for all users.

Leslie wanted her personal LOGIN script to consist of the following commands:

```
WRITE "Good %GREETING_TIME, Supervisor."
IF DAY_OF_WEEK = "MONDAY" AND HOUR24< "10" THEN BEGIN
WRITE "Remember the meeting at 10:00 am."
PAUSE
END
MAP DISPLAY OFF
MAP F:=SYS:
MAP G:=DATA:
MAP ROOT H:=DATA:\BUSINESS\IS\SUPERVISOR
MAP ROOT L:=DATA:\BUSINESS
MAP M:=DATA:\FORMS
MAP INS S1:=SYS:PUBLIC
MAP INS S2:=S1:IBM_PC\MSDOS\%OS_VERSION
MAP INS S3:=SYS:SOFTWARE\WP51
MAP INS S4:=SYS:SOFTWARE\SP
MAP INS S5:=SYS:SOFTWARE\DB
MAP DISPLAY ON
```

The command WRITE "Good %GREETING_TIME, Supervisor" will display the message enclosed in quotes on the console when Leslie logs in. The command %GREETING_TIME is a variable that will be replaced by the string GOOD MORNING, GOOD AFTERNOON, or GOOD EVENING, depending on the time of day. (Other variables available to your LOGIN scripts are discussed in Chapter 11.)

The command IF DAY_OF_WEEK = "MONDAY" AND HOUR24< "10" THEN BEGIN will check the variables DAY_OF_WEEK and the time; if the day is Monday and the time is before 10:00 a.m., the LOGIN process will display the reminder message. The PAUSE command will stop the LOGIN process until Leslie presses any key to continue. The

END statement marks the end of the instructions to be executed when it's Monday. If it is not Monday, or if it is later than 10:00 a.m., the LOGIN process will skip to the first instruction following the END statement.

The MAP DISPLAY OFF statement will prevent the drive mappings from being displayed as they are assigned. It minimizes the clutter on the screen. Leslie remembered that the SYSCON program maintains both the system and personal LOGIN script files. To enter her personal LOGIN script she used the SYSCON program as follows:

1   At the DOS prompt, she typed SYSCON and pressed [Enter]. The SYSCON program's Available Topics menu, shown in Figure 4-8, was displayed.

FIGURE 4-8: The SYSCON Available Topics menu

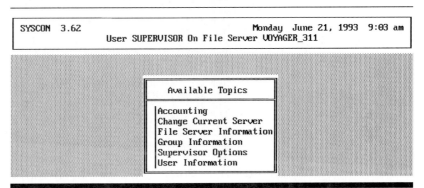

2   She used the ↓ (Down Arrow) key to highlight the User Information option and pressed [Enter]. A window showing all usernames was displayed.

3   She again used the arrow keys to highlight her SUPERVISOR username and pressed [Enter]. The User Information screen, shown in Figure 4-9, was displayed.

FIGURE 4-9: Leslie's SYSCON User Information screen

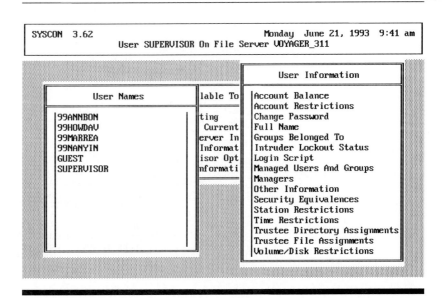

4 She then highlighted the Login Script option and pressed [Enter]. A blank screen was displayed.

5 She entered her LOGIN script commands, as shown in Figure 4-10. She pressed [Enter] after each LOGIN script statement.

FIGURE 4-10: The supervisor's personal LOGIN script screen

```
SYSCON  3.62                              Monday  June 21, 1993  9:04 am
                   User SUPERVISOR On File Server VOYAGER_311


┌────────────────────────────────────────────────────────────────────┐
│                   Login Script For User SUPERVISOR                   │
├────────────────────────────────────────────────────────────────────┤
│WRITE "Good %GREETING_TIME, Supervisor"                               │
│IF DAY_OF_WEEK = "MONDAY" AND HOUR24 < "10" THEN BEGIN                 │
│   WRITE "Remember the meeting at 10:00 am."                          │
│   PAUSE                                                              │
│END                                                                  │
│MAP DISPLAY OFF                                                      │
│MAP F:=SYS:                                                          │
│MAP G:=DATA:                                                         │
│MAP ROOT H:=SYS:SYSTEM                                               │
│MAP ROOT L:=DATA:BUSINESS\IS                                         │
│MAP M:=DATA:FORMS                                                    │
│MAP S1:=SYS:PUBLIC                                                   │
│MAP S2:=SYS:PUBLIC\IBM_PC\MSDOS\V5.00                                │
│MAP S3:=SYS:SOFTWARE\WP                                              │
│MAP S4:=SYS:SOFTWARE\SP                                              │
│MAP S5:=SYS:SOFTWARE\DB                                              │
│MAP DISPLAY ON                                                      │
└────────────────────────────────────────────────────────────────────┘
```

6 After entering the last statement, Leslie pressed the Esc key to save the LOGIN script program.

7 To exit SYSCON, Leslie used the shortcut method: she held down the Alt key while pressing [F10].

To test the supervisor's personal LOGIN script, Leslie logged out of the file server and then logged back in. The supervisor LOGIN script statements were executed, and after she typed the MAP command, she saw the drive mappings shown on the screen in Figure 4-11.

FIGURE 4-11: Leslie's screen after she logged in as supervisor and typed "MAP"

```
Enter your password:
Good morning, Supervisor
Remember the meeting at 10:00 am.
Strike any key when ready . . .

F:\>MAP

Drive  A:    maps to a local disk.
Drive  B:    maps to a local disk.
Drive  C:    maps to a local disk.
Drive  D:    maps to a local disk.
Drive  E:    maps to a local disk.
Drive  F: = VOYAGER_311\SYS:   \
Drive  G: = VOYAGER_311\DATA:   \
Drive  H: = VOYAGER_311\SYS:SYSTEM   \
Drive  L: = VOYAGER_311\DATA:BUSINESS\IS    \
Drive  M: = VOYAGER_311\DATA:   \FORMS
       ─────
SEARCH1:   = Z:. [VOYAGER_311\SYS:   \PUBLIC]
SEARCH2:   = Y:. [VOYAGER_311\SYS:   \PUBLIC\IBM_PC\MSDOS\V5.00]
SEARCH3:   = X:. [VOYAGER_311\SYS:   \SOFTWARE\WP]
SEARCH4:   = W:. [VOYAGER_311\SYS:   \SOFTWARE\SP]
SEARCH5:   = V:. [VOYAGER_311\SYS:   \SOFTWARE\DB]

F:\>
```

USING THE SESSION UTILITY

Leslie next planned to do some work in the SALES directory structure. She wanted to modify her L: drive mapping to point to the SALES directory area and add another search drive to the DATA:\BUSINESS\IS\ UTILITY subdirectory.

From her NetWare course, Leslie recalled that the SESSION utility is an "interactive" way to work with drive mappings — it uses menus and windows to allow the user to view and change the drive mappings without requiring him or her to know the syntax of the MAP command. Leslie decided to try using the SESSION utility to make some changes to her drive mappings. To add a new search drive, Leslie used the SESSION utility as follows:

1 She typed the command SESSION at the DOS prompt to display the screen shown in Figure 4-12.

FIGURE 4-12: The SESSION Available Topics menu

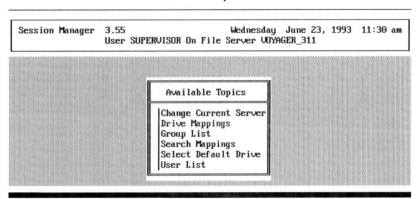

2 Next she selected the Search Mappings option. The screen shown in Figure 4-13 was displayed.

FIGURE 4-13: Leslie's Current Search Mappings screen

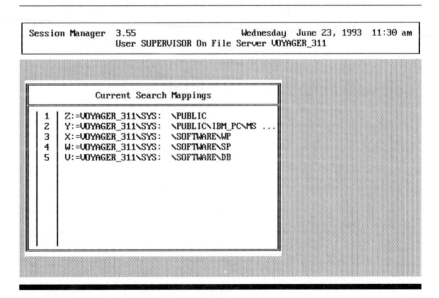

3 To add a new search drive mapping, Leslie pressed the Ins key. The SESSION utility responded by displaying "6" as the next search drive

number. She pressed [Enter] to make 6 the new search drive, then typed the path to the utilities directory, as shown in Figure 4-14.

FIGURE 4-14: Leslie's screen after she typed the path to her utilities

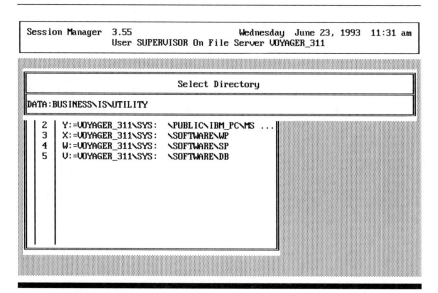

4 She then pressed [Esc] to return to the menu shown in Figure 4-12.

To change the mapping of drive L:, Leslie used the SESSION utility as follows:

1 She first highlighted the Drive Mappings option and pressed [Enter]. The Current Drive Mappings window shown in Figure 4-15 was displayed.

FIGURE 4-15: Leslie's Current Drive Mappings screen

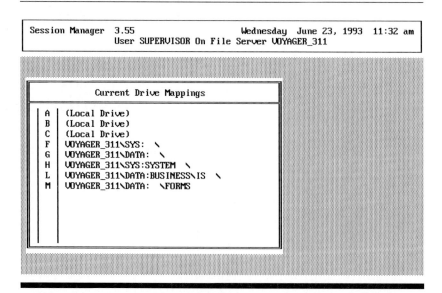

2 Next Leslie used the arrow keys to move the pointer bar to the L: drive mappings and pressed the F3 key. A window showing the current drive mapping was displayed.

3   She then modified the existing path to point to DATA:\SALES directory and pressed [Enter].

4   The SESSION utility responded by asking, "Do you want to map root this drive?" as shown in Figure 4-16. Leslie responded by typing "Y" and pressing [Enter].

FIGURE 4-16: Leslie's screen after she changed the L: drive mapping

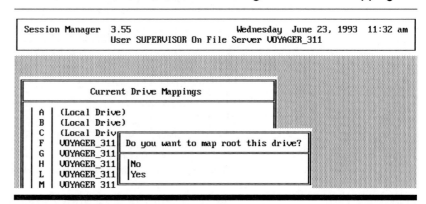

5   She then pressed the Esc key until she exited the SESSION utility.

After completing her work in the SALES directory structure, Leslie wanted to remove the search drive pointer to the utility directory and change the L: drive pointer back to the WORK subdirectory of the BUSINESS directory structure. Because she is planning to copy files from the WORK subdirectory into various users' home directories, she also wanted to establish a new drive pointer, I:, mapped to the DATA:\BUSINESS\USERS subdirectory. This will allow her to copy commands using the drive pointers rather than specifying the complete paths. To delete the search drive mapping, Leslie used the SESSION utility as follows:

1   She typed the command SESSION at the DOS prompt to display the screen shown in Figure 4-12.

2   Next she selected the Search Mappings option. The screen shown in Figure 4-13 was displayed.

3   Leslie then moved the pointer to the S6: drive mapping and pressed [Del]. The SESSION utility required her to press [Enter] again to confirm the deletion.

4   She then pressed [Esc] to return to the menu shown in Figure 4-12.

To add a new network drive pointer, Leslie used the SESSION utility as follows:

1   She first highlighted the Drive Mappings option and pressed the Enter key. The Current Drive Mappings window was again displayed.

2   She pressed [Ins], changed the drive letter to I:, and pressed [Enter].

3 She then typed the complete path to the BUSINESS\USERS directory, as shown in Figure 4-17, and pressed [Enter]. After she responded with a "Y" to the "Do you want to map root this drive?" question, the new mapping was displayed in the Current Drive Mappings window.

FIGURE 4-17: Leslie's screen after she used the Ins key to create the I: drive

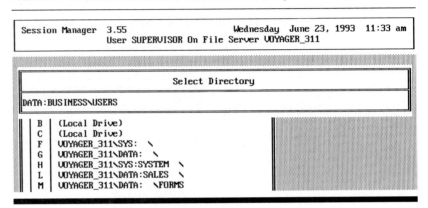

```
Session Manager   3.55                    Wednesday  June 23, 1993  11:33 am
                  User SUPERVISOR On File Server VOYAGER_311

┌──────────────────────────────────────────────────────────────────────────┐
│                            Select Directory                                │
├──────────────────────────────────────────────────────────────────────────┤
│DATA:BUSINESS\USERS                                                         │
├──────────────────────────────────────────────────────────────────────────┤
│  B │ (Local Drive)                                                         │
│  C │ (Local Drive)                                                         │
│  F │ VOYAGER_311\SYS:  \                                                   │
│  G │ VOYAGER_311\DATA:  \                                                  │
│  H │ VOYAGER_311\SYS:SYSTEM  \                                             │
│  L │ VOYAGER_311\DATA:SALES  \                                            │
│  M │ VOYAGER_311\DATA:  \FORMS                                            │
```

4 She then pressed [Esc] until she exited the SESSION utility.

Leslie learned how the SESSION command can also be used to see other users who are currently logged in, send messages to another user, or view existing user groups. In Chapter 5 you will follow Leslie as she sets up a security system for her network.

In this chapter the following NetWare commands were used to perform the functions described below.

MAP *drive:=*
[fileserver\volume:path]

In this chapter, this command was used to create new drive letters pointing to the directory location specified by the NetWare path. The *fileserver\volume:path* can include file server name, volume, directory, and subdirectory, as shown in the following examples. The file server name and volume are optional if they are the same as the default drive.

F:\SALES>MAP L:=VOYAGER_311\DATA:BUSINESS

Maps drive pointer L: to the business directory using the complete path.

F:\SALES>MAP L:=\BUSINESS

Also maps drive pointer L: to the BUSINESS directory because the default drive F: is currently on the DATA volume.

F:\SALES>MAP H:=L:IS

Maps H: to the BUSINESS\IS subdirectory

F:\SALES>MAP G:=

Maps drive pointer G: to the SALES directory (makes G: equal to the mapping of F:)

MAP ROOT *drive:=[path]*

The ROOT option creates a drive mapping that appears to DOS as the beginning of the volume. In this chapter, the ROOT option was used when a home directory to drive H was mapped:, and the user's local work directory to drive L:. Root drive mappings do not show the path to the directory on the DOS prompt, and therefore prevent the CD \ command from changing the drive mapping to another location.

MAP DEL *drive:*

This command is used to remove a network drive mapping.

MAP S#:=[path]

This command was used to create search drive mappings. The # must be replaced with a number from 1 to 16. Search drive mappings tell the NetWare shell where to look for a program or data file when that file is not in the current directory. When a program file cannot be found in the current directory, the shell will look in the directory specified by search drive 1 first; if the file is not found there, it will look in the directory specified by search drive 2, and so on. Search drives are normally mapped to the SYS:PUBLIC directory, the DOS directory, and any software subdirectories needed by the user.

MAP INS S#:=[path]

The INS option preserves existing search drives by renumbering them. For example, if you had two search drives, S1:=SYS:PUBLIC and

S2:=SYS:PUBLIC\DOS, the command MAP INS S1:=SYS:SOFT-WARE\WP would cause the S2:=SYS:PUBLIC\DOS drive to become S3:, and the S1=SYS:PUBLIC to become S2:. The MAP INS S1:=*[path]* command is often used when a temporary search drive is added to an existing list. The temporary search drive may later be deleted simply by typing the command MAP DEL S1:.

MAP NEXT *[path]*   While Leslie did not use this command, it can be used to map the next available drive letter to the specified directory path. For example, if you currently have drive mappings for F:, G: and H:, the MAP NEXT SYS:BUSINESS command would map I: to the SYS:BUSINESS directory.

LOGIN Script Commands   In this chapter you were introduced to the concept of using a LOGIN script to set up drive mappings for users whenever they log in. When a user logs in, NetWare first executes any commands in the system LOGIN script; it then checks for the existence of a personal LOGIN script in the user's mail subdirectory. If no personal LOGIN script is found, a default LOGIN script contained in the NETX.COM program is executed. In Chapter 11, you will learn more LOGIN script commands and create a system LOGIN script.

MAP DISPLAY *[off/on]*   The MAP DISPLAY OFF command prevents the results of each map operation from being displayed on the workstation when the user logs in. This will keep the display less cluttered, making it easier for the user to read more important messages. The *on* option causes the system to display the results of each map operation.

MAP drive:=*[path]*   The MAP command in a LOGIN script uses the same syntax as the standard MAP command.

WRITE *"message text"*   The WRITE command is used to display a message on the screen during the login process. Variables such as %GREETING_TIME may be inserted into the message string. It is important to type the variable name in all caps following the [%] symbol. LOGIN script variable names may be found in the Login Script section of the NetWare Installation Manual.

PAUSE   The PAUSE command causes the LOGIN script process to stop until the user presses the Enter key.

IF *[condition]* **THEN BEGIN END**   The IF DAY_OF_WEEK = "MONDAY" AND HOUR24< "10" command was used to check the DAY_OF_WEEK and HOUR24 variables in order to determine if the user was logging in before 10:00 a.m. on a Monday. When the condition is true, the statements between the

BEGIN and END commands will be executed. When the condition is false, the system skips to the statement following the END command.

The SYSCON Utility   In this chapter the SYSCON utility was used to enter a user LOGIN script for the supervisor account. This was done by selecting the User Information option from SYSCON's Available Topics main menu. When the username SUPERVISOR was highlighted and the Enter key was pressed, the User Information window was displayed. Selecting the Login Script option allows you to create or change the personal LOGIN script for the selected user. The Esc key is used to save the LOGIN script and return to the User Information window. Holding down the Alt key while pressing F10 allows you to quickly exit the SYSCON utility.

The SESSION Utility   In this chapter the SESSION utility was used to add and change both regular and search drive pointers. Regular drive pointers can be maintained by selecting the Drive Mapping option from SESSION's Available Topics menu. [F3] can be used to change an existing mapping, the Delete key can be used to delete a drive pointer, and the Ins key is used to create a new drive pointer. When a new drive pointer is addedor existing mapping is changed, the SESSION utility will ask if you want to make the new mapping a root mapping.

Search drive pointers are maintained by selecting the Search Mappings option from SESSION's Available Topics menu. As in regular drive mappings, [F3] can be used to change a mapping, the Delete key to remove, and the Ins key to create a new search pointer. If you assign a search drive number that is already in use, rather than replacing the existing search drive, the SESSION utility will insert the new pointer using that search number and automatically renumber the existing search drives.

1. _____ are the default local drive pointers.

   a. A: through C:
   b. A: through E:
   c. F: through Z:
   d. K: through Z:

2. _____ drive pointers are letters that are mapped to point at areas in the directory structure where data files are stored.

3. A _____ drive pointer appears to the user or application as if the default path is to the beginning of a drive or volume.

4. _____ drive mappings are used to allow a user located in a data directory to access software located in different directory.

5. _____ drive mappings affect the DOS path.

6. A maximum of _____ search drives can be assigned.

7. The first search drive is assigned to the drive pointer letter _____.

8. If you mapped three search drives S1, S2, and S3, what drive letter would be assigned to the S3 mapping? _____

9. Give two reasons a drive letter should be assigned to each volume on your file server.

10. Making the user home directory path a root drive pointer is important because _____ .

    Use the following diagram to answer questions 11 through 20:

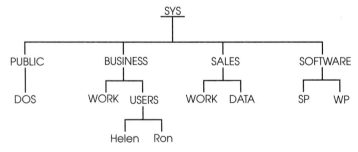

11. Write a MAP command to create a regular L: drive mapping to the business department's work directory.

12. Write a MAP command to insert a new search drive to the SP software directory between the existing S1 and S2 mappings.

13. Write a MAP command to remove the S4 search drive mapping.

14. Write a MAP command to create a "root" home directory for Helen.

15. Assuming you do not know the search drive number of the last search drive, write a MAP command that would add a search drive to the WP software after the last existing search drive number.

16. The _____ interactive NetWare utility can be used to enter or change personal LOGIN script files.

17. Personal LOGIN scripts are kept in the _____ directory.

18. The _____ interactive NetWare utility can be used to modify drive mappings.

19. Default LOGIN script commands are built into the _____.

20. On a separate sheet of paper, write a personal LOGIN script for Helen to do the following:
Display a greeting message with the greeting time.
Map S1 to the PUBLIC directory.
MAP S2 to the DOS directory.
MAP S3 to the WP software directory.
MAP her home directory.
MAP a drive to her WORK directory.
On Tuesdays, display a message that she has a meeting at 1:30 p.m.

SUPEROR TECHNICAL COLLEGE PROJECT 4

In this project you will apply the concepts and commands you learned in this chapter to planning and working with drive pointers for Superior Technical College. You will use the MAP and SESSION utilities to create, modify, and delete drive mappings for your user session. You will also use the SYSCON utility to create a personal LOGIN script, which will set up the drive mapping environment you have planned for your user account.

Assignment 4-1: **Plan Drive Pointer Usage**
Using your volume and directory worksheets as guides, determine a set of common network and search drive pointers that will be used by all Superior Technical College users to move around your directory structure. At a minimum your drive mapping plan should include the following:

■ Drive letter F: to the SYS volume

■ If your assigned file server has more than one volume, a drive letter assigned to each additional volume on your file server

■ A drive letter (H:) to be used for the user's home directory

■ A drive letter (L:) to the workgroup's shared work area

■ Search drive pointers for each application software subdirectory in the SYS:SOFTWARE directory

Record your drive pointer assignments under Assignment 4-1 on Student Answer Sheet 4. *Save a copy of these charts*; you will need to refer to them in later chapters.

Assignment 4-2: Use the MAP Command

❶ Log in to your assigned file server using the username assigned to you by your instructor. Record your username on Student Answer Sheet 4.

❷ Use MAP commands to establish the network drive pointers you defined in Assignment 4-1. Do not map search drives at this time. Record the MAP commands you use on Student Answer Sheet 4.

❸ Enter a MAP command to map drive pointer P: to the directory where you are planning to place the student service graduate system. Record the MAP command you use on Student Answer Sheet 4.

❹ Use the MAP > PRN command to obtain a hardcopy of your drive mappings. Attach the printout to Student Answer Sheet 4.

Assignment 4-3: Test the Search Drives

❶ Change to the P: drive. Enter the command **DB**, then press **[Enter]**. Record the message you receive on Student Answer Sheet 4.

❷ Use the MAP command to implement the search drive mappings you defined in Assignment 4-1. Record the MAP commands you enter on Student Answer Sheet 4.

❸ Use the MAP > PRN command to obtain a hardcopy of your drive pointer environment. Attach the printout to Student Answer Sheet 4.

❹ Enter the command **DB** and press **[Enter]**. If your search drive is working you should receive a message on the screen. Print your screen. Attach the printout to Student Answer Sheet 4. On Student Answer Sheet 4, describe why the DB command worked now but did not work in step 1.

Assignment 4-4: Use the CD Command with Search Drive Mappings
To see how the CD command can affect search drive mappings, perform the following steps:

❶ Change to drive letter Z:. Record the default path on Student Answer Sheet 4.

❷ Type **CD ** and press **[Enter]**. Record the results on Student Answer Sheet 4.

❸ Change back to drive letter F:. Type **MAP** and press **[Enter]**. Record the results on Student Answer Sheet 4.

❹ Change back to drive letter Z:. Type **CD \PUBLIC** and press **[Enter]**. Record your results on Student Answer Sheet 4.

❺ Change back to drive F: and type **MAP** and press **[Enter]**. Record the results and your observations on Student Answer Sheet 4.

Assignment 4-5: **Use Search Drives with the PATH Command**

In this assignment you will record observations you make regarding the way adding and deleting search drives affects the DOS path.

❶ Use the DOS PATH command to view the current DOS path. Record the current path on Student Answer Sheet 4.

❷ Use the MAP DEL command to delete search drive S3:. Record your command on Student Answer Sheet 4.

❸ Type the PATH command again and record the new path on Student Answer Sheet 4.

❹ Use the MAP INS command to add a new search drive, S4:, to the same path as the search drive you deleted in step 2. Record the MAP INS command you use on Student Answer Sheet 4.

❺ Use the PATH command to record the current path on Student Answer Sheet 4.

❻ On Student Answer Sheet 4, describe the way adding and deleting search drives affect the DOS path.

Assignment 4-6: **Include Drive Mappings in Your LOGIN Script**

❶ On Student Answer Sheet 4, write a personal LOGIN script that will welcome you to the network by saying Good morning, afternoon, or evening, depending on when you log in, along with your name.

❷ On Student Answer Sheet 4, write a personal LOGIN script that will automatically set up the drive mappings you defined in Assignment 4-1 whenever you log in.

❸ On Student Answer Sheet 4, write a personal LOGIN script that will have the computer remind you that you have a meeting at 10:00 a.m. on Mondays.

❹ On Student Answer Sheet 4, write a personal LOGIN script that will use the MAP command to display your drive mappings.

❺ Use the SYSCON command to enter your personal LOGIN script commands. Print the screen showing your personal LOGIN script commands. Record the command you used and attach the printout to Student Answer Sheet 4.

❻ Test your personal LOGIN script by doing the following:

■ Log out of the file server.

■ Log in to the file server.

■ Be sure your drive mappings are showing and print the screen. Attach your printout to Student Answer Sheet 4.

Assignment 4-7: **Use the SESSION Utility to Add New Search Drive Mappings**

In this assignment you will use the SESSION utility to add a search drive mapping to your utilities directory and change the default mapping of your L: drive pointer.

❶ From the DOS prompt start the SESSION utility. Select the Search Mappings option and use the Ins key to add a new search drive pointer to your utilities directory. Record the search drive number and drive pointer assigned to the new search drive on Student Answer Sheet 4.

❷ Print the screen showing your current search drive mappings. Attach the printout to Student Answer Sheet 4.

❸ Use the Esc key to return to the SESSION main menu screen. Select the Drive Mappings option and use the F3 key to change your L: drive pointer to map to the directory containing the subdirectories for the Trades and Industry division. Exit the SESSION utility. Use the MAP >PRN command to print a copy of your drive mappings. Attach the printout to Student Answer Sheet 4.

Assignment 4-8: **Use a Search Drive Mapping**
In addition to using a search drive to run programs from your utilities directory, in this assignment you will see how you can use the drive pointer assigned to the search drive to help you copy files into your utilities directory.

❶ Use the NCOPY A:\UTILITY*.* *[drive-pointer]* command to copy all the utility files from the \UTILITY directory of your student work diskette into the utility directory for the programmers. Replace *[drive-pointer]* with the letter assigned to your utilities directory search drive in Assignment 4-7, step 1. Record the NCOPY command you use on Student Answer Sheet 4.

❷ Change to drive H: and type the command **UTIL** and press **[Enter]**. If your search drive mapping works, you should receive a message. Record the message on Student Answer Sheet 4. Print the screen. Attach the printout to Student Answer Sheet 4.

Assignment 4-9: **Use the SESSION Utility to Create New Network Drive Mappings**
In this assignment you will remove the search drive mapping to your UTILITIES directory and create a new network drive mapping to help you copy files into the Educational Services subdirectories.

❶ From the DOS prompt start the SESSION utility. Select the Drive Mappings option and use the Ins key to create a new drive mapping for letter M:. Map drive pointer M: to your directory that contains the Educational Services program subdirectories. Print the screen showing your current drive mappings and attach it to Student Answer Sheet 4.

❷ Exit the SESSION utility. Use the NCOPY A:\OUTLINES*.ACC M:*[path]* command to copy all files with the extension .ACC into the accounting subdirectory. Replace the *[path]* with the name of your subdirectory for the accounting program. Record the NCOPY command you use on Student Answer Sheet 4.

❸ Use the NCOPY A:\OUTLINES*.CIS M:*[path]* command to copy all files with the extension .CIS into the computer information systems subdirectory. Replace *[path]* with the name of your subdirectory for the computer information systems program. Record the NCOPY command you use on Student Answer Sheet 4.

❹ Use the NDIR M:*.* /SUB > PRN command to list all files you have copied into the accounting and computer information systems subdirectories to the printer. Attach your printout to Student Answer Sheet 4.

Turn in Materials   Carefully write the correct step number on each of your printouts (from Assignments 4-2, 4-3, 4-6, 4-7, 4-8, and 4-9). Assemble the printouts in the correct order and attach them to Student Answer Sheet 4. Be sure to save a copy of the charts you completed for Assignment 4-1; you will need them in later chapters. If instructed, turn in the materials to your instructor on or before the scheduled due date.

Student Name: _____ Date: _____

Assignment 4-1: **Plan Drive Pointer Usage**

Network Drive Pointers

Letter	Path	Description

Search Drive Pointers

Number	Path	Description

Assignment 4-2: **Map Network Drive Pointers**

❶ Record your username here. _____

❷ Record the MAP commands you used to establish your network drive pointers.

❸ Record the MAP command used to map drive letter P: to the student service graduate system directory.

❹ Attach a printout of the results of the MAP >PRN command.

Assignment 4-3: **Test the Search Drives**

❶ Record the message you received after typing "DB" from the P: drive.

❷ Record the MAP commands you used to establish your search drive pointers.

❸ Attach a printout of the results of the MAP >PRN command.

❹ Attach a printout of the results of the DB command. In the space below, describe how the DB command worked after mapping your search drives.

Assignment 4-4: **Use the CD Command with Search Drive Mappings**

❶ Record the default path for drive letter Z.

❷ Record the results obtained after you type "CD\" and press [Enter].

❸ Record your results.

❹ Record your results.

❺ Record your results.

Assignment 4-5: **Use Search Drives with the PATH Command**

❶ Record the current DOS path.

❷ Record your MAP DEL command.

❸ Record the DOS path after you delete search drive 3.

❹ Record the MAP INS command you used to insert search drive 4.

❺ Record the DOS path after you insert search drive S4.

❻ In your own words, describe how deleting or adding a search drive changes the DOS path.

Assignment 4-6: **Include Drive Mappings in Your Personal LOGIN Script**

❶ Record your personal LOGIN script commands.

❷ Record your personal LOGIN script command.

❸ Record your personal LOGIN script command.

❹ Record your drive mappings.

⑤ Record your personal LOGIN script command. Attach your printout.

⑥ Attach a printout of your personal LOGIN commands after logging out, then logging in.

Assignment 4-7: **Use the SESSION Utility to Add New Search Drive Mappings**

❶ Record the search drive number and drive letter assigned.
Search drive number: _____
Drive pointer assigned: _____

❷ Attach a printout of your current search drive mappings.

❸ Attach a printout of your new drive mappings.

Assignment 4-8: **Use a Search Drive Mapping**

❶ Record the NCOPY command you used.

❷ Record the message you received after typing "UTIL" and pressing [Enter]. Attach a printout of your new search drive mapping.

Assignment 4-9: **Use the SESSION Utility to Create New Network Drive Mappings**

❶ Attach a printout showing your current drive mappings.

❷ Record the NCOPY command you used to copy the .ACC files into your accounting program subdirectory.

❸ Record the NCOPY command you used to copy the .CIS files into your computer information systems program subdirectory.

❹ Attach a printout showing all files you have copied into the ACC and CIS subdirectories.

In this chapter you will learn to:

- List the three levels of NetWare security

- Identify the three NetWare bindery files and their purposes

- Differentiate between workgroup and user account managers

- Describe the eight NetWare trustee rights and apply them to meet an organization's file security needs

- Determine user-effective rights in a given directory structure

- Use the Inherited Rights Mask to change user-effective rights

- Identify the common file attributes

- Use the Novell trustee file security worksheet to document trustee right assignments

SYSTEM SECURITY

You can compare a file server to a large data storage tank that contains many files and directories. Because some of these files may contain critical or confidential data, the network operating system must be able to restrict which users or computers on the network will be allowed to update or access the information on the file server. Restricting access to the server and protecting files are major functions of the security system.

To provide this protection, the NetWare security system consists of three levels: login security, trustee rights security, and file and directory attributes.

LOGIN SECURITY

The first level, **login security**, controls who can access the server by providing a login process that requires the potential user to supply a valid username and optional password. The network administrator can place additional restrictions on the password such as setting a minimum password length, determining how long a password can be used before it expires, requiring the user to enter a different or unique password each time the password expires, or limiting the number of grace logins. The number of grace logins determines how many times a user can log in after the password has expired. NetWare also allows the network administrator to restrict users to certain login times as well as requiring them to log in from a specific workstation.

NetWare keeps username, password, and login restrictions in **bindery files**, which consist of three hidden files, NET$OBJ.SYS, NET$PROG.SYS, and NET$VAL.SYS, stored in the SYS:SYSTEM directory. The NET$OBJ file contains the names of the users, groups, workgroups, file servers, print servers, or other entries that have been given a name. The NET$PROP file contains the properties or characteristics of each bindery object (for example, password requirement, account restrictions, account balances, and group members). The NET$VAL file contains the values assigned to an object's properties (for example, the actual password, the number of grace logins, or the time and station restrictions).

A user account can be assigned special privileges during the login process. The highest of these is the **supervisor equivalent**, which has all the rights of the SUPERVISOR account. Supervisor-equivalent users can be designated only by the supervisor.

The supervisor can also designate a workgroup manager account. A **workgroup manager** can create new users and groups, which can then be managed or deleted by the workgroup manager who created them. Creating workgroup managers is a way for the network administrator to delegate work to a capable user within a department.

A **user account manager** is similiar to a workgroup manager but has more limited capabilities. A user account manager can only manage and delete users and groups assigned by the supervisor.

A **console operator** gets full use of the FCONSOLE utility but cannot shut down the file server. Because the FCONSOLE functions are severely limited on NetWare 3.11 file servers, this designation is no longer very useful.

A **print queue operator** can manipulate jobs in the print queue by changing job printing sequence and priority and deleting jobs from the print queue.

A **print server operator** can manage the physical print server; the operator can stop a printer, change forms number, restart a printer, and advance a printer to the top of a new form.

TRUSTEE RIGHTS SECURITY

Once a user has logged in to the file server, the second level of security, **trustee rights security**, restricts what the user can do in the file system. The SUPERVISOR or supervisor-equivalent users are automatically given all rights to the entire file server's directory structure. However, in most organizations, a network administrator does not want all users to be able to access and change files without restrictions. Therefore, one important aspect of designing a security system is determining what files and directories users need to control and from what files and directories they should be restricted.

Application and system software files should be protected from accidental erasure. The server could also contain files that need to be protected from being changed or viewed by users who are not responsible for that information. For example, if you are responsible for maintaining the inventory files, what happens if someone else in the organization changes the price of an item incorrectly? Who will have to answer to the boss? In this case you would want to control who updates the file and monitor or audit the changes.

Other files on the server could contain confidential information and should be accessed only by one or two users. For example, salary and payroll information should not be available to user employees. When confidential information of this sort is to be placed on the file server, unauthorized users must be prevented from accessing or viewing these files.

In NetWare, security is placed in the file system using trustee right assignments, which define the access rights each user has to a directory or file. (If you are using NetWare 2.x, your instructor will give you more information on trustee rights.) Trustee assignments, which can be made to directories or files, include File Scan (F), Read (R), Write (W), Create (C), Erase (E), Modify (M), Access Control (A), and Supervisory (S) rights. Figure 5-1 on the following page contains a brief description of each access right.

Figure 5-1: NetWare access rights

Access Right	Effect in Directory	Effect in File
Read	Allows users to open and read files or run programs in the directory	Allows users to open and read files (even when revoked at directory level)
File Scan	Allows users to see files and subdirectories	Allows users to see filenames (even when revoked at the directory level)
Create	Allows users to create files and subdirectories	Allows users to salvage files if deleted
Erase	Allows users to delete files and subdirectories	Allows users to delete files (even when revoked at the directory level)
Write	Allows users to open and write to files in a directory	Allows users to open and write to files (even when revoked at the directory level)
Modify	Allows users to change the attributes of and rename any file or subdirectory	Allows users to change attributes or rename files (even when revoked at the directory level)
Access Control	Allows users to modify trustee assignments and the IRM of this directory along with files and subdirectories	Allows users to modify trustee assignments and the IRM (even when revoked at directory level)
Supervisory	Grants all rights to the directory and all subdirectories; this right cannot be revoked or redefined at a lower level. Only a supervisor equivalent can assign this right	Grants all rights to the file

Only the SUPERVISOR or equivalent user can grant the Supervisory right to a directory. The Supervisory right gives a user all rights to the directory and files as well as all rights to all subdirectories within that directory. The Supervisory right cannot be blocked or revoked at a lower level. The Supervisory right allows the network administrator to delegate the control of a directory structure to a workgroup manager.

When a directory trustee assignment is given to a user, the user will automatically inherit these rights to all subdirectories within that directory. When a different trustee assignment is made for that user in one of the subdirectories, the user's effective rights in that subdirectory will be changed to the new assignment.

Every directory has an **Inherited Rights Mask (IRM)**. This filter controls what rights will be passed from the higher level directory into that directory. When you create a directory, the IRM is set to allow users to inherit all their effective rights from the higher directory. If you want to prevent users from receiving certain inherited rights, you can remove the rights you do not want inherited from the IRM.

FILE AND DIRECTORY ATTRIBUTES

Once a user is given trustee rights to a directory, the third level of NetWare security, **file and directory attributes**, becomes important. Attributes are flags that may be placed on files or directories. Commonly used file attributes consist of Read Only (RO), Sharable (S), Delete Inhibit (DI), Rename Inhibit (RI), Hidden (H), System (SY), Purge (P), and Normal (N). These flags allow the files to be shared (S), protected from changes (RO), protected from deletion (DI), or hidden from view (H). If you are using NetWare version 2.x, your instructor will provide you with more information on attributes.

In this chapter's case you will walk through planning and documenting the security environment for PC Solutions. At the end of the case, you will be able to apply these concepts, as well as your own ideas, to defining and documenting the trustee security environment for Superior Technical College.

THE PC SOLUTIONS CASE

Once Leslie had established her directory structure she was ready to define her users and determine their trustee assignments. When discussing the network with the accounting users, Leslie noted that they were very concerned about protecting their data, especially payroll information, from other users. Leslie assured them that the Novell NetWare system provides many security features and that the data may be more secure on the file server than on their local PCs. After all, she explained, if someone had a key, what would prevent him or her from entering your office and accessing the data stored in your desktop PC? She further explained that with NetWare, information can be protected by password, station, and time restrictions.

DEFINING LOGIN SECURITY

Leslie's first move was to define the users and determine the security restrictions, if any, that should be placed on their accounts. She started by reviewing the organizational chart along with the processing specifications and storage requirements table she created earlier (see Figure 2-4). In addition, she found it helpful to talk with some of the users about their job functions. From this information she was able to use the Novell users worksheet to document her findings, as shown in Figure 5-2. Leslie remembered to keep each username to eight or fewer characters; this is necessary because SYSCON will create the user's home directory with the same name. It will also be important later when Leslie creates a system LOGIN script that needs to map a drive pointer to each user's home directory.

FIGURE 5-2: Users' worksheet for PC Solutions

Full Name	Username	Groups	Password Length/Days	Restrictions Time	Restrictions Station	Managed By	Workgroup Manager
Ned Lynch	99NEDLYN	Business	4/180 days	No	No	99MARREA 99LESSTE	N
Ann Bonny	99 ANNBON	Business	4/90 days	8:00–5:00	Yes	99LESSTE	N
George Moon	99GEOMOO	Sales	4/180 days	No	No	99MARREA 99LESSTE	N
Julie Elliot	99JULELL	Sales	4/180 days	No	No	99MARREA 99LESSTE	N
James Bligh	99JAMBLI	Sales	4/180 days	No	No	99MARREA 99LESSTE	N
Mary Read	99MARREA	Support	5/30 days	No	No	99LESSTE	Y
Edward Low	99EDWLOW	Business	4/180 days	No	No	99MARREA 99LESSTE	N
Ben Avery	99BENAVE	Business	4/180 days	No	No	99MARREA 99LESSTE	N
Rita Dunn	99RITDUN	Support	4/180 days	No	No	99MARREA 99LESSTE	N
Leslie Stevens	99LESSTE	Everyone	4/60 days	No	No	99LESSTE	Y
Nancy Yin	99NANYIN	Help Desk	4/180 days	No	No	99MARREA 99LESSTE	N
Howell Davis	99HOWDAV	Help Desk	4/180 DAYS	No	No	99MARREA 99LESSTE	N

Leslie decided to take Ron's advice and make each username consist of the first three letters of the user's first name followed by the first three letters of the user's last name. (The number that precedes the username identifies who created the user and is included to make the case similar to your student project.)

To provide additional protection to the payroll system files, Leslie placed time and station restrictions on Ann Bonny's account. Even if someone knew Ann's password, he or she would be required to log in from Ann's workstation during a normal working day. This extra security seemed to reassure Ann.

Leslie decided to make Mary Read a manager of all the users, with the exception of Leslie and Ann Bonny. Making Mary a user account manager will allow her to change the passwords, login restrictions, and LOGIN scripts of the users she manages. Because Mary has a good grasp of computers, Leslie planned to make her a workgroup manager and give her the basic training she will need to act as a backup network administrator. Because Mary is a workgroup manager, Leslie felt it was important to require her account to have longer passwords that expire more frequently.

DEFINING TRUSTEE SECURITY

Using the volume and directory worksheets along with the tables she completed earlier (see Chapter 2), Leslie was ready to define the access rights users need to perform their processing functions. As she did this, she completed the Novell trustee directory security worksheets shown in the figures that follow. Because of the limitations of the size of the charts, Leslie decided to place one workgroup on each worksheet.

The worksheet in Figure 5-3 is reserved for the group 99EVERY-ONE and any special assignments. The trustee rights to be granted to a user in a directory are indicated by placing the letters standing for each right to be granted under each user's name. For example, everyone is assigned the Read (R) and File Scan (F) rights in the FORMS directory.

FIGURE 5-3: Trustee directory security worksheet for PC Solutions

Directory Path	99EVERYONE	99MARREA	99LESSTE		
SYS:LOGIN	( )				
MAIL	(C)				
SYSTEM	(None)				
PUBLIC	(R F)				
MENUS	(R F)		S		
SYS:SOFTWARE	(R F)		S		
DATA:FORMS	(R F)	(R F C W M E)	S		
DATA			S		

In her NetWare class, Leslie learned that trustee rights "flow down" to all the subdirectories from the directory in which they are assigned. The effective rights a user has in a subdirectory may be a result of this "flow down" effect and are referred to as **inherited rights**. **Effective rights** are the actual rights a user has in a directory or file. Effective rights may be the result of a trustee assignment or inherited rights, or they may be a combination of a trustee assignment or inherited rights, along with any rights granted to a group of which the user is a member.

Using the inherited rights property, along with group rights, Leslie needed to assign the group 99EVERYONE Read (R) and File Scan (F) rights to the SYS:SOFTWARE directory. This will give all users the rights necessary to run the general-purpose application programs. Because Mary Read maintains the DATA:\FORMS directory, Leslie has assigned her the Supervisory right to this directory. This will allow Mary to manage this directory and to assign rights to other users.

Figure 5-4 shows the worksheet Leslie developed for the Business workgroup. Because Mary Read is a workgroup manager, Leslie has given her all rights, except Supervisory, to the BUSINESS directory. Because Leslie wanted Mary to be able to read files in the users' home directories, she has given her Read and File Scan rights to the BUSI-NESS\USERS subdirectory. This trustee assignment will override all the inherited rights she would otherwise get from being a trustee with all rights to the BUSINESS directory.

FIGURE 5-4: Trustee directory security worksheet for the Business workgroup

Directory Path	Business Group	99ANNBON	99NEDLYN	99EDWLOW	99MARREA	99BENAVE
BUSINESS\PAYROLL		R F C W M E				
BUSINESS\BUDGETS	R F		R F C W M E	R F C W M E		R F
BUSINESS\WORK	R F C W M E					
BUSINESS\GL	R F		R F C W M E			
BUSINESS\USERS					R F	
SALES\ORDERS			R F	R F		
BUSINESS					R F C W M E A	

Ann wants no one else to be able to read the payroll files, so Leslie will use the IRM to block the rights to the payroll subdirectory that Mary would normally inherit. If Leslie had given Mary the Supervisory right to the BUSINESS directory, she would not have been able to reassign her rights to the BUSINESS\USERS subdirectory or to block the Supervisory right using the IRM. Because SALES\ORDERS contains data used in generating accounting reports, Leslie assigned both Ned Lynch and Ed Low Read and File Scan rights to it.

The trustee right assignments shown in Figure 5-5 on the following page are for the Sales workgroup. As you can see, they are fairly simple. All Sales staff need to be able to enter information into the ORDERS system. After reading the installation documentation that came with the ORDERS software, Leslie found out that to enter orders, a user will need Read, Write, and File Scan rights to the SALES\ORDERS subdirectory. In addition to using the ORDERS system, each Sales employee will have all rights to his or her home directory and be able to exchange files using the SALES\WORK subdirectory. Because Mary Read is a workgroup manager, Leslie gave her the Supervisory right to the SALES directory.

FIGURE 5-5: Trustee directory security worksheet for the Sales workgroup

Directory Path	Sales Group	99MARREA				
SALES\WORK	R F C W M E					
SALES\ORDERS	R F W					
SALES		S				

Leslie also assigned Mary the Supervisory right to the SUPPORT directory, outlined in Figure 5-6, and she assigned Rita all rights except Supervisory and Access Control to the SUPPORT\CATALOG and SUPPORT\WPPOOL subdirectories. By withholding the Supervisory or Access Control rights from Rita, Leslie allowed her to work with files in these subdirectories but prevented her from assigning trustee rights to other users. Leslie knows that keeping to a minimum the number of users who can assign trustee rights will help her keep better track of who has rights to what directories.

FIGURE 5-6: Trustee directory security worksheet for the Support workgroup

Directory Path	99RITDUN	99MARREA				
SUPPORT\CATALOG	R F C W M E					
SUPPORT\WPPOOL	R F C W M E					
SUPPORT		S				

As Figure 5-7 shows, Leslie assigned the PC Help Desk staff access to the PROBLEMS subdirectory. Staff members have Read (R), File Scan (F), Create (C), Write (W), Modify (M), and Erase (E) rights, and Mary Read again has Supervisory status.

FIGURE 5-7: Trustee directory security worksheet for the Help Desk workgroup

Directory Path	99NANYIN	99HOWDAV	99MARREA			
HELPDESK\PROBLEMS	R F C W M E	R F C W M E				
HELPDESK			S			

DEFINING FILE ATTRIBUTE SECURITY

Leslie's next job was to define the file and directory attributes needed to allow users to share files safely. She used the Novell directories worksheet to help her document her requirements. The results of filling in this worksheet are shown in Figure 5-8. Leslie used empty brackets in the IRM column to indicate that all rights will be removed from the BUSINESS\PAYROLL directory's IRM. This will prevent Mary or any other user from inheriting rights to the payroll files.

FIGURE 5-8: Directories worksheet for PC Solutions

Directory Path	Directory Attributes	IRM	Filename	File Attributes
FORMS			*.*	S
MENUS			*.*	S
BUSINESS\IS\UTILITY			*.*	S RO
BUSINESS\GL			*.PRG	S RO
BUSINESS\AP			*.PRG	S RO
			*.FMT	
			*.FRM	S RO
BUSINESS\PAYROLL		( )	*.EXE	S RO
SALES\ORDERS			*.PRG	S RO
			*.FRM	S RO
			*.FMT	S RO

Leslie planned to flag all files in the FORMS and MENUS directories as Sharables to allow multiple users to access these files at the same time. Leslie could have made these files Read Only, but that would make it more difficult for Mary or Leslie to make changes to them.

Leslie planned to flag the files in the BUSINESS\IS\UTILITY subdirectory Sharable and Read Only. This will allow multiple users to run the files and prevent her from accidentally erasing files when she copies new programs into the utility directory.

Leslie felt she had made good progress with PC Solutions' security requirements, so she decided to take a break. When she gets back she'll tackle installing the application software, a process you will follow in Chapter 6.

1. List the three levels of NetWare security.

2. List three restrictions that can be placed on user passwords.

3. The _____ NetWare bindery file contains the usernames.

4. The _____ NetWare bindery file contains the user password.

5. A _____ can manage other users but is not able to create new users or groups.

6. A _____ user has the same rights as the supervisor.

7. Only the _____ can use FCONSOLE to shut down the file server.

8. The _____ can change the sequence of jobs to be printed.

9. Once a user has logged in to the file server, the second level of security, called _____ , restricts what the user can do in any given directory or file.

10. The _____ file attribute will protect a file from deletion while still allowing it to be changed.

11. The _____ file attribute is necessary if you want two or more users to have simultaneous access to the file.

12. Given that Joe has been given a trustee assignment of RFCWE to the BUSINESS directory, and a trustee assignment of RFW to the BUSINESS\SPDATA\BUDGETS subdirectory, what are Joe's effective rights in the BUSINESS\SPDATA subdirectory?

13. Given the information in Question 12, what are Joe's effective rights in the BUSINESS\SPDATA\BUDGETS subdirectory?

14. Assume all rights except Read and File Scan are removed from the IRM of the BUSINESS\SPDATA directory described in Question 12. What are Joe's effective rights in the BUSINESS\SPDATA subdirectory?

15. Given the information in Question 14, what are Joe's effective rights in the BUSINESS\SPDATA\BUDGETS subdirectory?

SUPERIOR TECHNICAL COLLEGE PROJECT 5

In this phase of the Superior Technical College network setup you are to define the three levels of NetWare security for your Superior Technical College system. You'll use this information in later lab projects when you create the network users and work with the file system, so keep a copy of Student Answer Sheet 5 if you need to hand it in to your instructor.

Assignment 5-1: **Define Login Security**

❶ Using the processing information along with the organizational chart and tables from Chapter 2, fill in the user's worksheet provided under Assignment 5-1 on Student Answer Sheet 5. Your instructor may supply you with additional information at this time through mock interviews or handouts. *Be sure to include your assigned student number ahead of each username you define.*

Assignment 5-2: **Define Trustee Security**

❶ Use the information from Assignment 5-1 along with the volume and directory worksheets you created in Chapter 2 to fill in the trustee directory security worksheet provided under Assignment 5-2 on Student Answer Sheet 5. Use one worksheet for each major workgroup, as demonstrated in the chapter.

Assignment 5-3: **Define File Attribute Security**

❶ Use the directories worksheet provided under Assignment 5-3 on Student Answer Sheet 5 to document any attributes or Inherited Rights Masks you want to use in your directory structure.

Turn in Materials If requested, turn in a copy of Student Answer Sheet 5 to your instructor on or before the scheduled due date. *Be sure to make a copy for yourself,* because you will be using these sheets to perform future Superior Technical College projects.

Student Name: _____ Date: _____

Assignment 5-1: Define Login Security

❶ Complete the information below.

Users worksheet for file server: _____

Full Name	Username	Groups	Password Length/Days	Time	Station	Manager	WGM?

Assignment 5-2: Define Trustee Security

❶ Complete the charts below for each workgroup.

Trustee directory security worksheet for file server: _____

Workgroup: _____

Trustee rights to be assigned to Groups or Users

Directory Path					

Trustee directory security worksheet for file server: _____

Workgroup: _____

Trustee rights to be assigned to Groups or Users

Directory Path						

Trustee directory security worksheet for file server: _____

Workgroup: _____

Trustee rights to be assigned to Groups or Users

Directory Path						

Trustee directory security worksheet for file server: _____

Workgroup: _____

Trustee rights to be assigned to Groups or Users

Directory Path						

Assignment 5-3:   Define File Attribute Security

❶   Complete the chart below.

Directories worksheet for file server: _____

Directory Path	Directory Attributes	IRM	Filename	File Attributes

INSTALLING SOFTWARE

In this chapter you will learn to:

- Identify three methods of software installation

- Follow standard Novell NetWare procedures to install an application package on a file server

- Use an INSTALL program to install program files into the software directory

- Use the FLAG command to make software files Sharable and Read Only

- Use the MAP command to establish a search drive mapping to the software directory

- Use the NDIR command to document installation

- Test your software installation

There are probably as many ways to install application software on a network as there are software packages to install. Before deciding to install a software package on a server, you must determine if the software is network compatible and check the copyright restrictions. If an application is going to be shared, you will probably need to obtain additional copies or negotiate a site license.

Network compatible means the software can be copied and run from a network drive. Not all software can be installed on a file server. For example, the installation program on some older application software writes directly to a local drive, making installation on a network mapped drive difficult, if not impossible.

The process of installing a network-compatible application on a file server can be broken down into one of three major categories: single-user installation, multiuser installation, and network-aware installation, in which the application package would automatically recognize the network and set up certain options and features for the user.

In the PC Solutions case you will see how Leslie installs an application that is network aware and an application that does not have a network installation option. At the end of the chapter, the Superior Technical College project will give you a chance to apply these concepts by installing two software simulations.

THE PC SOLUTIONS CASE

Leslie returned from her break ready to install the general ledger software. Because both the general ledger and order entry systems use the database software, Leslie must install the database system before installing these other applications. In her NetWare class, Leslie learned the basic steps involved in installing application software. She will follow these steps when installing the applications:

1. Determine the network compatibility and multiuser capability of the software

2. Create the necessary directory structure and drive mappings

3. Install the application software files

4. Flag application program files

5. Provide user access rights

6. Modify the CONFIG.SYS file

7. Test the application

INSTALLING A NETWORK-AWARE APPLICATION

Because both the general ledger and order entry systems use the database software, Leslie has obtained a network version of the database system along with a site license.

Creating the Necessary Directory Structure and Drive Mappings

According to the documentation that came with the database system, the INSTALL program will copy all the files from the diskettes into the directory path the user specifies. The installation instructions explained that the directory path must be specified using a drive pointer and cannot contain a NetWare volume name. From the installation instructions Leslie learned that because the database system keeps work files in the directory path specified during installation, each user of the database system must have the same drive letter mapped to the root of the volume where the database system is installed. Because Leslie wants to use the SYS:SOFTWARE\DB directory she created during the file server installation, she plans to use the F: drive pointer during the installation; all users will have the F: drive pointer mapped to the root of the SYS volume.

Installing the Application Software Files

From the installation documentation, Leslie learned that she must use the -N option of the install program to install the network version of the database system on her file server. Typing "INSTALL -N" and pressing [Enter] started the installation process. The install program first asked her for the directory path in which to install the program files. Next it asked her to insert disk 1 into drive A. After copying the files from disk 1, she inserted the other disks as requested. Within 15 minutes the installation program reported that the network version of the database was successfully installed.

Flagging Application Program Files

To allow multiple users to run the database software, the installation instructions told Leslie that she must flag all files in the DB directory to be Sharable (S). Since the database system updates work files that are kept in the SYS:SOFTWARE\DB directory, database system users will need trustee rights to write to this directory when running the database software. To protect database program files from being changed, the installation instructions recommended making Read Only (RO) all program files, *.COM, *.EXE, *.MSG, and *.OVL. To make the required files Sharable and Read Only, Leslie used the NetWare FLAG commands shown in Figure 6-1 on the following page.

To make it more difficult for anyone to copy the software onto diskettes, Leslie flagged the main program file, DBA.COM, to hide it, as shown in Figure 6-2 on the following page. To totally protect the file from being copied by anyone, even the SUPERVISOR, Leslie could have used the Execute Only (E) attribute. Once the Execute Only attribute is applied to a file, the attribute cannot be removed even by the SUPERVISOR. Leslie learned in class that not all software will run correctly when the Execute attribute is used. In Leslie's environment,

FIGURE 6-1: Leslie's screen after she mad all program files in the SOFTWARE\DB directory Sharable and Read Only

```
F:\>CD SOFTWARE\DB

F:\SOFTWARE\DB>FLAG *.COM  S RO
     DBA.COM                  [ Ro S - - - - - - - - -- -- -- DI RI ]

F:\SOFTWARE\DB>FLAG *.EXE  S RO
     DB.EXE                   [ Ro S - - - - - - - - -- -- -- DI RI ]
     PROTECT.EXE              [ Ro S - - - - - - - - -- -- -- DI RI ]

F:\SOFTWARE\DB>FLAG *.MSG  S RO
     DBASE.MSG                [ Ro S - - - - - - - - -- -- -- DI RI ]

F:\SOFTWARE\DB>FLAG *.OVL  S RO
     DBA.OVL                  [ Ro S - - - - - - - - -- -- -- DI RI ]

F:\SOFTWARE\DB>
```

FIGURE 6-2: Leslie's screen after she hid the DBA.COM program file

```
F:\SOFTWARE\DB>DIR *.COM

 Volume in drive F is SYS
 Volume Serial Number is 0900-7CD9
 Directory of F:\SOFTWARE\DB

DBA      COM       941 01-01-80  12:46a
        1 file(s)        941 bytes
                    39485440 bytes free

F:\SOFTWARE\DB>FLAG *.COM  H
     DBA.COM                  [ Ro S - - H - - - - - -- -- DI RI ]

F:\SOFTWARE\DB>DIR *.COM

 Volume in drive F is SYS
 Volume Serial Number is 0900-7CD9
 Directory of F:\SOFTWARE\DB

File not found

F:\SOFTWARE\DB>
```

she believed the Hidden (H) attribute will provide her with sufficient protection from illegal copying of the software.

Providing User Access Rights

To run the database software, users will need a search drive mapped along with the Read and File Scan rights to the SYS:SOFTWARE\DB directory. Because this particular database system updates temporary files in the DB directory to keep track of the number of users, users of this application will also need to have the Write (W) trustee right to the SYS:SOFTWARE\DB subdirectory. On her trustee directory worksheet Leslie planned to give everyone Read and File Scan access to the SYS:SOFTWARE directory. Because of the inheritance of effective rights, all users would get Read and File Scan rights to the SYS:SOFTWARE\DB subdirectory. To add the Write access right to the DB subdirectory, Leslie added a line to her trustee directory worksheet, as shown in Figure 6-3. She needed to reassign the group EVERYONE the Read and File Scan rights along with the Write right. Just assigning the Write right at the DB subdirectory level would have the effect of blocking the Read and File Scan rights. Leslie has already planned to provide all users with a search drive mapping to the SYS:SOFTWARE\DB directory, as explained in Chapter 4.

Modifying the CONFIG Files

The database documentation told Leslie that the system needs a minimum of 20 files and 15 buffers to operate. DOS needs a file handle requiring about 16 bytes for each file that is opened. Buffers are used to store information going to and from local disk drives; they can speed require about 500 bytes of the workstation's memory per buffer, but speed up accessing local disk drives. Note that most files will be on the file server, so the number of buffers will not affect reading and writing files to the file server. Since the software is installed in a network environment, Leslie decided to keep the number of buffers at a minimum and provide extra file handles. Keeping buffers to a minimum will make more memory available to her workstation. Leslie modifies the CONFIG.SYS of each workstation to contain:

FILES=40

BUFFERS=15

FIGURE 6-3: Leslie's trustee directory worksheet after she changed the rights to the SOFTWARE\DB directory

Directory Path	99EVERYONE	99MARREA	99LESSTE			
SYS:LOGIN						
MAIL	C					
SYSTEM	none					
PUBLIC	R F		S			
MENUS	R F		S			
SYS:SOFTWARE\DB	**R F W**					
SYS:FORMS	R F	R F C W M E	S			
DATA:BUSINESS			S			

Testing the Application

To make the changes to the CONFIG.SYS file effective in her system, Leslie needed to log out and reboot her workstation. After logging in she changed to her home directory on drive H:. Because of the search drive mappings in her personal LOGIN script, she has a search drive to the SYS:SOFTWARE\DB software directory as shown in Figure 6-4. She then was able to start the database software by typing "DBA" at the DOS prompt.

FIGURE 6-4: Leslie's screen showing her search drive mapping to SOFTWARE\DB

```
F:\>LOGIN SUPERVISOR
Enter your password:
Good afternoon, Supervisor

F:\>MAP

Drive  A:    maps to a local disk.
Drive  B:    maps to a local disk.
Drive  C:    maps to a local disk.
Drive  D:    maps to a local disk.
Drive  E:    maps to a local disk.
Drive  F: = VOYAGER_311\SYS:  \
Drive  G: = VOYAGER_311\DATA:  \
Drive  H: = VOYAGER_311\SYS:SYSTEM  \
Drive  L: = VOYAGER_311\DATA:BUSINESS\IS  \
Drive  M: = VOYAGER_311\DATA:  \FORMS
      ----
SEARCH1:  = Z:.  [VOYAGER_311\SYS:  \PUBLIC]
SEARCH2:  = Y:.  [VOYAGER_311\SYS:  \PUBLIC\IBM_PC\MSDOS\V5.00]
SEARCH3:  = X:.  [VOYAGER_311\SYS:  \SOFTWARE\WP]
SEARCH4:  = W:.  [VOYAGER_311\SYS:  \SOFTWARE\SP]
SEARCH5:  = V:.  [VOYAGER_311\SYS:  \SOFTWARE\DB]

F:\>DBA
F:\>
```

INSTALLING A SINGLE-USER APPLICATION

Determining Compatibility

The first application package Leslie planned to install, the general ledger application, was originally written by the Indianhead Computer Software Co. for use on a standalone computer. Leslie contacted Indianhead and checked the compatibility and legal requirements for installing the general ledger application on the file server. She explained to Bill, a programmer at Indianhead Computer Software, that both Ned Lynch and Ann Bonny need to access and maintain the general ledger files. Bill told Leslie that while the program will run on the network, the current version is not designed for multiuser access. He informed her that a new multiuser version of the software will be available soon.

Leslie asked Bill if making the general ledger files sharable would allow both Ned and Ann to access data. Bill explained that because this version of the package is not "multiuser," if two users update or view the files at the same time the program could crash or one user's changes could overwrite the changes made by another user, resulting in incorrect or incomplete information. Because Leslie does not want either of these problems, she decided to allow only one user to access the files at any one time. By leaving the files nonsharable, Leslie can prevent two users from accessing information at the same time.

Creating the Directory Structure

Leslie has already designed and created a directory for the general ledger package. After reading the installation instructions, she found that the INSTALL program will create a directory called GLSYSTEM on the root of the designated drive. She did not want the package installed on the root of her data volume, so she used the L: drive, a root drive mapped to the BUSINESS directory. Because a root drive mapping appears to be the beginning of the volume, the installation program will think it is creating the directory on the root, when actually the directory will be created in Leslie's BUSINESS directory. She also deletes her existing BUSINESS\GL directory because the INSTALL program will create its own directory called GLSYSTEM.

Installing Application Files

Next Leslie inserted the original copy of GL system diskette 1 into drive A: and ran INSTALL. The INSTALL program asked her on which drive she wanted to install the software. She entered "L:"; to her frustration, the INSTALL program responded with "Invalid drive message." Leslie reasoned that the installation program only accepts local drive letters such as C, D, or E. To make it work, Leslie decided to map drive D: to the DATA:\BUSINESS directory, as shown in Figure 6-5. Leslie was happy to see that this worked and that she can complete the installation process.

Figure 6-5: Leslie's screen after she mapped drive D: to the GL directory

```
F:\>MAP ROOT D:=DATA:BUSINESS

Drive D is in use by a local drive.
Do you want to assign it as network drive? (Y/N) Y
Drive   D: = VOYAGER_311\DATA:BUSINESS   \

F:\>MAP

Drive   A:    maps to a local disk.
Drive   B:    maps to a local disk.
Drive   C:    maps to a local disk.
Drive   D: = VOYAGER_311\DATA:BUSINESS   \
Drive   E:    maps to a local disk.
Drive   F: = VOYAGER_311\SYS:   \
Drive   G: = VOYAGER_311\DATA:   \
Drive   H: = VOYAGER_311\SYS:SYSTEM   \
        -----
SEARCH1:   = Z:. [VOYAGER_311\SYS:   \PUBLIC]
SEARCH2:   = Y:. [VOYAGER_311\SYS:   \PUBLIC\IBM_PC\MSDOS\V5.00]
SEARCH3:   = X:. [VOYAGER_311\SYS:   \SOFTWARE\WP]
SEARCH4:   = W:. [VOYAGER_311\SYS:   \SOFTWARE\SP]
SEARCH5:   = V:. [VOYAGER_311\SYS:   \SOFTWARE\DB]
```

Flagging Application Program Files

To list the files installed in the GLSYSTEM directory along with their attributes, Leslie next used the NDIR command, as shown in Figure 6-6. She noticed that the files were flagged as Read, Write, and Archive. Just as in DOS, the Archive attribute means the file has been changed but not backed up. Since the files are not flagged as Sharable, only one user at a time will be allowed to have access to the data. To protect the software programs from any accidents that might happen when Ned or Ann are working on the general ledger, Leslie used the FLAG

FIGURE 6-6: Leslie's screen after she used the NDIR command to list files in the GLSYSTEM directory

```
VOYAGER_311/DATA:BUSINESS\GLSYSTEM

Files:            Size     Last Updated        Flags          Owner
--------------  --------  --------------  ------------------  ---------
CONFIG    DB          13   4-03-90  8:13a [Rw-A-------------] SUPERVISO
CONFIG    GEN        817   4-08-91  9:10p [Rw-A-------------] SUPERVISO
ENDPER    PRG      2,072   1-01-80 12:19a [Rw-A-------------] SUPERVISO
GENDICT   DBF     19,853   4-08-91  9:10p [Rw-A-------------] SUPERVISO
GENDICT   NTX     10,240   4-08-91  9:10p [Rw-A-------------] SUPERVISO
GENEDIT   BAK        551   4-08-91  8:56p [Rw-A-------------] SUPERVISO
GENEDIT   TXT        585   4-08-91  8:58p [Rw-A-------------] SUPERVISO
GENINQ    SKL     11,392   6-18-86  5:30p [Rw-A-------------] SUPERVISO
GENLAYT   DBF     15,147   4-08-91  9:09p [Rw-A-------------] SUPERVISO
GENLAYT   NTX      6,144   4-08-91  9:09p [Rw-A-------------] SUPERVISO
GENMNT    SKL     19,200   6-18-86  5:30p [Rw-A-------------] SUPERVISO
GENREP    SKL      6,528   6-18-86  5:30p [Rw-A-------------] SUPERVISO
GENSKEL   DBF         99   4-08-91  9:10p [Rw-A-------------] SUPERVISO
GENTEXT   DBF        195   4-08-91  9:10p [Rw-A-------------] SUPERVISO
GL_MAINT  PRG     18,904   2-06-90 12:11a [Rw-A-------------] SUPERVISO
GL_RMENU  PRG      1,849   9-30-90 11:58p [Rw-A-------------] SUPERVISO
GLAUDIT   BAK      6,909   4-18-90  1:43p [Rw-A-------------] SUPERVISO
GLAUDIT   PRG      6,469   4-08-91  9:10p [Rw-A-------------] SUPERVISO
GLBACKUP  DBF      3,266   1-01-80 12:17a [Rw-A-------------] SUPERVISO

Strike any key for next page or C for continuous display...
```

*.PRG RO command to make all the .PRG files Read Only.

Providing for User Access

Looking back at her trustee directory worksheet, Leslie checked to be sure she had given the users of the general ledger system the necessary rights to access the GLSYSTEM directory. She noticed that she forgot to give Ben Avery Read and File Scan access to this directory. She corrected her trustee directory worksheet to give Ben access and changed the name of the directory listed to GLSYSTEM, as shown in Figure 6-7.

FIGURE 6-7: Leslie's trustee directory worksheet, corrected to add Ben Avery to the GLSYSTEM directory

Directory Path	Business Group	99ANNBON	99NEDLYN	99EDWLOW	99MARREA	99BENAVE
BUSINESS\ PAYROLL		R F C W M E				
BUSINESS\ BUDGETS	R F		R F C W M E	R F C W M E		R F
BUSINESS\ WORK	R F C W M E					
BUSINESS\ GLSYSTEM	**R F**		**R F C W M E**			**R F**
BUSINESS\ USERS					R F	
SALES\ ORDERS			R F	R F		
BUSINESS					R F C W M E A	

Configuration Files and Testing

The documentation states that the application will use the database system and needs a minimum of 20 files and 15 buffers to operate. Leslie has already met these requirements; she is ready to try running the application. To test the program, Leslie changed to drive L: and used the CD command to change to the GLSYSTEM subdirectory. Because she has a search drive still mapped to the SYS:SOFTWARE\DB subdirectory, she can run the application by entering the command DBA GLMENU, as described in her software documentation.

In Chapter 7, you'll follow Leslie as she creates users and groups for her PC Solutions network.

In this chapter the following NetWare commands were used to perform the functions described below.

FLAG *filename attribute*   This command was used to make the files specified Sharable or Read Only by setting the attributes. The optional dash [-] ahead of the attribute will remove the attribute setting. Valid attributes are:

- Normal: Sets file attributes to Nonsharable, Read Write
- Sharable
- Read Only: Also turns on DI and RI
- Delete Inhibit
- Rename Inhibit
- Hidden
- System: Used on system files such as the Bindery

NDIR   This command was used to list file directory information, including the file attributes.

LISTDIR /S   This command was used to list the structure of a directory area. The /S option lists all subdirectories in the directory's structure.

1. List three levels of network compatibility.

2. Which of following would be an acceptable location to install a word processing program that will be used by several users in your company? For each unacceptable directory, describe why you feel that directory path would not work.
   a. The root of the SYS volume

   b. In SYS:SYSTEM\WP

   c. In SYS:PUBLIC

   d. In SYS:WP

3. Write a NetWare command to make sharable all files in the DATA:SALES\ORDERS directory with the extension .PRG.

4. If you install a database application that is designed to be used on a standalone PC on the file server, state one reason you should not make the database files Sharable.

5. Write the NetWare command to protect database program files from being changed.

6. To make it more difficult for users to copy program files from the file server using DOS commands, you should use the _____ file attribute.

7. To prevent all users, including the SUPERVISOR, from being able to copy files from the file server, you should use the _____ attribute.

8. Describe why all program files in the SYS:SOFTWARE\WP directory should be made Sharable.

9. When would you not want to make program files Sharable?

10. At a minimum, what rights do users usually need to run programs in a shared software directory?

SUPERIOR TECHNICAL COLLEGE PROJECT 6

Now it's time to install application software on your Superior Technical College network. Lee Olsen, Virg Kent, Ruth Olsen, and Clara Villa want to use a graphics program to produce the school brochures and catalogs.

Assignment 6-1: Install Network-Aware Software

❶ Create a special-purpose SOFTWARE directory for Virg's graphics package within your Superior Technical College structure. Within the directory create WP, SP, and DB subdirectories. Use the LISTDIR /S > PRN command to print your Superior Technical College directory structure. Attach the printout to Student Answer Sheet 6.

❷ Be sure your student work diskette is in a diskette drive. Change to that drive. The \GRAPHICS directory of your student work diskette contains a simulation of the process of installing a network version of a graphics package. Use the CD \GRAPHICS command to change to the \GRAPHICS directory of the drive containing your student diskette. Type **INSTALL** and press **[Enter]**. The INSTALL program will display the installation startup instructions. To start the INSTALL process, reenter the INSTALL command. When it asks you to insert disk number 1 or 2, leave your student work diskette in the drive and press **[Enter]**. All files will be copied into the path specified on the INSTALL program. Use the FLAG command to flag all files to be Sharable. Record the FLAG command you use on Student Answer Sheet 6.

❸ Use the FLAG command to hide the GRAPHICS.COM program. Record the FLAG command you use on Student Answer Sheet 6.

❹ Use the NDIR > PRN command to obtain a printout showing the contents of your GRAPHICS directory. Attach this printout to Student Answer Sheet 6.

❺ Modify your Chapter 5 trustee directory security worksheet to include a trustee assignment that will give Lee, Virg, Clara and Ruth the rights necessary to run the graphics package. Attach a copy of the modified trustee directory security worksheet to Student Answer Sheet 6.

Assignment 6-2: Install a Single-User Application

In this assignment you will install the Student Services GRADUATE placement system into your directory structure. This application was originally written for use on a standalone PC. There is no copyright problem in placing it on your file server. This is not a multiuser application, so only one user may update the database at any one time.

❶ Use the LISTDIR /S > PRN command to obtain a printout of your Superior Technical College directory structure. Highlight the directory where you plan to install the graduate placement system. Attach the printout to Student Answer Sheet 6.

❷ Change to the drive containing your student work diskette and use the command CD \GRADUATE to change to the graduate system. Use the TYPE README.TXT command to view installation instructions. Use the MAP command to create a root drive pointer to the directory that is to contain the GRADUATE subdirectory. Be sure the drive letter you use for the mapping is one of the valid drive letters specified in README.TXT. (If you have already created a subdirectory for the graduate placement system that does not have a drive letter specified in the README.TXT file, you must rename or remove the existing directory before continuing with the installation of this application.) Record your MAP command on Student Answer Sheet 6.

❸ Use the command specified in the README.TXT file to install the application on your mapped drive. Flag all .BAS program files to be Sharable and Read Only. Do *not* allow the *.DBF and *.NDX files to be Sharable. Record the command you use on Student Answer Sheet 6.

❹ Use the NDIR > PRN command to print a hard copy of the contents of the graduate application subdirectory. Attach a copy of your printout to Student Answer Sheet 6. Be sure your trustee directory security worksheet provides all users with the rights necessary to run the graduate placement application.

Assignment 6-3: **Install a Multiuser Application**
In this assignment you will install the testing software into your Superior Technical College directory structure in the subdirectory you defined for it in Chapter 2.

❶ On your printout from Assignment 6-2, step 1, highlight the directory where you plan to install the testing application. Change to the drive containing your student work diskette, and use the command CD \TESTING to change to the testing system. Use the TYPE README.TXT command to view installation instructions. Use the SESSION utility to change the root drive pointer created in Assignment 6-2, step 2, to the directory that is to contain the testing application subdirectory. Print the SESSION utility's Drive Mapping screen showing the corrected drive mapping. Attach this printout to Student Answer Sheet 6.

❷ Use the command specified in the README.TXT file to install the application on your mapped drive. Flag all files to be Sharable. Use the NDIR > PRN command to print the contents of the testing application subdirectory. Attach a copy of your printout to Student Answer Sheet 6. Be sure your trustee directory security worksheet provides all users with the rights necessary to run the testing application.

Turn in Materials Assemble the following materials in the appropriate sequence: Student Answer Sheet 6, printouts from Assignments 6-1, 6-2, and 6-3. Write on each printout the step in which it was generated. Turn in the materials to your instructor on or before the specified deadline.

Student Name: _____ Date: _____

Assignment 6-1:   **Install Network-Aware Software**

❶   Attach a printout of the results of the LISTDIR/S > PRN command.

❷   Record the FLAG command you used to make all files in your SOFTWARE\DB directory Sharable.

_____

❸   Record the FLAG command you used to hide the DBA program.

_____

❹   Attach a printout showing the results of the NDIR > PRN command.

❺   Attach a copy of the modified trustee directory security worksheet.

Assignment 6-2:   **Install a Single-User Application**

❶   Attach a printout of the result of the LISTDIR/S > PRN command.

❷   Record your MAP command. _____

❸   Record the FLAG command you used to make all the .BAS program files in your graduate placement directory Sharable and Read Only.

_____

❹   Attach a printout of your graduate application subdirectory.

Assignment 6-3:   **Install a Multiuser Application**

❶   Attach a printout of the SESSION utility's Drive Mapping screen showing your highlighted drive mapping for the testing application directory.

❷   Attach a printout showing the contents of the testing application directory.

In this chapter you will:

- Use SYSCON accounting functions to monitor file server usage

- Get information using the Supervisory option of SYSCON

- Use SYSCON to create groups and add members

- Use SYSCON to create users and home directories

- Use SYSCON to assign user account restrictions and user trustee rights

- Use SYSCON to create a workgroup manager and a user account manager

- Use the USERDEF utility to create templates and users

- Test your user accounts by logging in as a new user and listing trustee rights

CREATING USERS AND GROUPS

SYSCON, which stands for SYStem CONfiguration, is the main supervisory utility used to create and maintain users and groups. Users can be created with other utilities, but only SYSCON can be used to create and maintain user groups. In addition, SYSCON can be used to control network accounting and maintain the file server's startup file.

NetWare Accounting allows the NetWare administrator to charge users for various services such as disk blocks read or written, disk space used, file server services, and login time. In addition to charging for these services, NetWare also allows the administrator to print daily and weekly totals for each service. By setting charge rates for each desired type of service, the administrator can select which services are to be charged to the users and determine the ratio of how many units of service it takes to make one charge unit. For example, a ratio of 1/10 in disk blocks read would mean that 10 blocks read would equal 1 unit of charge. A unit of charge can stand for any monetary value determined by the administrator.

NetWare Accounting is maintained by adjusting the balance information on each user's account according to the charge ratio of the service used. When the user's account balance becomes zero or negative, the user will not be able to log in until the balance is restored. Usage totals are tracked in the SYSTEM directory in a file named NET$ACCT.DAT. The contents of this file can be summarized and printed using the ATOTAL.EXE program. An audit of all user login and usage data can obtained from this file by running the PAUDIT.EXE program.

The NET$REC.DAT is a conversion table used by the PAUDIT and ATOTAL programs to translate the NET$ACCT.DAT information. Although you can erase the NET$ACCT.DAT file to reset weekly totals, the NET$REC.DAT file must be left in the SYSTEM directory.

In this chapter you will follow Leslie through the process of using the SYSCON utility to create users and groups for PC Solutions. She will also use SYSCON to assign user account restrictions and trustee rights and to make user account and workgroup managers.

SYSCON, although one of the most powerful utilities, does require several steps to create users. The USERDEF utility is designed to streamline the process of creating users by allowing you to create user templates. In this chapter you will see how to apply the USERDEF utility to creating users by implementing departmental templates.

The USERDEF utility, along with certain functions of SYSCON, can be used only by the SUPERVISOR or a supervisor-equivalent user. In this chapter you will also see how to use the supervisory functions of SYSCON, such as Accounting.

All NetWare menu utilities have certain function keys that are used for common purposes. The F1 key may be used for additional help information on a certain screen. The F3 key is used to change the value of an entry. For example, you can use F3 in SYSCON to change a user's login name. In FILER you can use the F3 key to change the name of a highlighted directory. The F5 key is used to mark items. If you wanted to delete three user accounts in SYSCON, you could highlight each username and press the F5 key. After all three usernames have been marked, press the Del key and SYSCON will remove all the marked users. A similar method can be used to remove a number of files or subdirectories using the FILER utility.

THE PC SOLUTIONS CASE

Leslie was ready to set up the file server environment for PC Solutions users. To do this, she used the powerful NetWare menu utilities SYSCON and USERDEF. Leslie planned to start by using SYSCON to set up accounting on the file server, then create user groups and any special users. Because of the USERDEF utility's ability to use templates for each workgroup, Leslie planned to use it to create users in the Business, Sales, and Help Desk departments. Templates allowed her to set up common parameters, such as group membership, home directory area, and user account security, that will apply to all users created with that department's template.

USING NETWARE ACCOUNTING

Although Leslie did not plan to bill her users for access time, she wanted to be able to track file server usage to document the growth of the network and plan for future needs. These records will be useful when she needs to justify to Ben the purchase of another disk drive or more memory for the file server. The number of file server requests, along with the number of disk blocks read or written, will tell her how heavily the file server is being used each week. The disk storage information will help her plan for additional disk space requirements needed in the future. Leslie planned to keep this information on a spreadsheet and then produce a graph showing growth of file server usage over a period of time.

To keep track of and print these totals, Leslie must have at least one charge ratio defined in one of the five accounting areas. Because she wanted to create a year-to-date log showing how many hours each user was logged in to the file server, she decided to set up a 1/60 charge ratio in the Connect Time Charge Rates option. This ratio will cause NetWare to deduct 1 unit of charge from the user's account balance for each 60 minutes of connect time.

To set up the Accounting feature, Leslie logged in as SUPERVISOR and ran SYSCON. She next selected the Accounting option from SYSCON's Available Topics menu. SYSCON asked if she wanted to install Accounting, as shown on the SYSCON Available Topics screen in Figure 7-1 on the following page. She selected Yes and pressed [Enter]. In a few seconds the NetWare Accounting feature was enabled on her server and she received the Accounting menu shown in Figure 7-2 on the following page.

FIGURE 7-1: The SYSCON Available Topics menu

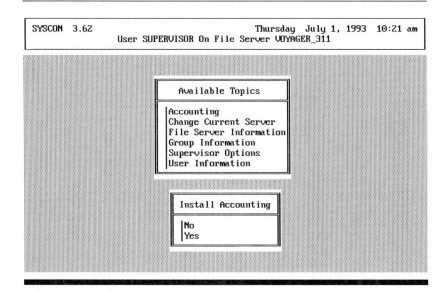

```
SYSCON  3.62                            Thursday  July 1, 1993  10:21 am
                   User SUPERVISOR On File Server VOYAGER_311

                          ┌──────────────────────┐
                          │   Available Topics   │
                          ├──────────────────────┤
                          │Accounting            │
                          │Change Current Server │
                          │File Server Information│
                          │Group Information     │
                          │Supervisor Options    │
                          │User Information      │
                          └──────────────────────┘

                          ┌──────────────────────┐
                          │  Install Accounting  │
                          ├──────────────────────┤
                          │No                    │
                          │Yes                   │
                          └──────────────────────┘
```

FIGURE 7-2: The Accounting menu after Accounting is installed

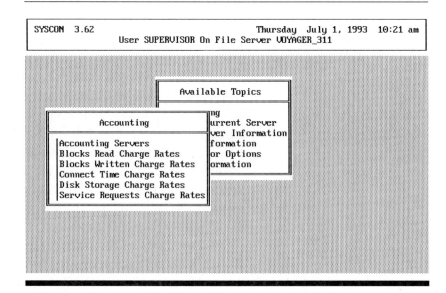

```
SYSCON  3.62                            Thursday  July 1, 1993  10:21 am
                   User SUPERVISOR On File Server VOYAGER_311

                          ┌──────────────────────┐
                          │   Available Topics   │
          ┌───────────────┴──────────┐           │
          │        Accounting        │ng         │
          ├──────────────────────────┤urrent Server│
          │Accounting Servers        │ver Information│
          │Blocks Read Charge Rates  │formation  │
          │Blocks Written Charge Rates│or Options │
          │Connect Time Charge Rates │ormation   │
          │Disk Storage Charge Rates │───────────┘
          │Service Requests Charge Rates│
          └──────────────────────────┘
```

To set up the connect time charge ratio, Leslie did the following:

1. She highlighted the Connect Time Charge Rates option and pressed [Enter]. The Connect Time Charge Rates screen shown in Figure 7-3 appeared. The charges are broken down by half-hour time slots for each day of the week. Whenever a user logs in to the file server, the system checks the charge rate table to determine the charge ratio for that day and time. In the figure, a 1 indicates no charge. Because Leslie was interested in keeping track of the hours of connect time, she needed to enter a charge rate.

FIGURE 7-3: The Connection Time Charge Rate screen before any changes are made

```
SYSCON   3.62                           Thursday  July 1, 1993  10:21 am
                     User SUPERVISOR On File Server VOYAGER_311

                                      Sun   Mon   Tue   Wed   Thu   Fri   Sat
        Connect Time Charge Rates   8:00am  1    1    1    1    1    1    1
                                    8:30am  1    1    1    1    1    1    1
                                    9:00am  1    1    1    1    1    1    1
Sunday                              9:30am  1    1    1    1    1    1    1
8:00 am To 8:29 am                 10:00am  1    1    1    1    1    1    1
                                   10:30am  1    1    1    1    1    1    1
Rate  Charge     Rate  Charge      11:00am  1    1    1    1    1    1    1
  1  No Charge     11               11:30am  1    1    1    1    1    1    1
  2                12               12:00pm  1    1    1    1    1    1    1
  3                13               12:30pm  1    1    1    1    1    1    1
  4                14                1:00pm  1    1    1    1    1    1    1
  5                15                1:30pm  1    1    1    1    1    1    1
  6                16                2:00pm  1    1    1    1    1    1    1
  7                17                2:30pm  1    1    1    1    1    1    1
  8                18                3:00pm  1    1    1    1    1    1    1
  9                19                3:30pm  1    1    1    1    1    1    1
 10                20                4:00pm  1    1    1    1    1    1    1
        (Charge is per minute)       4:30pm  1    1    1    1    1    1    1
```

2. To create a new charge rate for all days and times, she pressed the F5 key and used the arrow keys to block all entries from 8:00 a.m. through 7:30 a.m. She then pressed the Enter key. SYSCON displayed the Select Charge Rate window shown on the left in Figure 7-4.

FIGURE 7-4: Setting the Connect Time Charge ratio

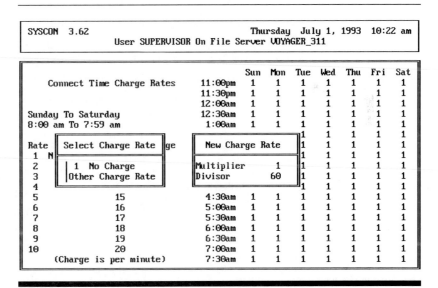

```
SYSCON   3.62                           Thursday  July 1, 1993  10:22 am
                     User SUPERVISOR On File Server VOYAGER_311

                                      Sun   Mon   Tue   Wed   Thu   Fri   Sat
        Connect Time Charge Rates   11:00pm  1    1    1    1    1    1    1
                                    11:30pm  1    1    1    1    1    1    1
                                    12:00am  1    1    1    1    1    1    1
Sunday To Saturday                  12:30am  1    1    1    1    1    1    1
8:00 am To 7:59 am                   1:00am  1    1    1    1    1    1    1
                                                   1    1    1    1    1
Rate  | Select Charge Rate |ge     | New Charge Rate |  1    1    1    1    1
  1  N                                              1    1    1    1    1
  2    | 1  No Charge     |         Multiplier    1 |  1    1    1    1    1
  3    | Other Charge Rate|         Divisor     60 |  1    1    1    1    1
  4                                                 1    1    1    1    1
  5                15                4:30am  1    1    1    1    1    1    1
  6                16                5:00am  1    1    1    1    1    1    1
  7                17                5:30am  1    1    1    1    1    1    1
  8                18                6:00am  1    1    1    1    1    1    1
  9                19                6:30am  1    1    1    1    1    1    1
 10                20                7:00am  1    1    1    1    1    1    1
        (Charge is per minute)       7:30am  1    1    1    1    1    1    1
```

3. Next, she highlighted the Other Charge Rate option and pressed [Enter]. The New Charge Rate window shown to the right of the Select Charge Rate window in Figure 7-4 was displayed.

4. She then entered the charge ratio of 1/60 and pressed the Esc key to save the rate of 1 for the multiplier and 60 for the divisor. The updated Connect Time Charge Rates screen shown in Figure 7-5 on the following page was displayed. The charge ratio of 1/60 means that for each 60 minutes of use, the system will accumulate 1 unit of charge.

FIGURE 7-5: The new Connect Time Charge Rates screen after Leslie changed the rate

```
SYSCON  3.62                              Thursday  July 1, 1993  10:22 am
                    User SUPERVISOR On File Server VOYAGER_311

                                             Sun  Mon  Tue  Wed  Thu  Fri  Sat
        Connect Time Charge Rates    11:00pm  1    1    1    1    1    1    1
                                     11:30pm  1    1    1    1    1    1    1
                                     12:00am  1    1    1    1    1    1    1
   Saturday                          12:30am  1    1    1    1    1    1    1
   7:30 am To 7:59 am                 1:00am  1    1    1    1    1    1    1
                                      1:30am  1    1    1    1    1    1    1
   Rate  Charge      Rate  Charge     2:00am  1    1    1    1    1    1    1
     1   1/60         11               2:30am  1    1    1    1    1    1    1
     2               12               3:00am  1    1    1    1    1    1    1
     3               13               3:30am  1    1    1    1    1    1    1
     4               14               4:00am  1    1    1    1    1    1    1
     5               15               4:30am  1    1    1    1    1    1    1
     6               16               5:00am  1    1    1    1    1    1    1
     7               17               5:30am  1    1    1    1    1    1    1
     8               18               6:00am  1    1    1    1    1    1    1
     9               19               6:30am  1    1    1    1    1    1    1
    10               20               7:00am  1    1    1    1    1    1    1
         (Charge is per minute)       7:30am  1    1    1    1    1    1    1
```

5. She then used the Esc key to return to the Accounting menu shown in Figure 7-2.

6. Pressing [Esc] again returned her the SYSCON Available Topics menu. Accounting is now up and running on her file server.

Note: All the other charge rate options except Disk Storage Charge Rates use the same method to change or set charge rates. The Disk Storage Charge Rates option uses a slightly different screen, as shown in Figure 7-6. To set up the charge ratio for disk storage, Leslie would select the time of day when you want the system to examine the storage used by each user and total it. Because this task takes some processing time, it is a good idea to have the server do this outside normal work hours. To indicate this time and charge rate, Leslie would move the cursor down to the desired day and time and press the 1 key. The number 1 stands for the first charge rate. Since there is no charge ratio for rate 1, the system asks for the multiplier and divisor rates as it did for the connect time charge rates. Leslie could enter the desired ratio, or press the Esc key twice to accept the 1/1 ratio, with the result shown in Figure 7-6.

At the end of each week, Leslie can now log in as SUPERVISOR, go to the SYS:SYSTEM directory, and use the ATOTAL program to print a summary of her file server usage, as shown in Figure 7-7. Accounting total

FIGURE 7-6: The Disk Storage Charge Rates screen

```
SYSCON  3.62                              Thursday  July 1, 1993  10:22 am
                    User SUPERVISOR On File Server VOYAGER_311

                                          Sun  Mon  Tue  Wed  Thu  Fri  Sat
     Disk Storage Charge Rates    4:30pm
                                  5:00pm
                                  5:30pm
   Sunday                         6:00pm
   10:00 pm To 10:29 pm           6:30pm
                                  7:00pm
   Rate  Charge     Rate  Charge  7:30pm
     1   1/1         11            8:00pm
     2              12            8:30pm
     3              13            9:00pm
     4              14            9:30pm
     5              15           10:00pm   1
     6              16           10:30pm
     7              17           11:00pm
     8              18           11:30pm
     9              19           12:00am
    10              20           12:30am
        (Charge is per block-day) 1:00am
```

FIGURE 7-7: Leslie's screen after she ran the weekly ATOTAL program

```
H:\>ATOTAL

ACCOUNTING SERVICES TOTAL UTILITY, Version 2.02

07/01/1993:
    Connect time:         4    Server requests:    21255
    Blocks read:        298    Blocks written:        61
    Blocks/day:           0

Totals for week:
    Connect time:         4    Server requests:    21255
    Blocks read:        298    Blocks written:        61
    Blocks/day:           0


H:\>
```

information is stored in the NET$ACCT.DAT file. At the end of each week, Leslie planned to erase this file. If there is no NET$ACCT.DAT file, NetWare Accounting will create a new file, effectively resetting the totals for the next week.

USING SYSCON SUPERVISOR OPTIONS

Before creating new users, Leslie wanted to set the default account restrictions values that SYSCON will use for each user she created. Setting these defaults will save her time because she will not repeatedly have to enter these values for each user. To set default account restrictions, Leslie did the following:

1. She highlighted the Supervisor Options of the SYSCON menu and pressed [Enter]. The Supervisor Options menu shown in Figure 7-8 was displayed.

FIGURE 7-8: The Supervisor Options menu

```
┌─────────────────────────────────────────────────────────────────┐
│ SYSCON  3.62                          Thursday  July 1, 1993  10:25 am │
│              User SUPERVISOR On File Server VOYAGER_311            │
└─────────────────────────────────────────────────────────────────┘

              ┌─ Available Topics ─┐
              │Accounting│    ┌──────── Supervisor Options ────────┐
              │Change Cur│    │                                    │
              │File Serve│    │Default Account Balance/Restrictions│
              │Group Info│    │Default Time Restrictions           │
              │Supervisor│    │Edit System AUTOEXEC File           │
              │User Infor│    │File Server Console Operators       │
              └──────────┘    │Intruder Detection/Lockout          │
                              │System Login Script                 │
                              │View File Server Error Log          │
                              │Workgroup Managers                  │
                              └────────────────────────────────────┘
```

2. To access the default values, she highlighted the Default Account Balance/Restrictions option and pressed [Enter]. The Default Account Balance/Restrictions screen was displayed.

3. Leslie then changed these values to the settings shown in Figure 7-9 on the following page. These values will apply to any new users she creates. Existing users are *not* affected by changing the default values. A description of each default is available by pressing the F1 key.

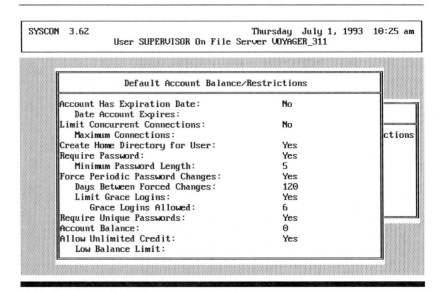

```
SYSCON  3.62                          Thursday  July 1, 1993  10:25 am
                    User SUPERVISOR On File Server VOYAGER_311


               Default Account Balance/Restrictions

      Account Has Expiration Date:        No
          Date Account Expires:
      Limit Concurrent Connections:       No
          Maximum Connections:                              ctions
      Create Home Directory for User:     Yes
      Require Password:                    Yes
          Minimum Password Length:        5
      Force Periodic Password Changes:     Yes
          Days Between Forced Changes:     120
          Limit Grace Logins:             Yes
              Grace Logins Allowed:        6
      Require Unique Passwords:            Yes
      Account Balance:                     0
      Allow Unlimited Credit:              Yes
          Low Balance Limit:
```

4. After checking the values, Leslie pressed [Esc] to save the changes and return to the Supervisor Options menu shown in Figure 7-8.

Leslie next wanted to document the contents of the AUTOEXEC file, which contains commands the file server will execute when it is started. To view the contents of the AUTOEXEC file, Leslie selected the Edit System AUTOEXEC File option of the Supervisor Options menu and pressed [Enter]. The AUTOEXEC file Jake created for her when he installed NetWare on the server appeared, as shown in Figure 7-10. She could use this option to modify or add commands, such as loading a print server, but at this time she pressed the Print Screen key to print the contents of the file for future reference.

To increase security, Leslie wanted to prevent unauthorized users from attempting to log in to the network by guessing a user's password. To do this, NetWare provides a feature called **intruder detection/lockout**. When intruder detection/lockout is on and someone tries to guess a user's password more than the predetermined number of times in a given time period, the user account will be locked for the time period selected. This protection applies to the SUPERVISOR account as well. To turn on intruder detection/lockout, Leslie highlighted the Intruder Detection/Lockout option of the Supervisor Options menu and pressed [Enter]. She then filled out the Intruder Detection/Lockout screen, as shown in Figure 7-11. Now if someone tries to guess a user's password more than seven times in a 30-minute period, the user's account will be locked out for 15 minutes. Pressing [Esc] saved the intruder lockout information and returned Leslie to the Supervisor Options menu.

```
SYSCON  3.62                          Thursday  July 1, 1993  10:25 am
                    User SUPERVISOR On File Server VOYAGER_311


                       System AUTOEXEC File

file server name VOYAGER_311
ipx internal net 1
load SMCPLUSS port=300 mem=CC000 int=A frame=ETHERNET_802.3
bind IPX to SMCPLUSS net=DAD
mount all
load remote pass
load rspx
load monitor
```

FIGURE 7-11: Leslie's Intruder Detection/Lockout screen

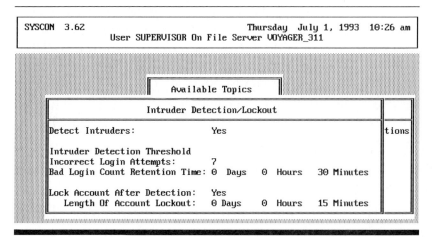

```
SYSCON  3.62                        Thursday  July 1, 1993  10:26 am
            User SUPERVISOR On File Server VOYAGER_311

                      ┌──────────────────────────┐
                      │     Available Topics     │
              ┌───────┴──────────────────────────┴──┐      ┌──────┐
              │       Intruder Detection/Lockout     │      │tions │
              ├──────────────────────────────────────┤      └──────┘
  Detect Intruders:            Yes
  
  Intruder Detection Threshold
  Incorrect Login Attempts:      7
  Bad Login Count Retention Time: 0  Days   0  Hours    30 Minutes
  
  Lock Account After Detection:  Yes
     Length Of Account Lockout:  0  Days   0  Hours    15 Minutes
```

The System Login Script option on the Supervisor Options menu will allow Leslie to set up and maintain a system LOGIN script of commands that will be executed by all users upon logging into the file server. She planned to implement the system LOGIN script commands soon.

Jake told Leslie that it is important to periodically use the View File Server Error Log option, also on the Supervisor Options menu, to track file server messages and look for problems. The file server error log lists any error messages or warnings issued since the error log was last cleared. It specifies the date and time of the error or warning and identifies the nature of the message. (The NetWare System Messages manual contains explanations of the messages.)

Because Mary Read periodically hires part-time staff to help her during the busy fall season, Leslie would like to allow Mary to create and manage these temporary employee accounts. To do this, Leslie planned to make Mary Read a workgroup manager. Before NetWare 2.2, it would have been necessary to make Mary's account a supervisor-equivalent to allow her to create users. But now, as a workgroup manager, Mary has the right to create new users and manage or delete the user accounts she creates. A workgroup manager does not have rights to manage or change other user accounts. Leslie will make Mary a workgroup manager later, after she has created Mary's user account.

To exit the Supervisor Options menu and return to SYSCON's Available Topics menu, Leslie pressed the Esc key.

CREATING GROUPS

In the workgroup table Leslie created in Chapter 2, she defined four groups: BUSINESS, SALES, HELPDESK, and SUPPORT (refer to Figure 2-3). To create these groups Leslie selected the Group Information option from SYSCON's Available Topics menu and pressed [Enter]. Next she pressed the Ins key and entered the name of a new group, as shown in Figure 7-12. The new group was then added to the list of existing groups.

FIGURE 7-12: Creating a new group

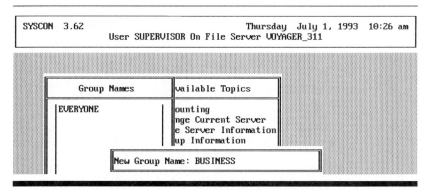

```
SYSCON  3.62                        Thursday  July 1, 1993  10:26 am
            User SUPERVISOR On File Server VOYAGER_311

        ┌───────────────────┬───────────────────┐
        │    Group Names    │vailable Topics    │
        ├───────────────────┼───────────────────┤
        │ EVERYONE          │ounting            │
        │                   │nge Current Server │
        │                   │e Server Information
        │                   │up Information     │
        │         ┌─────────┴──────────────────────┐
        │         │New Group Name: BUSINESS         │
        │         └─────────────────────────────────┘
```

CREATING USERS

As administrative assistant, Mary Read works for both the Sales and Business Departments. Leslie planned to give Mary's account workgroup manager privileges as well as assign her control of other users' accounts. Leslie wanted to create a user account for herself to use for nonsupervisory functions, so she will use the SUPERVISOR username only when it is required to perform a specific function. Because Leslie's and Mary's user accounts do not fit into one of Leslie's USERDEF department templates, Leslie decided to create usernames for Mary and herself using the SYSCON utility. She will then create the users in the Sales and Business Departments with templates from USERDEF. To create Mary's username with SYSCON, Leslie did the following:

1. She first selected the User Information option from SYSCON's Available Topics menu and pressed [Enter]. A window appeared, showing existing usernames.

2. To create a new user, Leslie pressed [Ins] and entered Mary Read's username, as shown in Figure 7-13, then pressed [Enter].

FIGURE 7-13: Creating a new user account for Mary Read

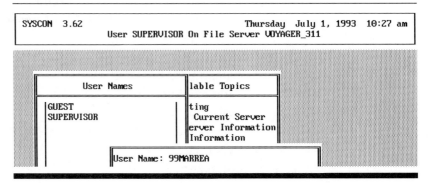

3. When SYSCON asked for the path to Mary's home directory, Leslie responded by typing DATA:SUPPORT/99MARREA, as shown in Figure 7-14. SYSCON next asked if she wanted to create this directory. If there is already a directory for 99MARREA, SYSCON will display an error message and create Mary's username without giving her rights to the specified home directory. Leslie would then have to give Mary rights to her home directory later through a separate trustee assignment. For this reason Leslie did not create the home directories in Chapter 3.

FIGURE 7-14: Entering the new user's home directory path

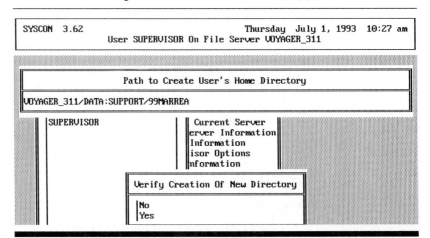

4. Leslie repeated the above process to create a username 99LESSTE for herself. After creating her username, Leslie pressed [Esc] to return to SYSCON's Available Topics menu.

ADDING A USER TO A GROUP

According to the workgroup table Leslie created in Chapter 2 (see Figure 2-3), Mary Read needs to be a member of the Business, Sales, and Support workgroups. To make Mary a member of these groups, Leslie did the following:

1. She highlighted the User Information option from the SYSCON Available Topics menu and pressed [Enter]. The User Names window showing all existing users was displayed.

2. Next she highlighted Mary's username, 99MARREA, in the User Names window and pressed [Enter]. The User Information menu shown in Figure 7-15 was then displayed.

FIGURE 7-15: The User Information menu

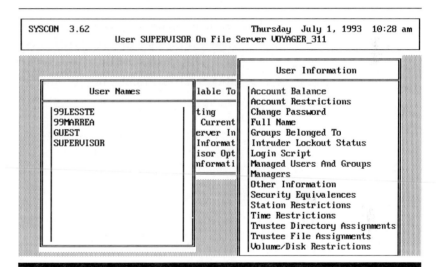

3. From the User Information window, Leslie selected the Groups Belonged To option, as shown on the right in Figure 7-16. SYSCON displayed a window of the groups to which Mary Read belongs. Mary is a member of the group EVERYONE. Whenever a new user is created, NetWare automatically makes that user a member of the group EVERYONE.

4. To make Mary a member of the other groups, Leslie pressed the Ins key. A list of groups Mary does not belong to is displayed to the left of the Groups Belonged To screen, as shown in Figure 7-16 on the following page.

FIGURE 7-16: Leslie's screen before she selected the groups for Mary Read's account

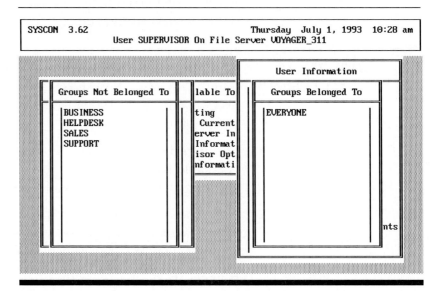

```
SYSCON  3.62                              Thursday  July 1, 1993  10:28 am
                          User SUPERUISOR On File Server UOYAGER_311

                                               User Information
         Groups Not Belonged To      lable To   Groups Belonged To
           BUSINESS                  ting        EUERYONE
           HELPDESK                    Current
           SALES                     erver In
           SUPPORT                   Informat
                                     isor Opt
                                     nformati

                                                                       nts
```

5. Leslie used the arrow keys to highlight a group and then pressed the F5 key until she marked the BUSINESS, SALES, and SUPPORT groups; then she pressed [Enter]. The Groups Belonged To window was updated to show the newly selected groups.

6. She then pressed [Esc] twice to return to the User Names window.

7. Leslie then repeated the above process to add her name, 99LESSTE, to the appropriate groups.

MAKING TRUSTEE ASSIGNMENTS

To grant Mary the trustee rights defined on the trustee directory security worksheet she created in Chapter 5, Leslie did the following:

1. She first highlighted the User Information option of the Available Topics menu and pressed [Enter]. The User Names window was displayed, showing the existing users.

2. Leslie then highlighted the 99MARREA username and pressed [Enter]. The User Information window shown in Figure 7-15 was displayed.

3. Next she highlighted the Trustee Directory Assignments option and pressed [Enter]. The screen shown in Figure 7-17 was displayed.

FIGURE 7-17: Adding a new trustee assignment to Mary's user account

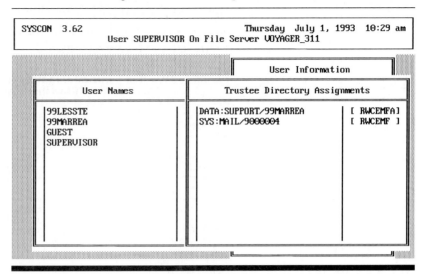

4. To enter a new trustee assignment, Leslie pressed [Ins]. The SYSCON utility opened a window asking for the path to the directory where the trustee right was to be granted.

5. Leslie entered the path to the BUSINESS directory. When a path is entered, NetWare will accept either a backslash (\) or a slash (/) as a separator between subdirectory levels. (If Leslie had not remembered the exact path, she could have used [Ins] at this time and selected the path one level at a time starting with the file server and DATA volume.) When Leslie pressed [Enter], the new trustee assignment was added to the list, with Read and File Scan rights.

6. To give Mary all rights except SUPERVISOR to the BUSINESS directory, Leslie highlighted the BUSINESS directory trustee rights and pressed [Enter].

7. She then pressed [Ins] to add other rights. The Trustee Rights Not Granted window shown in Figure 7-18 appeared.

FIGURE 7-18: The Trustee Rights Not Granted window

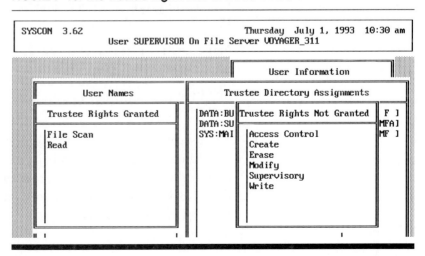

8. To select rights to add, Leslie used the arrow keys to highlight each right and pressed [F5]. After she selected all rights except Supervisory, she pressed [Enter]. The new rights for DATA:BUSINESS were added to the list, as shown in Figure 7-19.

FIGURE 7-19: Leslie's Trustee Directory Assignments screen after she added all rights to the Trustee Rights Granted window

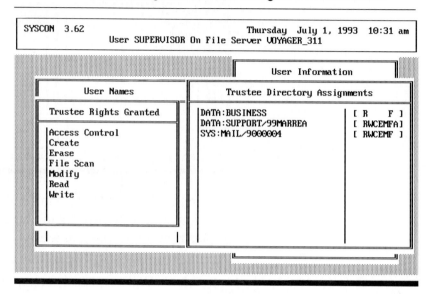

9. To save the new rights Leslie pressed [Esc]. The trustee assignment for the BUSINESS directory was changed to include the new rights.

10. Leslie repeated steps 3 through 9 for each of Mary's other trustee assignments, then pressed [Esc] until she returned to the Available Topics menu.

MAKING A WORKGROUP MANAGER

Because Mary Read will need to create and delete user accounts for her temporary employees, Leslie needed to give her workgroup manager status. To add Mary as a workgroup manager, Leslie did the following:

1. She first highlighted Supervisor Options from the Available Topics menu and pressed [Enter]. The Supervisor Option window shown in Figure 7-8 was displayed.

2. Next Leslie selected the Workgroup Managers option to open a window showing all existing workgroup managers.

3. She then pressed [Ins] to add a new workgroup manager to the list. SYSCON displayed a window of existing users and groups.

4. She used the arrow keys to highlight Mary's username and her own username and pressed [Enter]. Mary's and Leslie's usernames were now added to the list of workgroup managers, as shown in Figure 7-20. Both Leslie's and Mary's accounts now have privileges to create and manage new users and groups.

**FIGURE 7-20: Leslie's screen after she selected herself and Mary Read
to be workgroup managers**

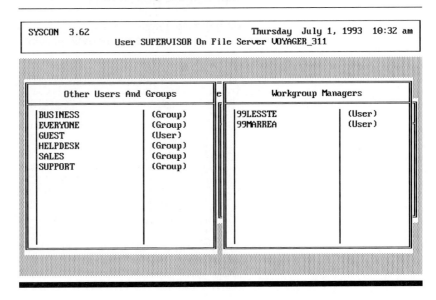

```
SYSCON   3.62                               Thursday  July 1, 1993  10:32 am
                        User SUPERVISOR On File Server VOYAGER_311

        ┌───────── Other Users And Groups ─────────┐e┌──── Workgroup Managers ────┐
        │ BUSINESS              (Group)             │ │ 99LESSTE         (User)    │
        │ EVERYONE              (Group)             │ │ 99MARREA         (User)    │
        │ GUEST                 (User)              │ │                            │
        │ HELPDESK              (Group)             │ │                            │
        │ SALES                 (Group)             │ │                            │
        │ SUPPORT               (Group)             │ │                            │
        │                                           │ │                            │
        │                                           │ │                            │
        └───────────────────────────────────────────┘ └────────────────────────────┘
```

5. To exit SYSCON quickly, Leslie held down [Alt] and pressed [F10].

**CREATING TEMPLATES
WITH USERDEF**

In her NetWare class, Leslie learned that the USERDEF utility can
simplify the task of creating users by allowing the supervisor to define
and use templates that contain account information common to all
users in a department. However, only the supervisor or a supervisor-
equivalent user can use the USERDEF utility; workgroup managers are
restricted to creating users with SYSCON.

   Leslie decided to use templates to help her create users in PC
Solutions' major workgroups. A template contains such information as
home directory location, groups to which the users belong, account
balance information, and password requirements. To use USERDEF to
create a template for the Business Department, Leslie did the following:

1. She typed the command USERDEF from the DOS prompt and pressed
    [Enter]. The USERDEF Available Options menu shown in Figure 7-21
    was displayed.

FIGURE 7-21: The USERDEF Available Options menu

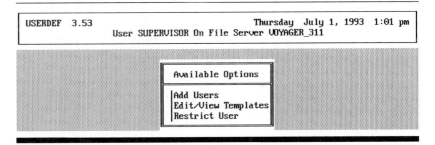

```
USERDEF   3.53                              Thursday  July 1, 1993  1:01 pm
                        User SUPERVISOR On File Server VOYAGER_311


                              ┌── Available Options ──┐
                              │ Add Users             │
                              │ Edit/View Templates   │
                              │ Restrict User         │
                              └───────────────────────┘
```

2. To create a new template, Leslie highlighted the Edit/View Templates
    option and pressed [Enter]. A window showing any existing templates
    was displayed.

3. She then pressed [Ins] and typed "BUSINESS" for the name of her new template, as shown in Figure 7-22.

FIGURE 7-22: Leslie's screen after she pressed (Ins) and typed the name of the new template

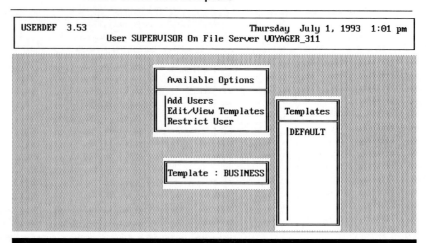

4. When she pressed [Enter], the template BUSINESS window, shown in Figure 7-23, was displayed.

FIGURE 7-23: Leslie's screen after she created the BUSINESS template

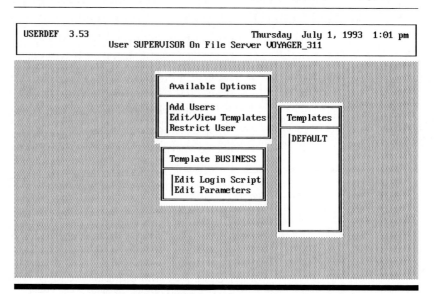

5. Next Leslie highlighted the Edit Parameters option and filled out the Parameters for Template BUSINESS screen, as shown in Figure 7-24. A description of each field can be obtained by press the F1 key.

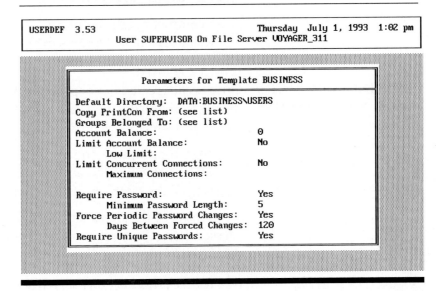

```
USERDEF  3.53                              Thursday  July 1, 1993  1:02 pm
                      User SUPERVISOR On File Server VOYAGER_311

                       Parameters for Template BUSINESS

          Default Directory:   DATA:BUSINESS\USERS
          Copy PrintCon From: (see list)
          Groups Belonged To: (see list)
          Account Balance:                    0
          Limit Account Balance:              No
                Low Limit:
          Limit Concurrent Connections:       No
                Maximum Connections:

          Require Password:                   Yes
                Minimum Password Length:      5
          Force Periodic Password Changes:    Yes
                Days Between Forced Changes:   120
          Require Unique Passwords:           Yes
```

6. Leslie entered the path where she wanted the Business Department users' home directories located in the Default Directory field.

7. In the Groups Belonged To list, Leslie entered the names of all the groups to which new users in the Business Department will belong. To add groups to this list, Leslie highlighted the option and pressed [Enter]. Then she pressed [Ins] and selected the groups from those displayed in the Existing Groups window. Pressing [Esc] returned her to the Parameters for Template BUSINESS window.

8. In the Account Balance field, Leslie entered a zero. NetWare Accounting will deduct one unit (hour) for each 60 minutes of connect time. By looking at the negative number in a user's balance field, Leslie will be able to determine the number of hours the user has been connected to the file server. Leaving the "No" in the Limit Account Balance field will allow the user to have unlimited credit. This will allow the user to log in with a zero or negative balance.

9. Leslie required all users to have a password of at least five bytes. The password will expire after 120 days; at that time, the user will have to invent a new password, one that is unique from any of the user's previous passwords. When a password expires, a user is given several grace login times before the account is disabled. Because passwords are required, each new user created with this template will be given his or her username as an expired password.

10. After filling in the screen, Leslie pressed [Esc] to save her entries and return to the Template BUSINESS window shown in Figure 7-23.

11. Because she did not plan to enter personal LOGIN scripts at this time, Leslie pressed [Esc] again to return to the Templates window. The BUSINESS and DEFAULT templates were displayed in the Templates window.

12. She then repeated steps 3 through 10 to set up templates for the Sales and PC Help Desk departments.

13. After completing all templates, Leslie pressed [Esc] to return to the USERDEF Available Options menu.

CREATING NEW USERS WITH USERDEF Once Leslie created her department templates, she was ready to create the users for the Business and Sales Departments. To use USERDEF to create the users for the Business Department, Leslie did the following:

1. She first highlighted the Add Users option from the USERDEF Available Options menu and pressed [Enter]. The templates window showing all the templates created was displayed.

2. Next, she used the arrow keys to highlight the BUSINESS template and pressed [Enter]. A list of current users, shown in Figure 7-25, was displayed.

FIGURE 7-25: Leslie's USERDEF screen after she chose to add users with the BUSINESS template

```
USERDEF   3.53                              Thursday  July 1, 1993  1:03 pm
                    User SUPERVISOR On File Server VOYAGER_311

                                    ┌─────────────────────┐
                                    │  Available Options  │
                                    ├─────────────────────┤
                      ┌───────────┐ │Add Users            │
                      │ Templates │ │Edit/View Templates  │
                      ├───────────┤ │Restrict User        │
                      │BUSINESS   │ └─────────────────────┘
                      │DEFAULT    │ ┌─────────────────────────────────┐
                      │           │ │              Users              │
                      │           │ ├─────────────────────────────────┤
                      │           │ │99LESSTE                         │
                      │           │ │99MARREA                         │
                      │           │ │GUEST                            │
                      │           │ │SUPERVISOR                       │
                      └───────────┘ └─────────────────────────────────┘
```

3. To create a new user, Leslie pressed [Ins]. USERDEF asked for new user's full name.

4. Leslie entered the full name of the first user in the Business workgroup. After she entered the full name, USERDEF asked for the username. USERDEF assumes the first name as the username, so Leslie needed to backspace to type the username she defined on the user worksheet, created in Chapter 5. When she pressed [Enter], the new username showed up in the right-hand column of the Users list with the word "new" in parentheses.

5. Leslie repeated steps 3 and 4 until she entered all users in the Business Department.

6. After all usernames were entered, Leslie pressed [Esc]. USERDEF then asked if she wanted to create the new users using the template BUSINESS, as shown in Figure 7-26.

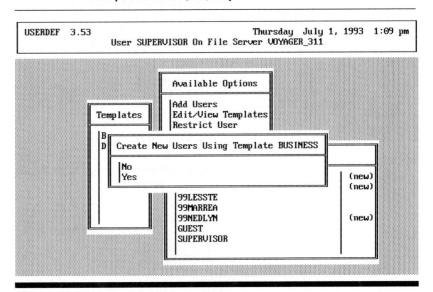

7. She responded by pressing [Enter]. USERDEF then created the new users and displayed the results, as shown in Figure 7-27. Because passwords were required in the template, each user was assigned his or her username for a password.

FIGURE 7-27: Leslie's USERDEF result screen after she created the Business Department users

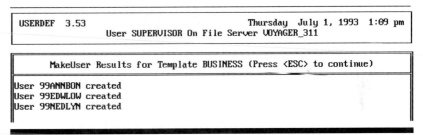

8. After verifying that the user accounts were created, Leslie pressed the [Esc] key twice to return to the Templates selection window.

9. She then repeated steps 2 through 8 for each of the other departments.

10. After all users accounts were created, Leslie exited USERDEF by holding down [Alt] while pressing [F10].

ASSIGNING USER ACCOUNT BALANCES

Because Leslie used the accounting balance to keep track of each user's connection time, she periodically needed to set this number back to zero. Rather than having to do this for each user, she selected a number of users and set the account balance for all at the same time. To assign a new account balance to multiple users, Leslie did the following:

1. She started SYSCON and selected User Information from the menu.

2. She used the arrow keys and the F5 key to highlight each of her user accounts. After all usernames were highlighted, she pressed [Enter];

SYSCON displayed the Set User Information window. This screen allows her to set other restrictions for all the marked users. The F1 key can be used to display a description of each field shown.

3. Leslie highlighted the Account Balance option and pressed [Enter]. The Set Marked Users Account Balance window, shown in Figure 7-28, appeared. Notice that the users have unlimited credit. Leslie selected this option in the template used to create the users. Without unlimited credit, users would be locked out of the system when they had depleted their account balances.

FIGURE 7-28: Leslie's screen allowing unlimited credit to all marked users

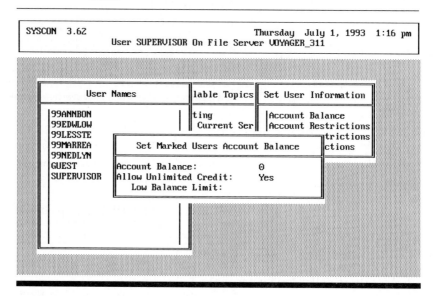

4. To set a new balance for all selected users, Leslie changed the Account Balance line to zero and pressed [Esc].

5. SYSCON then asked if she wanted to change all marked users to these settings. Leslie selected Yes and pressed [Enter]. The Account Balance field was set for each of Leslie's users.

6. Leslie pressed [Esc] until she returned to SYSCON's Available Topics menu.

ASSIGNING USERS TO A USER ACCOUNT MANAGER

As a workgroup manager, Mary is able to manage only the usernames she creates. However, Leslie wanted Mary to manage the user accounts defined as managed by Mary on the users' worksheet Leslie developed in Chapter 5. In addition, Leslie would like Mary to collect the connection time data for her by going to each user's information screen and recording the account balance. Each negative unit of account balance will correspond to one hour of connection time for that user. To allow Mary to manage the other users and record their account balances, Leslie needed to make Mary an account manager of these users. To make Mary a user account manager, Leslie did the following:

1. First she selected the User Information option from the Available Topics menu.

2. Next she used the arrow keys to highlight Mary's username and pressed [Enter]. The User Information option menu appeared.

3. Leslie then selected the Managed Users and Groups option from the User Information menu and pressed [Enter]. SYSCON displayed a window showing all users currently managed by Mary. The group EVERYONE is included because Mary is a workgroup manager and therefore NetWare must be able to add any new users she creates to the group EVERYONE. Note that making someone a manager of a group does not mean they can manage all users in that group.

4. To add more users, Leslie pressed [Ins]. A window of existing usernames was displayed, as shown in Figure 7-29.

FIGURE 7-29: Leslie's screen making Mary Read a user account manager

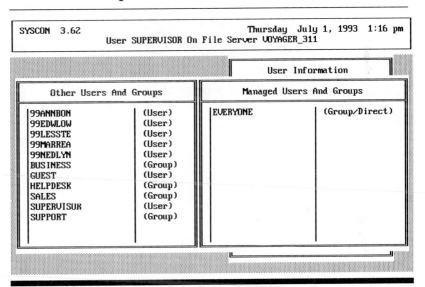

5. To mark all usernames, Leslie used the arrow keys to highlight each username and then pressed [F5] to mark that user. After all usernames were marked, she pressed [Enter] to add the selected users to the window of users managed by Mary.

6. Leslie exited SYSCON by holding down [Alt] while she pressed [F10].

Leslie has put in full morning creating users and workgroups. In Chapter 8 we'll follow her as she performs a number of file- and directory-related functions on the PC Solutions network.

In this chapter, the SYSCON and USERDEF utilities were used to perform the following functions.

SYSCON SYSCON contains functions for assignment and control of users, groups, security, and managers, as shown in Figure 7-30. The following user setup tasks were performed in this chapter using SYSCON:

FIGURE 7-30: The SYSCON menu and its submenus

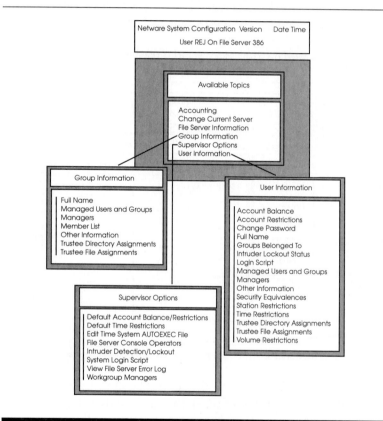

- Install and configure accounting
- Set system defaults for creating users
- Edit or view the file server's AUTOEXEC file
- Enable intruder detection and lockout
- Create users and configure user accounts
- Create groups and assign members
- Make trustee right assignments
- Designate workgroup and user account managers

SYSCON can also be used to do the following:

- Assign password, station, and time restrictions
- Create and maintain system and user LOGIN scripts

USERDEF The USERDEF utility, illustrated in Figure 7-31, is used to create multiple users with the same characteristics. Templates contain the characteristics to be used when creating users. A template can be created for each group of users requiring special characteristics.

FIGURE 7-31: The USERDEF menu

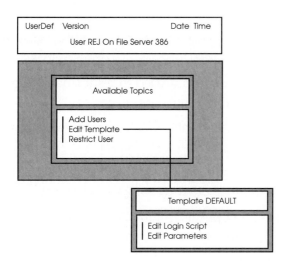

In this chapter, Leslie used USER-DEF to do the following:

■ Create templates for each department

■ Set up home directories

■ Assign account and disk space restrictions

■ Assign password restrictions

1. What is the name of the file used to keep accounting usage totals? Where is the file located?

2. The _____ program is used to print a daily and weekly summary of the accounting usage data.

3. The _____ Accounting file contains translation tables and must not be deleted.

4. A _____ can create and manage new users and groups but cannot manage other existing user accounts.

5. Only the supervisor or supervisor-equivalent user can use the _____ utility to create new users.

6. List any utilities that can be used to create new groups:

7. The _____ key is used to provide help information on the current screen.

8. The _____ key may be used to select multiple objects from a NetWare utility window.

9. If you wanted to change a username in SYSCON, you would first select the User Information option from the Available Topics menu. When the User Names window was displayed, you would highlight the username you wanted to change and press the _____ key.

10. Write a charge ratio that would provide one unit of charge for each half hour of connect time.

11. The _____ charge rate involves setting up a time and day you want the system to examine and total disk storage.

12. When using SYSCON, you can set the default account restrictions by using the _____ option of the Available Topics menu.

13. *True or false:* Setting up intruder detection is an option that must be performed during file server installation.

14. *True or false:* You can use SYSCON to change the file server's startup file.

15. Name one function that SYSCON can do that USERDEF cannot when a user's account balance is set up.

16. Which of the following can be done by USERDEF but not by SYSCON?
    a. Grant trustee assignments
    b. Make a user a member of a group
    c. Set up a user LOGIN script
    d. Copy PRINTCON jobs from another user

17. Which of the following can be done by SYSCON but not by USERDEF?
    a. Grant trustee assignments
    b. Make a user a member of a group
    c. Set up a user LOGIN script
    d. Copy PRINTCON jobs from another user

18. Which of the following is NOT contained on the USERDEF template?
    a. Account balance
    b. Groups
    c. Station restrictions
    d. Password restrictions

19. When users are created using USERDEF, what password is given to them if passwords are required?
    a. None
    b. PASS
    c. Their usernames
    d. They must provide one before they are allowed to log in

20. In NetWare 2.2 and above, a user who is allowed to manage user accounts that he or she did not create is called a _____.
    a. Hacker
    b. Workgroup manager
    c. User account manager
    d. Supervisor-equivalent

SUPERIOR TECHNICAL COLLEGE PROJECT 7

To perform USERDEF or the supervisory functions of SYSCON, you will need to log in with a username that has supervisory equivalency. However, because of the security requirements on your assigned file server, you may be restricted from performing supervisory functions in your Superior Technical College project. Therefore, this project has been divided into two sets of exercises, one requiring supervisor equivalency and one that can be done as a workgroup manager. Your instructor will inform you which set of exercises you will do on your file server. In either project set, you will create user accounts and perform other activities necessary to set up the user environment for your Superior Technical College project. Do the assignments in one of the two sections, not both.

The assignments in Section 1 require you to log in to your file server with a username that has supervisor equivalency. Your instructor will provide you with instructions on how or if you can do this section.

Section 2 assignments do not require supervisor equivalency. They may be done by logging in using your normal username, which has workgroup manager equivalency. If the file server you are working on contains sensitive information, you may be restricted from using supervisory functions. In that case, your instructor will inform you to skip Section 1 and go to Section 2. Use the same Student Answer Sheet whether you do Section 1 or Section 2.

Section 1: **Supervisor Equivalency Required**

Log in to your assigned file server using the supervisor-equivalent name supplied by your instructor.

Assignment 7-1: **Use NetWare Accounting**

Dave Johnson would like to see a report each week showing file server usage. To provide this information you must do the following:

❶ In the tables on Student Answer Sheet 7, record the requested charge rate information for the Blocks Read Charge Rates, Disk Storage Charge Rates, and Service Requests Charge Rates.

❷ Use the ATOTAL command to print a file server usage report to the printer. Attach the printout to Student Answer Sheet 7.

❸ Use the NDIR command to obtain a printout of the directory containing the NetWare Accounting files; highlight the names of the Accounting files. Attach your printout to Student Answer Sheet 7.

❹ On Student Answer Sheet 7, identify which file you would back up and erase at the end of each week to reset weekly report totals.

Assignment 7-2: **Use Supervisor Options**

❶ On Student Answer Sheet 7, record the SYSCON default restrictions for your file server. For the sake of other students, do not change these defaults.

❷ Use the correct Supervisor option to view the AUTOEXEC command(s) used when you boot your file server. Record the commands on Student Answer Sheet 7.

❸ Fill out the Intruder Detection/Lockout table on Student Answer Sheet 7.

❹ On Student Answer Sheet 7, record the usernames of all workgroup managers on your file server.

Assignment 7-3: **Create Groups**

To separate your users during the login process and allow you to provide rights to all your Superior Technical College staff, you need to create a group called ##EVERYONE. (The ## represents your assigned student number.) Because you are a workgroup manager, you will be able to create your users and perform the step given below:

❶ Log in using your assigned username. Use SYSCON to create your ##EVERYONE group along with all the groups you defined on your user worksheet. Record this information on Student Answer Sheet 7. Be sure to precede each group with your assigned student number.

Assignment 7-4: **Create Users**

Use SYSCON to create usernames and home directories for Virg Kent and yourself. Be sure to use your assigned student number as the first two characters of these usernames.

❶ Record the usernames and the paths to home directories on Student Answer Sheet 7.

Assignment 7-5: **Add Users to Groups**

❶ Use SYSCON to make Virg Kent and your username members of your ##EVERYONE group. Add Virg and yourself to any other groups to which you assigned them on your user worksheet. On Student Answer Sheet 7, record the groups to which you assign Virg.

Assignment 7-6: **Use SYSCON to Make Trustee Assignments**

❶ Use SYSCON to assign Virg Kent the trustee rights you defined for her on your trustee directory security worksheet. Be sure to give her the rights she needs to maintain files in your FORMS directory. Because she often helps users in the Instructional Services department, give Virg the trustee rights she needs to work with any files or subdirectories and assign ANY rights within the Student Services directories. Now log in as Virg Kent. Change to your Superior Technical College directory and use the LISTDIR /E /S > PRN command to print all Virg's effective rights. Use the WHOAMI /G > PRN command to print the groups she belongs to. Attach the printouts to Student Answer Sheet 7.

Assignment 7-7: **Create Workgroup Managers**

❶ Make Virg Kent and your username workgroup managers. Print the SYSCON screen showing all workgroup managers. Highlight the usernames you just added. Attach the printout to Student Answer Sheet 7.

❷ On Student Answer Sheet 7, describe the process you used to make Virg Kent a workgroup manager.

Assignment 7-8: **Create Department Templates**

❶ On Student Answer Sheet 7, fill in a template form for each of your department workgroups.

❷ Use the USERDEF utility to create the templates you have defined. Use the print screen function to document each USERDEF template you create. Attach your printout to Student Answer Sheet 7.

Assignment 7-9: **Create Department Users**

❶ Using the templates you created in Assignment 7-8, create the user accounts for each workgroup as defined on your user worksheet. Print the screen showing the USERDEF results for each group of users created. Attach the printouts to Student Answer Sheet 7.

Assignment 7-10: **Assign User Account Balances**

❶ Use the SYSCON utility to give each of your users unlimited credit status. Be sure to include Virg Kent and yourself. On Student Answer Sheet 7, describe why giving an account unlimited credit status may be important.

Assignment 7-11: **Assign Users to a User Account Manager**

❶ Make your username a manager of all the users you have created with SYSCON and USERDEF. Make Virg Kent a manager of all users in your Instructional Services department. Log out of the file server. Now log in as Lee Olsen. Print Lee Olsen's login screen. Attach the printout to Student Answer Sheet 7.

❷ Use the WHOAMI /A > PRN command to print information about Lee's account. Attach the printout to Student Answer Sheet 7.

❸ Run SYSCON and select User Information. Call up Lee's user information and print the screen showing who his account manager is. Attach the printout to Student Answer Sheet 7.

Turn in Materials Assemble Student Answer Sheet 7 and the printouts from Assignments 7-1, 7-4, 7-6, 7-7, 7-8, 7-9, and 7-11. If instructed, turn in the materials to your instructor on or before the scheduled due date.

Section 2: **Workgroup Manager or Supervisor Equivalency Required**
Log in to your file server using your username.

Assignment 7-1: **Use NetWare Accounting**

❶ Your instructor will demonstrate how to set up Accounting and give you the information you need to fill in the charts on Student Answer Sheet 7.

❷ On Student Answer Sheet 7, list and describe the function of the ATOTAL and PAUDIT programs.

❸ On Student Answer Sheet 7, list the Accounting file you could back up and erase to reset totals for the week.

Assignment 7-2: **Use Supervisor Options**

❶ On Student Answer Sheet 7, record the SYSCON default restrictions your instructor demonstrated for your file server.

❷ Your instructor will demonstrate using the Edit AUTOEXEC file to display your file server's startup commands. On Student Answer Sheet 7, record the command in the AUTOEXEC file of your server.

❸ Using the information displayed by your instructor, fill out the Intruder Detection/Lockout table on Student Answer Sheet 7.

❹ On Student Answer Sheet 7, record the usernames of all workgroup managers on your file server.

Assignment 7-3: **Create Groups**

To separate your users during the login process and allow you to provide rights to all your Superior Technical College staff, you need to create a group called ##EVERYONE. (The ## represents your assigned student number.) Because you are a workgroup manager, you will be able to create your users and perform the steps given below:

❶ Log in using your assigned username. Use SYSCON to create your ##EVERYONE group along with all the groups you defined on your user worksheet. Record this information on Student Answer Sheet 7. Be sure to precede all your group names with your assigned two-digit student number.

Assignment 7-4: **Create Users**

❶ Use SYSCON to create usernames and home directories for Virg Kent and yourself. Be sure to use your assigned student number as the first two characters. Record the usernames on Student Answer Sheet 7.

Assignment 7-5: **Add Users to Groups**

❶ Use SYSCON to make Virg Kent and your username members of your ##EVERYONE group. Add Virg and yourself to any other groups to which you assigned them on your user worksheet. On Student Answer Sheet 7, record groupt to which you assign Virg.

Assignment 7-6: **Use SYSCON to Make Trustee Assignments**

❶ Use SYSCON to assign Virg Kent the trustee rights you defined for her on your trustee directory security worksheet. Be sure to give her the rights she needs to maintain files in your FORMS directory. Because she often helps users in the Instructional Services department, give Virg the trustee rights she needs to work with any files or subdirectories and assign ANY rights within the Student Services directories. Now log in as Virg Kent. Change to your Superior Technical College directory and use the LISTDIR /E /S > PRN command to print all Virg Kent's effective rights. Use the WHOAMI /G > PRN command to print the groups she belongs to. Attach your printout to Student Answer Sheet 7.

Assignment 7-7: **Create Workgroup Managers**

❶ Your instructor will demonstrate using SYSCON to create workgroup managers.

❷ On Student Answer Sheet 7, describe the process necessary to make Virg Kent a workgroup manager.

Assignment 7-8: **Create Workgroup Templates**

❶ On Student Answer Sheet 7, fill in a template form for each of your department workgroups.

Assignment 7-9: **Create Department Users**

❶ Using the templates you created in Assignment 7-8, create the user accounts for each workgroup as defined on your user worksheet using the SYSCON utility. Print the SYSCON user window showing your newly created users. Attach the printouts to Student Answer Sheet 7.

Assignment 7-10: **Assign User Account Balances**

❶ Use the SYSCON utility to give each of your users unlimited credit status. Be sure to include Virg Kent and yourself. On Student Answer Sheet 7, describe why giving an account unlimited credit status may be important.

Assignment 7-11: **Assign Users to a User Account Manager**

❶ Make your username a manager of all the users you have created with SYSCON and USERDEF. Make Virg Kent a manager of all users in your Instructional Services department. Log out of the file server. Now log in as Lee Olsen. Print Lee Olsen's login screen. Attach the printout to Student Answer Sheet 7.

❷ Use the WHOAMI /A > PRN command to print information about Lee's account. Attach the printout to Student Answer Sheet 7.

❸ Run SYSCON and select User Information. Call up Lee's user information and print the screen showing who his account manager is. Attach the printout to Student Answer Sheet 7.

Turn in Materials Assemble Student Answer Sheet 7 and the printouts from Assignments 7-4, 7-6, and 7-11. If instructed, turn in the materials to your instructor on or before the scheduled due date.

Student Name: _____ Date: _____

Assignment 7-1:   **Use NetWare Accounting**

❶   When filling out the following tables, record the charge rate number and multiplier/divisor ratio, as well as the time and date for that charge rate. Record the time "7:00-5:00" or "All Day" and place an "X" under each day for which the rate and time is effective.

Charge Method: Blocks Read

#	Rate Ratio	Time	Sun	Mon	Tue	Wed	Thu	Fri	Sat

Charge Method: Disk Storage

#	Rate Ratio	Time	Sun	Mon	Tue	Wed	Thu	Fri	Sat

Charge Method: Service Requests

#	Rate Ratio	Time	Sun	Mon	Tue	Wed	Thu	Fri	Sat

❷   If you have supervisor equivalency, attach the ATOTAL printout. If you do not have supervisor equivalency, describe the function of the ATOTAL and PAUDIT programs.

❸   If you have supervisor equivalency, attach the NDIR printout highlighting Accounting files. If you do not have supervisor equivalency, skip this step.

❹   Which file could you back up and erase at the end of each week?

Assignment 7-2: **Use Supervisor Options**

❶ Record SYSCON default restrictions below.

```
                      Default Account Balance/Restrictions
Account Has Expiration Date:
   Date Account Expires:
Limit Concurrent Connections:
   Maximum Connections:
Create Home Directory for User:
Require Password:
   Minimum Password Length:
Force Periodic Password Changes:
   Days Between Forced Changes:
   Limit Grace Logins:
      Grace Logins Allowed:
Require Unique Passwords:
Account Balance:
Allow Unlimited Credit:
   Low Balance Limit:
```

❷ In the space below, record the AUTOEXEC file commands or contents.

❸ Record the intruder information below.

```
                        Intruder Detection/Lockout

Detect Intruders:

Intruder Detection Threshold

Incorrect Login Attempts:

Bad Login Count Retention Time:      ____Days          ____Hours          ____Minutes

Lock Account After Detection:

   Length of Account Lockout:        ____Days          ____Hours          ____Minutes
```

❹ Record the usernames of all workgroup managers on your file server.

Assignment 7-3: **Create Groups**

❶ Record your groups and members.
Group Name: _____
   Members:

Group Name: _____
    Members:

Group Name: _____
    Members:

Group Name: _____
    Members:

Group Name: _____
    Members:

Assignment 7-4:   **Create Users**

❶   Record Virg Kent's username: _____
Home directory path: _____
Record your username: _____
Home directory path: _____

Assignment 7-5:   **Add Users to Groups**

❶   Record the groups to which you assigned Virg.

Assignment 7-6:   **Use SYSCON to Make Trustee Assignments**

❶   Attach the LISTDIR /E /S and WHOAMI /G printouts.

Assignment 7-7:   **Create Workgroup Managers**

❶   If you have supervisor equivalency, attach a printout showing all workgroup managers. If you do not, skip to step 2.

❷   In the space below, describe the process you used to make Virg Kent a workgroup manager.

Assignment 7-8:   **Create Department Templates**

❶   Complete the following template forms for each of your department workgroups.

```
 Parameters for Template _____          Parameters for Template _____
Default Directory: _____         Default Directory: _____


Copy PrintCon From: (see list)                  Copy PrintCon From: (see list)
Groups Belonged To: _____         Groups Belonged To: _____


Account Balance:              1000    1000      Account Balance:              1000
Limit Account Balance:                No        Limit Account Balance:                No
     Low Limit:                       0              Low Limit:                       0
Limit Concurrent Connections:         No        Limit Concurrent Connections:         No
     Maximum Connections:        _____               Maximum Connections:        _____


Require Password:              ____              Require Password              ____
     Minimum Password Length:  ____                  Minimum Password Length:  ____
Force Periodic Password Changes:  ____          Force Periodic Password Changes:  ____
     Days Between Forced Changes: ____               Days Between Forced Changes: ____
Require Unique Passwords:      ____              Require Unique Passwords:      ____
```

```
 Parameters for Template _____          Parameters for Template _____
Default Directory: _____         Default Directory: _____


Copy PrintCon From: (see list)                  Copy PrintCon From: (see list)
Groups Belonged To: _____         Groups Belonged To: _____


Account Balance:              1000    1000      Account Balance:              1000
Limit Account Balance:                No        Limit Account Balance:                No
     Low Limit:                       0              Low Limit:                       0
Limit Concurrent Connections:         No        Limit Concurrent Connections:         No
     Maximum Connections:        _____               Maximum Connections:        _____


Require Password:              ____              Require Password              ____
     Minimum Password Length:  ____                  Minimum Password Length:  ____
Force Periodic Password Changes:  ____          Force Periodic Password Changes:  ____
     Days Between Forced Changes: ____               Days Between Forced Changes: ____
Require Unique Passwords:      ____              Require Unique Passwords:      ____
```

❷ If you have supervisor equivalency, attach a printout of each USERDEF template. If you do not, skip this step.

Assignment 7-9: **Create Department Users**

❶ Attach printout showing the SYSCON user window.

Assignment 7-10: **Assign User Account Balances**

❶ In the space below, describe a benefit of giving a user unlimited credit.

Assignment 7-11: **Assign Users to a User Account Manager**

❶ Attach Lee Olsen's login screen printout.

❷ Attach the WHOAMI /A printout.

❸ Attach the printout showing Lee Olsen's account manager.

In this chapter you will use the FILER utility to:

• Change the current directory path

• Assign directory trustee rights

• Create a directory structure

• Copy and rename files

• Work with file and directory attributes

• Set the option that will allow you to

view hidden directories

• Determine who has rights in a specific

directory

• Set the Inherited Rights Mask of a

directory

WORKING

WITH

FILER

The FILER menu utility is an important tool for working with the NetWare file system. Although many of FILER's functions can also be performed by other commands or utilities, certain functions, such as deleting an entire directory structure, viewing who has rights in a certain subdirectory, and setting common attributes on multiple files, can be done only from the FILER utility.

In this chapter you will learn how to use the FILER utility to perform many file system management tasks. In addition to performing network file security functions such as assigning trustee rights, file attributes, and viewing user effective rights, you will use FILER to perform DOS functions, such as making, renaming, or deleting directories and copying files. Like working with any other complex utility, it takes time and practice to become comfortable with FILER.

In addition to their primary purpose, NetWare utilities often duplicate features for the user's convenience. For example, FILER's major use is working with the NetWare directory and file system, including assigning trustees and Inherited Rights Masks to directories and files. SYSCON's primary use is creating and managing users and groups. For expedience, SYSCON can also be used to create home directories and assign trustee rights in the directory structure. In this way, the user can avoid switching back and forth between utilities when performing overlapping activities.

In this chapter you will see how FILER can be applied to the PC Solutions network to perform many file- and directory-related functions. At the end of the chapter, you will use the FILER utility to perform functions necessary to set up and maintain the network file system for Superior Technical College.

THE PC SOLUTIONS CASE

Leslie was ready to assign the trustee rights users will need to work in the directory structure. Because FILER is designed to work efficiently with the directory structure, she decided to use FILER rather than SYSCON to assign the trustee rights. Leslie knows that in NetWare 3.11 or higher, FILER has an option that allows her to view user-effective rights in a directory. This function will be useful in checking the security of certain directories such as PAYROLL.

STARTING FILER

To make the directory trustee assignments, Leslie referenced the trustee directory security worksheets she created in Chapter 5. In Chapter 7, Leslie used SYSCON to assign the trustee rights for the SYS volume shown in Figure 5-2. As you'll see, Leslie used the FILER utility to enter trustee assignments defined for the Business workgroup.

Because a supervisor-equivalent username is necessary for viewing all users who have effective rights in a directory as well as changing file owner and creation dates, Leslie logged in to the file server as

SUPERVISOR, typed "FILER," and pressed the Enter key. The FILER Available Topics menu, shown in Figure 8-1, was displayed. Notice that the current directory path shown on the top the FILER screen is pointing to the SYS volume.

FIGURE 8-1: FILER's Available Topics menu

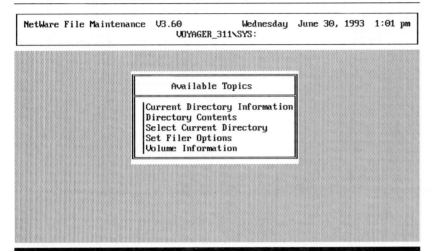

ASSIGNING TRUSTEES TO A SUBDIRECTORY

To make the trustee assignments she documented on the trustee directory security worksheet for the Business workgroup, as shown in Figure 5-3, Leslie first wanted to change her current directory to the DATA:BUSINESS directory. This will allow her to quickly make trustee assignments for each of the subdirectories. Let's follow the steps Leslie took to change to the BUSINESS directory and make the trustee assignments for the PAYROLL subdirectory.

1. To change her current directory to the BUSINESS workgroup directory, Leslie highlighted the Select Current Directory option and pressed [Enter]. She then entered the path to the BUSINESS directory, as shown in Figure 8-2. After she pressed the Enter key the new path was displayed at the top of the FILER screen.

FIGURE 8-2: Leslie's FILER screen after she typed the path to the Business directory

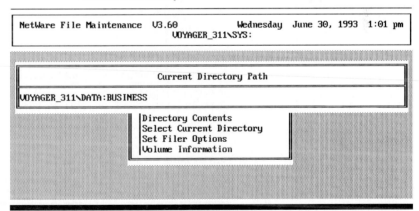

2. She selected the Directory Contents option and pressed [Enter]. The Directory Contents screen for the BUSINESS directory, shown in Figure 8-3 on the following page, was displayed.

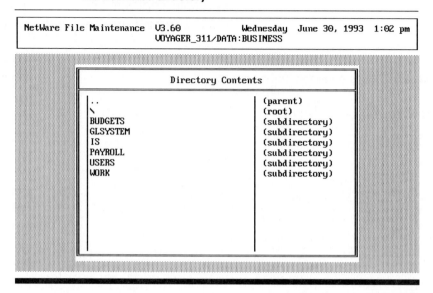

3. To make the trustee assignments shown on the trustee directory
security worksheet for the PAYROLL subdirectory, Leslie highlighted
the PAYROLL subdirectory and pressed the Enter key. The
Subdirectory Options screen, shown in Figure 8-4, was displayed.

FIGURE 8-4: Leslie's Subdirectory Options screen for the PAYROLL
subdirectory

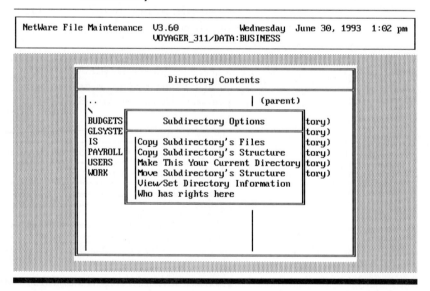

4. To enter trustee rights, she highlighted the View/Set Directory
Information option and pressed [Enter]. The Directory Information for
PAYROLL window, shown in Figure 8-5, was displayed.

FIGURE 8-5: Leslie's Directory Information for PAYROLL window

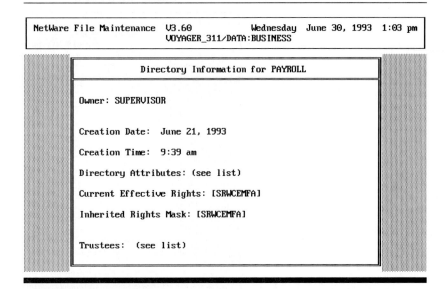

```
NetWare File Maintenance   V3.60          Wednesday   June 30, 1993   1:03 pm
                           VOYAGER_311/DATA:BUSINESS

                        Directory Information for PAYROLL

         Owner: SUPERVISOR

         Creation Date:   June 21, 1993

         Creation Time:   9:39 am

         Directory Attributes: (see list)

         Current Effective Rights: [SRWCEMFA]

         Inherited Rights Mask: [SRWCEMFA]


         Trustees:  (see list)
```

5. To make or change trustee assignments for this subdirectory, Leslie next highlighted the Trustees: (see list) option and pressed [Enter]. The screen of existing trustees for this directory, shown in Figure 8-6, was displayed. No existing trustees were shown.

FIGURE 8-6: Leslie's screen showing no existing trustees for the PAYROLL subdirectory

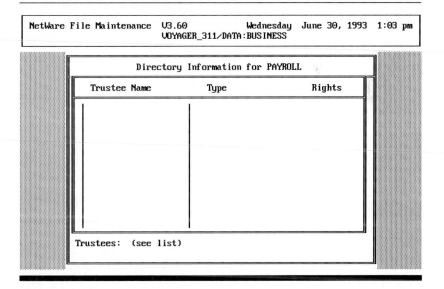

```
NetWare File Maintenance   V3.60          Wednesday   June 30, 1993   1:03 pm
                           VOYAGER_311/DATA:BUSINESS

                        Directory Information for PAYROLL

         Trustee Name            Type            Rights




         Trustees:  (see list)
```

6. To add a directory trustee, Leslie pressed the Ins key. A window of existing users and groups was displayed. She next highlighted 99ANNBON and pressed [Enter]. Ann's username was added as a trustee of the directory with Read and File Scan rights, as shown in Figure 8-7 on the following page.

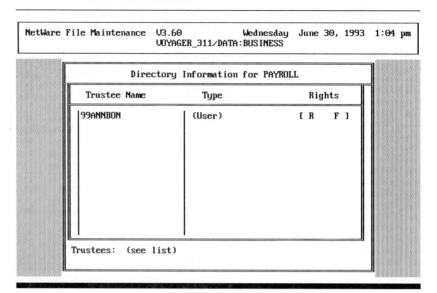

```
NetWare File Maintenance  V3.60           Wednesday  June 30, 1993  1:04 pm
                          VOYAGER_311/DATA:BUSINESS

          ┌──────────────────────────────────────────────────┐
          │         Directory Information for PAYROLL         │
          │  ┌────────────────┬──────────────┬─────────────┐  │
          │  │ Trustee Name   │ Type         │ Rights      │  │
          │  ├────────────────┼──────────────┼─────────────┤  │
          │  │ 99ANNBON       │ (User)       │ [ R    F ]  │  │
          │  │                │              │             │  │
          │  │                │              │             │  │
          │  │                │              │             │  │
          │  │                │              │             │  │
          │  │                │              │             │  │
          │  │                │              │             │  │
          │  │                │              │             │  │
          │  └────────────────┴──────────────┴─────────────┘  │
          │  Trustees:  (see list)                            │
          └──────────────────────────────────────────────────┘
```

7. To give Ann additional rights, Leslie pressed [Enter]. The Trustee Rights window for the highlighted user, shown on the right side of Figure 8-8, was displayed. She again used the Ins key, this time to display the Other Rights window shown on the left in Figure 8-8.

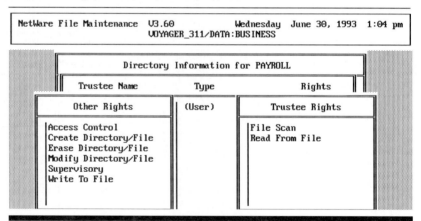

```
NetWare File Maintenance  V3.60           Wednesday  June 30, 1993  1:04 pm
                          VOYAGER_311/DATA:BUSINESS

      ┌──────────────────────────────────────────────────────┐
      │          Directory Information for PAYROLL            │
      │┌──────────────────┬──────────────┬──────────────────┐│
      ││ Trustee Name     │ Type         │ Rights           ││
      │├──────────────────┼──────────────┼──────────────────┤│
      ││ Other Rights     │ (User)       │ Trustee Rights   ││
      │├──────────────────┼──────────────┼──────────────────┤│
      ││ Access Control   │              │ File Scan        ││
      ││ Create Directory/File           │ Read From File   ││
      ││ Erase Directory/File            │                  ││
      ││ Modify Directory/File           │                  ││
      ││ Supervisory      │              │                  ││
      ││ Write To File    │              │                  ││
      │└──────────────────┴──────────────┴──────────────────┘│
      └──────────────────────────────────────────────────────┘
```

8. She then used the arrow keys along with the F5 key to highlight and mark the Create Directory/File, Erase Directory/File, Modify Directory/File, and Write To File rights as defined on her trustee directory security worksheet. Then she pressed [Enter]. The selected rights were added to the Trustee Rights window, which already contained File Scan and Read From File.

9. To save these rights and return to the Trustee Window, Leslie pressed the Esc key. The new trustee assignment was displayed, as shown in Figure 8-9.

FIGURE 8-9: Leslie's screen after she added the Create, Erase, Modify and Write rights to the trustee 99ANNBON

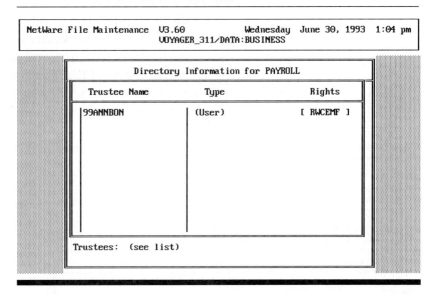

FIGURE 8-9: Leslie's screen after she added the Create, Erase, Modify and Write rights to the trustee 99ANNBON

```
NetWare File Maintenance   V3.60           Wednesday  June 30, 1993  1:04 pm
                           VOYAGER_311/DATA:BUSINESS

                       Directory Information for PAYROLL

        Trustee Name            Type              Rights

       99ANNBON               (User)            [ RWCEMF ]




       Trustees:  (see list)
```

10. Because there were no more trustees for this directory, Leslie pressed the Esc key until she returned to the Directory Contents screen shown in Figure 8-3.

This process can be used to make the trustee assignments for the Sales and Support workgroups. Leslie next repeated steps 3 through 9 to assign trustees for each of the other subdirectories defined on the trustee directory security worksheet for the Business workgroup. After all trustee assignments were complete, Leslie used the Esc key to return to FILER's Available Topics menu.

Rather than assigning rights to a subdirectory by going through the Directory Contents option, Leslie could use FILER to make trustee assignments for the current directory by highlighting the Current Directory Information topic and pressing [Enter]. A screen similar to the one shown in Figure 8-5 would appear. Trustee assignments to the current directory could then be made by following steps 5 through 9. This technique is useful when you want to make a trustee assignment to the current directory path as displayed in the FILER header box at the top of the screen.

REMOVING AND CREATING DIRECTORY STRUCTURES WITH FILER

Leslie next wanted to make a new directory structure for the Help Desk department. To do this she first wanted to remove the existing HELP-DESK directory structure. To use FILER to remove the HELPDESK directory structure, Leslie first highlighted the Select Current Directory option from FILER's Available Topics menu and pressed [Enter]. When FILER asked for the Current Directory Path, she used the Backspace key to change the entry to DATA.

After changing the current directory, Leslie next highlighted the Directory Contents option and pressed [Enter]. FILER opened a window showing all the directories on the DATA volume. To remove the

HELPDESK structure, Leslie highlighted the directory HELPDESK and pressed the Delete key.

FILER next asked her to select either Delete Entire Subdirectory Structure or Delete Subdirectory's Files Only. She chose to delete the entire subdirectory structure and pressed the Enter key. Before deleting the structure, FILER asked her for a confirmation, as shown in Figure 8-10. She responded with "Y," and the existing HELPDESK structure and any files were deleted.

FIGURE 8-10: Leslie's screen before she deleted the HELPDESK directory structure

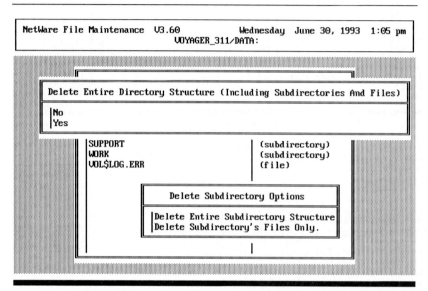

To add a new directory called HELPDESK, she pressed the Ins key and entered "HELPDESK." After she pressed [Enter], the HELPDESK directory appeared in the Directory Contents window.

To create the subdirectories of HELPDESK, Leslie made the HELPDESK directory her current directory by selecting it and then highlighting the Make This Your Current Directory option from the Subdirectory Options menu (shown in Figure 8-4). To create the subdirectories, Leslie again used the Ins key to enter each directory name.

To go back to the DATA volume she highlighted the two dots (..) at the top of the list, which represent the parent directory, and pressed [Enter]. FILER then asked if the parent directory was to be the current directory. Leslie responded "Yes" by pressing the Enter key. She then pressed the Esc key until she returned to FILER's Available Topics menu.

COPYING FILES USING FILER

The SOFTWARE\SP directory contained some files that Ed Low wanted copied into his BUDGETS directory. The worksheet files he wanted all contain the last two digits of the year (91, 92, or 93) as part of the filename. Because these files were mixed in the directory with other files using the same extension, Leslie wanted to use FILER to selectively copy the worksheet files into the BUDGETS directory.

Let's follow Leslie's steps as she used FILER to copy the desired budget worksheet files from the SOFTWARE\SP directory into the BUDGETS directory.

1. First Leslie used the Select Current Directory option of the Available Topics menu to enter the path to the SYS:SOFTWARE\SP directory.

2. Next she highlighted the Directory Contents option and pressed [Enter]. The Directory Contents window showing all subdirectories and files was displayed.

3. Leslie used the arrow keys and the F5 key to mark each of the files she wanted to copy. When all files were marked, she pressed the Enter key. FILER displayed the Multiple File Operations menu shown in the middle of the screen in Figure 8-11.

FIGURE 8-11: Leslie's Multiple File Operations screen

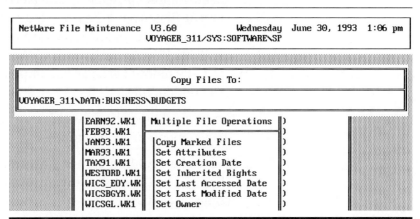

4. She highlighted the Copy Marked Files option and pressed [Enter]. FILER next asked for the path to copy the files to.

5. Leslie erased the existing path and typed the path to the BUDGETS directory, as shown on the top of Figure 8-11.

6. When she pressed [Enter], FILER copied the marked files into the BUDGETS directory. Leslie then pressed the Esc key until she returned to the Available Topics menu.

RENAMING FILES AND DIRECTORIES

Ed wanted his earnings files to have similar names. Currently the 1991 file is named TAX91.WK1 and the 1992 file is named EARN92.WK1. He asked Leslie to change the file named TAX91.WK1 to EARN91.WK1. To do this, Leslie first used the Select Current Directory option of the Available Topics menu to change to the BUDGETS directory. In addition, Leslie decided to change the name of the WORK subdirectory in the BUSINESS directory to SHARED.

To rename a file, Leslie highlighted the Directory Contents option of the Available Topics menu and pressed [Enter]. The Directory Contents window displayed all subdirectories and files in the BUDG-ETS subdirectory. Leslie then highlighted the filename TAX91.WK1 and pressed [F3]. She then used the Backspace key to erase the current name and typed "EARN91.WK1." When she pressed [Enter], the name of the selected file was changed.

To rename a subdirectory, Leslie again highlighted the Directory Contents of the Available Topics menu option and pressed [Enter]. The Directory Contents window displayed all subdirectories and files in the BUDGETS subdirectory. Leslie then highlighted the subdirectory name WORK and pressed [F3]. She then used the Backspace key to erase the current name and typed "SHARED." When she pressed [Enter], the name of the selected subdirectory was changed.

SETTING FILE ATTRIBUTES

Ed Low also mentioned that all files from past years should be protected so they cannot be changed or deleted. The current year's files should also be protected against being deleted, but Leslie needed to allow changes to those. To protect the past year's files from modification, Leslie decided to flag them as Read Only. She planned to use the Delete Inhibit flag available on NetWare 3.11 and higher to prevent the current files from being deleted while still allowing changes. (Your instructor can provide you with a list of all file and directory attributes available in your version of NetWare.)

Let's follow Leslie as she imposes the Read Only attribute on the 1993 budget files.

1. Leslie first used the Select Current Directory option of the Available Topics menu to change to the BUDGETS directory.

2. Next she highlighted the Directory Contents option and pressed [Enter]. The Directory Contents window showing the budget files she copied was displayed.

3. Using the arrow keys along with the F5 key, Leslie highlighted all the files containing a year prior to 1993 and pressed [Enter]. The Multiple File Operations menu, like the one shown in Figure 8-11, was displayed.

4. She highlighted the Set Attributes option and pressed [Enter]. The Other File attributes window was displayed. This window showed the new attribute settings for the group of selected files. The new attributes will replace any existing attributes for the files in the group.

5. To select attributes, Leslie pressed the Ins key and highlighted the Read Only attribute shown in Figure 8-12.

FIGURE 8-12: Leslie's screen after she pressed the Ins key to select the Read Only attribute for old budget files

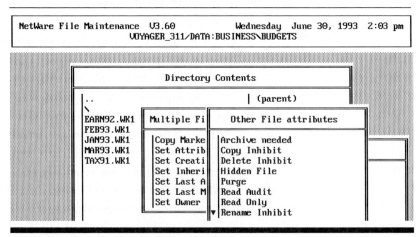

6. Pressing [Enter] added this attribute to the attribute window. Notice that when she selected the Read Only attribute, the Delete Inhibit and Rename Inhibit attributes were also added by default, as shown in Figure 8-13.

FIGURE 8-13: Leslie's screen after she added the Read Only attribute to the File Attributes window

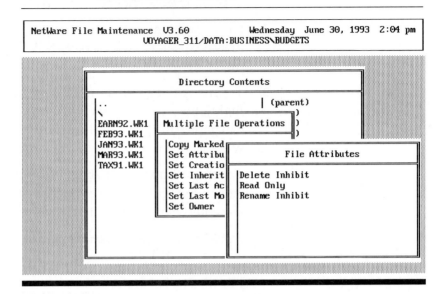

```
NetWare File Maintenance  V3.60        Wednesday  June 30, 1993  2:04 pm
                  VOYAGER_311/DATA:BUSINESS\BUDGETS
```

```
                        Directory Contents
    ..                              | (parent)
    \                                         )
    EARN92.WK1   Multiple File Operations     )
    FEB93.WK1                                  )
    JAN93.WK1    Copy Marked
    MAR93.WK1    Set Attribu          File Attributes
    TAX91.WK1    Set Creatio
                 Set Inherit   Delete Inhibit
                 Set Last Ac   Read Only
                 Set Last Mo   Rename Inhibit
                 Set Owner
```

7. When she pressed the Esc key, FILER asked her to "Set Marked Files to Specified Attributes." Leslie responded by typing "Y" and pressing the Enter key. FILER then set all the marked files to the specified attributes.

8. Pressing the Esc key again returned her to the Directory Contents window.

9. Leslie repeated this process to add only the Delete Inhibit attribute to the current budget spreadsheet files.

SETTING DIRECTORY ATTRIBUTES

Normally NetWare 3.11 and higher will keep all deleted files available for salvaging until the system needs the storage space. When the server needs more disk space, the space used by the oldest deleted files will be reused first. Although this is useful for data files, it is not necessary for temporary files, because they will not need to be salvaged. Setting the **purge attribute** for the directory containing temporary files avoids this problem.

The NetWare 2.1x through 3.12 menu system creates and deletes temporary files in the default directory where it is run. Because Leslie planned to have all users run the menu system from the MENUS directory she designed in Chapter 2, she wanted to avoid having the temporary menu files take up space in the salvage pool. Setting the purge attribute on the MENUS directory tells NetWare to remove deleted files and make their space immediately available to the system.

To avoid confusion and possible misuse, Leslie also wanted to prevent users from seeing the MENUS directory. She can do this by using the Hidden attribute to hide the directory from DOS commands and application programs. Let's follow Leslie's steps as she used FILER to set the Purge and Hidden attributes for the MENUS directory.

1. First she used the Select Current Directory option of the Available Topics menu to change to the MENUS directory.

2. Next she highlighted the Current Directory Information option and pressed [Enter]. The Directory Information screen for the MENUS directory was displayed.

3. To change directory attributes for the current directory, Leslie highlighted the Directory Attributes option and pressed [Enter]. The Current Attributes window showing any current directory attributes was displayed.

4. To add new attributes, she pressed [Ins]; the Other Attributes window shown in Figure 8-14 was displayed. (To remove an existing attribute she could have highlighted it with the arrow keys and pressed [Del].)

FIGURE 8-14: Leslie's screen showing other attributes for the MENUS directory

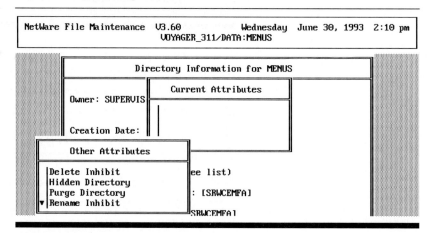

5. Using the arrow keys along with the F5 key, she marked the Purge and Hidden attributes and pressed [Enter]. The new attributes were then added to the Current Attributes window.

6. She then used the Esc key to return to the Available Topics menu.

SETTING FILER OPTIONS
Once Leslie hid the MENUS directory, it no longer appeared on her Directory Contents screen when she looked at the contents of the DATA volume. Viewing Hidden or System directories is an option that can be changed with FILER. In addition to directory and file search attributes, FILER contains several parameters that can be customized for your needs. These options are not saved and must be reset each time FILER is run.

Let's follow Leslie's steps as she changed FILER options to allow her to see hidden files and directories.

1. First she selected the Set Filer Options from the Available Topics menu and pressed [Enter]. FILER then displayed the Filer Settings window shown in Figure 8-15.

FIGURE 8-15: The Filer Settings screen after Leslie selected Set Filer Options

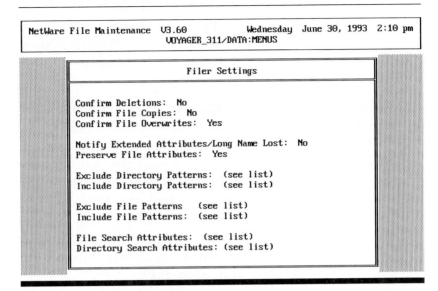

```
NetWare File Maintenance   V3.60        Wednesday  June 30, 1993  2:10 pm
                           VOYAGER_311/DATA:MENUS
```

```
                          Filer Settings

  Confirm Deletions:  No
  Confirm File Copies:  No
  Confirm File Overwrites:  Yes

  Notify Extended Attributes/Long Name Lost:  No
  Preserve File Attributes:  Yes

  Exclude Directory Patterns:  (see list)
  Include Directory Patterns:  (see list)

  Exclude File Patterns   (see list)
  Include File Patterns:  (see list)

  File Search Attributes:  (see list)
  Directory Search Attributes: (see list)
```

2. To allow her to view the Hidden directories, she highlighted the Directory Search Attributes: (see list) field and pressed [Enter]. The Directory Search Attributes window was displayed. The window was empty, indicating that directories with special attributes such as Hidden or System will not be displayed.

3. To add the Hidden attribute to this list, Leslie pressed the Ins key to display the Other Attributes window, as shown in Figure 8-16.

FIGURE 8-16: Leslie's Other Attributes screen after she selected Directory Search Attributes and pressed (Ins)

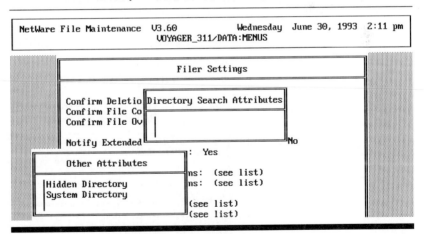

```
NetWare File Maintenance   V3.60        Wednesday  June 30, 1993  2:11 pm
                           VOYAGER_311/DATA:MENUS
```

```
                          Filer Settings

  Confirm Deletio │Directory Search Attributes│
  Confirm File Co │                           │
  Confirm File Ov │                           │
                  │                           │
  Notify Extended └───────────────────────────┘No

   ┌──────────────────┐     :  Yes
   │ Other Attributes │   ns:  (see list)
   ├──────────────────┤   ns:  (see list)
   │Hidden Directory  │
   │System Directory  │     (see list)
   │                  │     (see list)
   └──────────────────┘
```

4. Next she highlighted the Hidden Directory attribute and pressed [Enter]. The Hidden Directory attribute was added to the Directory Search Attributes window.

5. To continue, she used the Esc key to save the changes and return to the Available Topics menu. Then when she viewed the contents of the DATA volume, the Directory Contents window showed the MENUS directory.

The Filer Settings screen also contains options that allow Leslie to specify whether she wants file deletions, copies, or overwrites to be confirmed. She could also use this screen to specify what directory or file patterns she wants to use to include or exclude certain directories or files from FILER's displays and copy operations.

LISTING USERS WITH EFFECTIVE RIGHTS IN A DIRECTORY (NETWARE 3.11 AND HIGHER)

Remembering how sensitive Ann Bonny is about payroll security, Leslie needed to make sure that Ann is the only user with rights to the PAYROLL directory. She recalled that in NetWare 3.11 and 3.12, a supervisor-equivalent user can use FILER to list all users who have rights to a subdirectory. These rights may come from a direct trustee assignment, be inherited from a parent directory, or be a result of a user being a member of a group that has rights to the directory. Because this option is found only in the Subdirectory Options menu, Leslie needed to change her current directory to the parent of the subdirectory she wanted to check.

Let's follow Leslie's steps as she used FILER to determine who has rights to the PAYROLL subdirectory.

1. To change to the parent directory of the PAYROLL subdirectory, she first used the Select Current Directory option of the Available Topics menu to enter the path to the BUSINESS directory.

2. Next she highlighted the Directory Contents option and pressed [Enter]. The Directory Contents window showing all subdirectories and files in the BUSINESS directory was displayed.

3. To see who has rights in the PAYROLL subdirectory, Leslie highlighted PAYROLL and pressed [Enter]. A Subdirectory Options menu like the one shown in Figure 8-4 was displayed.

4. She selected the Who has rights here option and pressed [Enter]. The window showing all users who have effective rights to this directory, as shown in Figure 8-17, was displayed.

FIGURE 8-17: Leslie's screen showing all users who have rights to the PAYROLL subdirectory

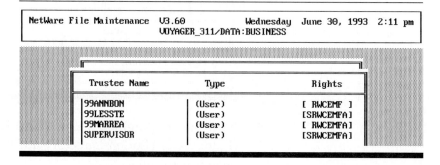

```
NetWare File Maintenance   V3.60          Wednesday   June 30, 1993   2:11 pm
                         VOYAGER_311/DATA:BUSINESS
```

Trustee Name	Type	Rights
99ANNBON	(User)	[RWCEMF]
99LESSTE	(User)	[SRWCEMFA]
99MARREA	(User)	[RWCEMFA]
SUPERVISOR	(User)	[SRWCEMFA]

5. After viewing the results, Leslie pressed the Esc key until she returned to the Available Topics menu.

Of course, SUPERVISOR and supervisor-equivalent usernames are listed, and the workgroup manager name, 99LESSTE, is listed because it has been given the Supervisory right to the DATA directory. However, Leslie was initially surprised to see Mary Read's username in the list. She then remembered that she gave Mary all rights except Supervisory to the BUSINESS directory. Therefore, Mary has inherited her effective rights into the PAYROLL subdirectory. Leslie could change this by either granting Mary another trustee assignment containing no rights to the PAYROLL directory or using the NetWare 3.11 Inherited Rights Mask (IRM) to block any effective rights in the parent BUSINESS directory from being transferred to the PAYROLL subdirectory. The advantage of the IRM approach is that it will also block other users from accidentally gaining inherited rights to this directory in the future.

CHANGING THE INHERITED RIGHTS MASK (NETWARE 3.11 OR HIGHER)

Leslie decided to change the IRM to prevent users such as 99MARREA from inadvertently inheriting rights into the PAYROLL subdirectory from a parent directory. When the PAYROLL subdirectory was first created, its IRM contained all rights. To block inherited rights, Leslie needed to remove rights from the Inherited Rights Mask of the PAYROLL subdirectory. This will block any users from gaining access to the PAYROLL subdirectory except supervisor-equivalent users with a specific trustee assignment to PAYROLL, or any users, such as 99LESSTE, who have been granted the supervisory right in a parent directory.

Let's follow Leslie's steps as she used FILER to remove all rights from the IRM of the PAYROLL subdirectory.

1. First she used the Select Current Directory option of the Available Topics menu to make the PAYROLL subdirectory the current directory path. (She could also do this by selecting the BUSINESS directory and then selecting the PAYROLL subdirectory from the Directory Contents window. However, in this case it is faster to go directly to the PAYROLL subdirectory.)

2. Next she highlighted the Current Directory Information option and pressed [Enter]. A Directory Information screen similar to the one shown in Figure 8-14 was displayed.

3. To change the IRM, Leslie highlighted the Inherited Rights Mask and pressed [Enter]. The Inherited Rights window listing all the inheritable rights, as shown in Figure 8-18 on the following page, was displayed.

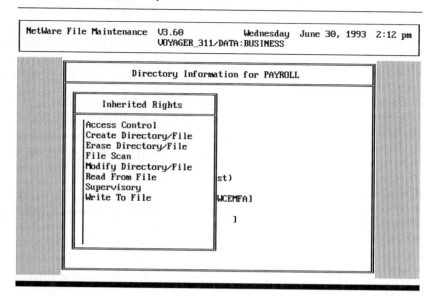

4. To block all rights except Supervisory (remember that the Supervisory right cannot be blocked), she used the arrow keys along with the F5 key to highlight and mark the rights to be removed.

5. To remove the selected rights, Leslie pressed the Del key. After she confirmed the deletion, the selected rights were removed from the Inherited Rights window.

6. After she pressed the Esc key to save the changes, the Directory Information for PAYROLL screen was updated with the new Inherited Rights Mask, as shown in Figure 8-19.

FIGURE 8-19: Leslie's Directory Information screen for the PAYROLL
subdirectory after she removed all rights except
Supervisory

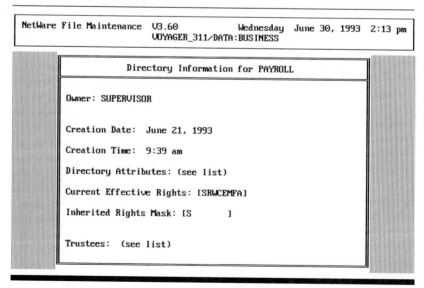

FIGURE 8-20: Leslie's screen after she used the TLIST command to check trustee assignments for the Business workgroup

```
F:\BUSINESS>TLIST

VOYAGER_311\DATA:BUSINESS
User trustees:
  99MARREA                          [ RWCEMFA]
No group trustees.

F:\BUSINESS>TLIST PAYROLL

VOYAGER_311\DATA:BUSINESS\PAYROLL
User trustees:
  99ANNBON                          [ RWCEMF ] ANN BONNY
No group trustees.

F:\BUSINESS>TLIST BUDGETS

VOYAGER_311\DATA:BUSINESS\BUDGETS
User trustees:
  99NEDLYN                          [ RWCEMF ] NED LYNCH
  99EDWLOW                          [ RWCEMF ] EDWARD LOW
  -----
Group trustees:
  BUSINESS                          [ R    F ]

F:\BUSINESS>
```

FIGURE 8-21: Leslie's screen after she used the LISTDIR /R command to view the Inherited Rights Masks in the BUSINESS directory

```
F:\BUSINESS>LISTDIR /R

Sub-directories of VOYAGER_311/DATA:BUSINESS
Inherited    Directory
------------------------------------------------
[SRWCEMFA]   ->IS
[SRWCEMFA]   ->GLSYSTEM
[S      ]    ->PAYROLL
[SRWCEMFA]   ->BUDGETS
[SRWCEMFA]   ->USERS
[SRWCEMFA]   ->WORK
6 sub-directories found

F:\BUSINESS>
```

FIGURE 8-22: Leslie's screen after she logged in as 99EDLOW and used the LISTDIR /S /E command to view the effective rights in DATA:BUSINESS

```
F:\BUSINESS>LOGIN 99EDWLOW
Enter your password:
Device LPT1: re-routed to queue CLASSROOM on server VOYAGER_311.

Password for user 99EDWLOW on server VOYAGER_311 has expired.
   You have 5 grace login(s) left to change your password.
Would you like to change your password? (Y/N) N

F:\BUSINESS\USERS\99EDWLOW>LISTDIR DATA:BUSINESS /S /E

The sub-directory structure of VOYAGER_311/DATA:BUSINESS
Effective    Directory
------------------------------------------------
[ R    F ]   ->GLSYSTEM
[ RWCEMF ]   ->BUDGETS
[        ]   ->USERS
[ RWCEMFA]   -> 99EDWLOW
[ RWCEMF ]   ->WORK
5 sub-directories found

F:\BUSINESS\USERS\99EDWLOW>
```

DOCUMENTING THE WORK

Before she headed for home, Leslie wanted to check some of the work she did with FILER. First she exited the FILER utility by holding down the Alt key and pressing [F10]. This is a shortcut method that saved having to press the Esc key several times.

To check trustee assignments made for the Business workgroup, Leslie used the TLIST commands shown in Figure 8-20. To check the changes she made to the IRM of the PAYROLL directory, Leslie used the LISTDIR /R command, as shown in Figure 8-21.

Next she wanted to log in as some of her new users and check their trustee assignments and effective rights. Figure 8-22 shows the results of Leslie logging in as user 99EDWLOW. Notice that when she logged in, the system displayed a message saying that the user's password is expired and that the user has a limited number of grace logins. Because Leslie wanted the users to establish their own passwords in the future, she answered "N" when the system asked if she wanted to change the password. Leaving the password expired will allow Ed to specify his own password when he first logs in.

As shown in Figure 8-22, the LISTDIR DATA:BUSINESS /S /E command lists Ed's effective rights in the Business Department's subdirectory structure. These rights can be from a direct trustee assignment, being a member of a group, or inherited rights from a parent directory.

FIGURE 8-23: Leslie's screen after she used the WHOAMI /R command to view all trustee assignments for 99EDLOW

```
F:\BUSINESS\USERS\99EDWLOW>WHOAMI /R
You are user 99EDWLOW attached to server VOYAGER_311, connection 1.
Server VOYAGER_311 is running NetWare v3.11 (100 user).
Login time: Wednesday  June  30, 1993  2:14 pm
[          ]   SYS:
[ R    F ]   SYS:LOGIN
[ R    F ]   SYS:PUBLIC
[    C   ]   SYS:MAIL
[ RWCEMF ]   SYS:MAIL/8000003
[ R    F ]   SYS:SOFTWARE
[          ]   DATA:
[ R    F ]   DATA:BUSINESS/GLSYSTEM
[ RWCEMF ]   DATA:BUSINESS/BUDGETS
[ RWCEMFA]   DATA:BUSINESS/USERS/99EDWLOW
[ RWCEMF ]   DATA:BUSINESS/WORK


F:\BUSINESS\USERS\99EDWLOW>
```

The WHOAMI /R command shown in Figure 8-23 displays all the trustee assignments made for Ed or one of the groups to which he belongs.

The network seems to be coming together; in Chapter 9 Leslie's goal will be to finish getting the file system ready for her users.

In this chapter the FILER utility was used to perform the following file system maintenance functions.

Adding Trustees To a Directory

You can use either the Current Directory Information or Directory Contents options of the Available Topics menu. If using the Directory Contents option you need to select the subdirectory you want to work with. Highlight the Trustees: (see list) option and press [Enter]. Use the Ins key to select trustees from a list of users and groups.

You can modify a trustee's rights by highlighting the trustee and pressing the Enter key. You can then use the Ins or Del keys to add or remove access rights. The Esc key will update the rights for the selected trustee.

Creating and Removing Directory Structures

If necessary use the Select Current Directory option of the Available Topics menu to enter the path to the parent directory. Use the Directory Contents option to display a list of existing subdirectories and files. Use the Ins key to create a new directory. To remove a directory, highlight the directory to be removed and press the Del key. Enter whether you want to delete the entire structure or only the files. Enter "Y" to confirm the deletion process.

Copying Files

FILER can be used to copy files by first using the Select Current Directory option of the Available Topics menu to enter the path to the directory containing the files to be copied. Next use the Directory Contents option to display all subdirectories and files. Mark each file you want to copy using the F5 key. Press [Enter] to obtain the Multiple File Operation menu. Select the Copy Marked Files option and enter the target path.

Setting File Attributes

FILER can be used to set file attributes by first using the Select Current Directory option of the Available Topics menu to enter the path to the directory containing the files to be flagged. Next use the Directory Contents option to display all subdirectories and files. Mark each file you want to flag using the F5 key and press [Enter] to obtain the Multiple File Operation menu. Select the Set Attributes option to open the File Attributes window. Use the Ins key to open the Other Attributes window and then mark the desired attributes using the F5 key. Press [Enter] and then [Esc] to set the marked files to the selected attributes.

Setting Directory Attributes

FILER can be used to set directory attributes by first using the Select Current Directory option of the Available Topics menu to enter the path to the directory to be flagged. Next use the Current Directory Information option to open the Directory Information screen.

Highlight the Directory Attributes: (see list) option and press [Enter] to open the Directory Attributes window. Use the Ins key to open the Other Attributes window and then mark the desired attributes using the F5 key. Press [Enter] and then [Esc] to set the new attributes.

Listing Users with Effective Rights In a Directory (NetWare 3.11 and Higher)

If you have supervisor equivalency and NetWare 3.11 or higher, you can use FILER to see who has effective rights in a specific subdirectory. To do this, first use the Select Current Directory option of the Available Topics menu to select the parent directory or volume root that contains the directory you want to check. Next select the Directory Contents option and highlight the desired subdirectory from the Directory Contents window. Select the Who has rights here option and press [Enter] to see a list of all users who have effective rights in the selected subdirectory.

Changing the Inherited Rights Mask

To change the IRM of a directory, first use the Select Current Directory option of the Available Topics menu to enter the path to the desired directory. Next use the Current Directory Information option to display the Directory Information window. Highlight the Inherited Rights Mask field and press [Enter]. The Inherited Rights window displays the effective rights the directory can currently inherit from the parent. You can now use the Del key to remove rights or the Ins key to add rights to the list. When a directory is created, the IRM contains all rights. The Supervisory right cannot be deleted.

TLIST *[path]*

Used to obtain a list of all trustees for the directory specified by path.

LISTDIR /R

Run from the F:\BUSINESS prompt to obtain a list of all subdirectories within the BUSINESS directory, along with their associated IRMs.

LISTDIR *[path]* **/S /E**

Used to obtain the effective rights in each of the subdirectories of the DATA:BUSINESS directory for the currently logged-in user.

WHOAMI /R

Used to list all the trustee assignments for the currently logged in user. The list includes trustee assignments made to any group to which the user belongs.

1. In addition to FILER, the _____ menu utility can also be used to assign trustee rights and create directories.

2. _____ is necessary for viewing a user's effective rights in a subdirectory.
    a. The Supervisory right   c. Workgroup manager status
    b. Supervisor equivalency   d. The Access Control right

3. The _____ key can be used to mark and add multiple rights from the Other Rights window.

4. When a user is first added as a trustee to a directory, he or she is given _____ rights by default.

5. When deleting a directory with FILER, what two options are you given?

6. When using FILER to copy files, you need to use the Select Current Directory option to change to the directory _____.
    a. To which the files will be copied
    b. Containing the source files to copy

7. The _____ key can be used to rename a file or directory.

8. In NetWare 3.11, what other attributes are added along with the Read Only attribute?

9. The _____ directory attribute prevents deleted files in a directory from being salvaged.

10. The _____ option from FILER's Available Topics menu is used to view who has rights to a specific directory.

11. List four of the options on the Subdirectory Options menu.

12. List four of the options on the Multiple File Operations menu.

13. List four settings that can be controlled from Set Filer Options.

14. What rights are contained in the IRM of a newly created directory?

SUPERIOR TECHNICAL COLLEGE

PROJECT 8

Now it's time to set up the network file system for Superior Technical College. To do so, you'll use FILER and the trustee directory security worksheets you completed in Project 5. Before you begin, pull together your copies of the Project 5 worksheets; you'll need them as you work through the assignments below.

Assignment 8-1: **Start FILER**

Log in to your assigned file server using the supervisor-equivalent name supplied by your instructor. If you are unable to log in as a supervisor equivalent because of file server security, you will still be able to do all assignments except Assignment 8-9 using your normal ##ADMIN username, which has workgroup manager privileges.

Now start FILER. Change your current directory to point to your Superior Technical College directory. Follow the steps below to use FILER's selection process to build the directory path.

❶ Highlight the Select Current Directory option and press **[Enter]**. Press **[Backspace]** to remove the current entry from the path box. Press **[Ins]**. A window showing the existing file server contents will be displayed. Record the contents of your file server window under Assignment 8-1 on Student Answer Sheet 8.

❷ Select your assigned file server and press **[Enter]**. A window showing all volumes on your assigned file server will be displayed. Record the contents of the volume window on Student Answer Sheet 8.

❸ Select the volume containing your assigned work area and press **[Enter]**. A window showing all directories in which you have access rights will be displayed. Record the contents of the directory window on Student Answer Sheet 8.

❹ Select your directory and press **[Enter]**. Press **[Esc]** to exit the selection process. Press **[Enter]** to change your current path to the one shown in the Current Directory Path box. Record the path name on Student Answer Sheet 8.

Assignment 8-2: **Assign Trustees**

Use FILER to assign trustees to each of your directories and subdirectories as specified on your trustee directory security worksheets completed in Project 5. Repeat Assignment 8-2, steps 1 through 3, for each of your trustee worksheets.

❶ Highlight the Select Current Directory option and enter the path to the directory shown on your trustee directory security worksheet. Attach a copy of your trustee directory worksheet to Student Answer Sheet 8.

If your trustee worksheet defines trustee assignments for the current directory path, do the following (otherwise skip to step 2). To add trustees to the current directory path as displayed in FILER's header screen, select the Current Directory Information option from FILER's Available Topics menu. Highlight the Trustees: (see list) field and press **[Enter]**. Press **[Ins]** and select a new trustee username to add to the trustee window. The user will be given Read and File Scan rights by default. To grant additional rights, press **[Enter]** to display the existing Trustee Rights window. Next press **[Ins]** to display the Other Rights window. Now use the arrow keys to highlight a desired right and press **[F5]** to mark it. Do this for each right you want to add to the Trustee Rights window. When you have finished marking rights, press **[Esc]**. Press **[Esc]** again to update the rights and return to the Trustees window. Repeat this process for each trustee.

❷ To add trustee rights to subdirectories of the current directory, select the Directory Contents option from the Available Topics menu. Highlight the subdirectory in which you want to add trustee assignments and press **[Enter]**. Highlight the Trustees: (see list) field and press **[Enter]**. Press **[Ins]** and select a new trustee username. The user will be given Read and File Scan rights by default.

❸ To grant additional rights, press **[Enter]** to display the existing Trustee Rights window. Next press **[Ins]** to display the Other Rights window. Now use the arrow keys to highlight a desired right and press **[F5]** to mark it. Do this for each right you want to add to the Trustee Rights window. When you have finished marking rights, press **[Esc]**. Press **[Esc]** again to update the rights and return to the Trustees window. Repeat this process for each trustee you want to add to the current directory. When you have finished entering all trustees for this subdirectory, press **[Esc]** to return to the Directory Contents window. Repeat the process to add trustees to a different subdirectory.

Assignment 8-3: **Create a Directory Structure with FILER**

The GRADUATE system has an option to archive reports in a subdirectory called REPORTS*year*. You need to create a REPORTS subdirectory structure within your GRADUATE directory, as shown in Figure 8-24.

FIGURE 8-24: The REPORTS subdirectory structure

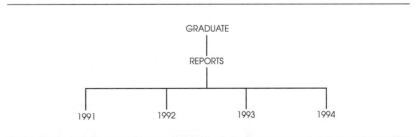

Use FILER to create this structure by following the steps below.

❶ Use the Select Current Directory option from FILER's Available Topics menu to set your current directory path to point to your GRADUATE placement system. Record the path setting on Student Answer Sheet 8.

❷ Select the Directory Contents option from FILER's Available Topics menus. The Directory Contents window showing any subdirectories and files in your GRADUATE directory will be displayed.

❸ Press **[Ins]**, enter **REPORTS** for the name of the new subdirectory, and press **[Enter]**. The REPORTS subdirectory should now appear in your Directory Contents window.

❹ Highlight the REPORTS subdirectory and press **[Enter]**. The Subdirectory Options menus will be displayed.

❺ Highlight the Make this your Current Directory option and press **[Enter]**.

❻ Press **[Ins]** four times to create the 1991, 1992, 1993, and 1994 subdirectories.

❼ Dora Bergson should be given all rights to the REPORTS subdirectory. Follow the steps in Assignment 8-2, step 2, to make Julie a trustee of the REPORTS directory.

Assignment 8-4: **Use FILER to Copy Files**

There are several files in the SOFTWARE.CTS\SP directory that John Rose would like copied into the BUDGETS directory area you created. These files all contain a year, such as 01, 02, or 03, as part of the filename. Use FILER to select these files and copy them into the BUDGETS directory you created for John and Lee. To use FILER to copy these files, do the following:

❶ Use the Select Current Directory option of the Available Topics menu to enter the path to the SYS:SOFTWARE\SP subdirectory. Use the Directory Contents option to view the contents of the SOFTWARE\SP directory. Use the arrow keys along with the F5 key to mark each of the files that contain 01, 02, or 03 as part of their filename. Record the filenames to be copied on Student Answer Sheet 8.

❷ After marking all the desired filenames, press **[Enter]**. The Multiple File Operations menu will be displayed.

❸ Highlight the Copy Marked Files option and press **[Enter]**. Enter the path to your BUDGETS directory. Instead of typing the complete path, let FILER build the path for you. To do this, follow steps 4 through 9.

❹ Press **[Backspace]** to erase the current path, then press **[Ins]**.

❺ Highlight your file server and press **[Enter]**.

❻ Choose your volume from the Volumes window and press **[Enter]**.

❼ Highlight your ##ADMIN directory and press **[Enter]**.

❽ Select the correct directory and subdirectory path leading to your BUDGETS subdirectory area. To end the selection process, press **[Esc]**. The path will be displayed in the Current Directory Path window.

❾ Press **[Enter]** to copy the files to the directory specified by this path.

Assignment 8-5: **Rename Files and Directories**

There is an inconsistency in the BUDGET worksheet filenames. Change the names of the worksheet files EARN01.WK1 and TAX02.WK1 to BUDGETxx.WK1 and BUDGETyy.WK1, where *xx* represents last year and *yy* represents two years ago. Change all worksheet filenames containing "00" by replacing "00" with the current year. To change filenames with FILER, follow the steps below.

❶ Use the Select Current Directory option of the Available Topics menu to enter the directory path to the budget files you copied in Assignment 8-4. Select the Directory Contents option to display the Directory Contents window showing your budget files. Highlight a file whose name needs to be changed and press **[F3]**. Record the old names of each file you will change on Student Answer Sheet 8. Press **[Backspace]** to erase the current name and enter the corrected name. Press **[Enter]** to rename the file. Repeat the process until you have made the necessary name changes. Record the new filenames on Student Answer Sheet 8.

❷ Use FILER to change the name of the STCFORMS directory to FORMS. Record each FILER option you use on Student Answer Sheet 8.

Assignment 8-6: **Set File Attributes**

John Rose said if possible he would like to protect all the current year's worksheets from being deleted, while at the same time allowing them to be changed and updated. He wants to protect all the previous year's files from being modified or erased. Now you'll use FILER to set the attributes to provide this level of file security. If you are using an older version of NetWare, make all the files Read Only. If using NetWare 3.11 or 3.12, flag the current year's files to be Delete Inhibit and Rename Inhibit, and the previous year's files to be Read Only. To use FILER to set the Read Only file attribute, follow the steps below.

❶ From the Directory Contents window, use the arrow keys and [F5] to mark each of the previous year's files and press **[Enter]**. If using a version of NetWare prior to 3.11, also highlight the current year's files. Highlight the Set Attributes option and press **[Enter]**. Press **[Ins]** to display the Other Attributes window. Record each of the attributes shown in the Other Attributes window on Student Answer Sheet 8.

❷ Highlight the Read Only attribute and press **[Enter]**. Record the contents of the File Attributes window on Student Answer Sheet 8. Press **[Esc]** to apply the selected attributes to the files.

❸ If you are using NetWare 3.11 or higher, use the following process to set the Delete-Inhibit and Rename-Inhibit attributes for all the current year's files. From the Directory Contents window, use the arrow keys along with the F5 key to mark each of the previous year's files and press

[Enter]. If using a version of NetWare prior to 3.11, also highlight the current year's files. Highlight the Set Attributes option and press [Enter]. Press [Ins] to display the Other Attributes window. Highlight the Delete-Inhibit and Rename-Inhibit attributes and press [Enter]. Record the contents of the File Attributes window on Student Answer Sheet 8. Press [Esc] to apply the selected attributes to the files.

Assignment 8-7: Set Directory Attributes

The NetWare menu system can be set up to create and erase temporary files in the MENUS directory. To cut system overhead and provide longer protection for salvaging good files, determine the necessary directory attribute to cause files erased from the MENUS directory to be immediately removed from the system. Then follow the steps below.

❶ Record the attributes you plan to use under Assignment 8-7 of Student Answer Sheet 8. Because other users may be given rights to create and erase files in the MENUS directory, you should make this directory more secure by hiding it from DOS commands and applications.

❷ To use FILER to set these attributes on your MENUS directory, choose the Select Current Directory option of the Available Topics window to enter the path to your MENUS directory. Highlight the Current Directory Information option and press [Enter]. The Directory Information screen will be displayed. Highlight the Directory Attributes field and press [Enter]. The Current Attributes window showing any existing attributes will be displayed. Press [Ins] to open the Other Attributes window. Record each of the attributes shown in the Other Attributes window on Student Answer Sheet 8. (Be sure to use the arrow keys to scroll through and display all other attributes.) Use the arrow keys and the F5 key to mark each desired attribute and then press [Enter] to add the selected attributes to the Current Attributes window.

❸ Verify that your MENUS directory is hidden by returning to the Directory Contents window to view all directories in your work area. The MENUS directory should not be included in the list. Print the Directory Contents screen and attach it to Student Answer Sheet 8.

Assignment 8-8: View Hidden Directories

❶ To change the FILER settings to allow you to view hidden directories, select Set Filer Options and press [Enter]. The Filer Settings window will be displayed. Highlight the Directory Search Attributes field and press [Enter]. The Directory Search Attributes window will be displayed. Record all the possible directory search attributes on Student Answer Sheet 8.

❷ Press [Ins] to open the Other Attributes window. Highlight the Hidden Directory attribute and press [Enter]. The Hidden Directory attribute will be added to the Directory Search Attributes window. Press [Esc] until you return to the Available Topics menu. Use the Directory Contents option to verify that you can now see the hidden MENUS directory. Print the screen and attach it to Student Answer Sheet 8.

Assignment 8-9: **List Users with Effective Rights in a Directory**
(Requires NetWare 3.11 and Higher)

If you do not have supervisor equivalency or are using an older version of NetWare, you will not be able to perform this assignment; if so, skip to Assignment 8-10.

Julie is worried about someone tampering with the reports archived by the GRADUATE system. While users should be able to read the reports, she wants Dora Bergson to be the only user with rights to update them. To use FILER to determine what users have effective rights in the GRADUATES\REPORTS directory, follow the steps below.

❶ Use the Select Current Directory option to enter the path to your GRADUATE placement system. Record the path name on Student Answer Sheet 8.

❷ Highlight the Directory Contents option and press **[Enter]**. The Directory Contents window showing all subdirectories and files in your GRADUATE placement directory will be displayed. Highlight the REPORTS subdirectory and press **[Enter]**. The Subdirectory Options menus will be displayed. Select the Who has rights here option and press **[Enter]**. Print the screen and attach the printout to Student Answer Sheet 8.

❸ On Student Answer Sheet 8, record each user, his or her rights, and how the rights to this directory were obtained.

❹ Press **[Esc]** to return to the Available Topics menu.

Assignment 8-10: **Change the Inherited Rights Mask**
(Requires NetWare 3.11 or Higher)

To protect the archived reports directory from being modified and still provide multiple users with the right to enter data into the GRADUATE system, you will need to restrict the Inherited Rights Mask of the the REPORTS directory to allow only Read and File Scan rights.

To use FILER to remove all rights from the Inherited Rights Mask except for Read, File Scan, and Supervisory, follow the steps below.

❶ Use the Select Current Directory option of the Available Topics menu to enter the path to your GRADUATE placement\REPORTS subdirectory. Select the Current Directory Information option to open the Directory Information for the REPORTS window. Highlight the Inherited Rights Mask field and press **[Enter]**. The Inherited Rights window showing all access rights will be displayed. Use the arrow keys along with the F5 key to mark all rights including Supervisory. Press **[Del]**. Note any message on Student Answer Sheet 8.

❷ Use the arrow keys along with the F5 key to mark all rights except Supervisory, Read, and File Scan. Press **[Del]**. Describe your results on Student Answer Sheet 8.

❸ Press **[Esc]** to return to the Available Topics menu.

❹ If you have supervisor equivalency, repeat the steps under Assignment 8-9 to display who has rights in the REPORTS directory.

Assignment 8-11: **Check Your Work**

❶ Exit FILER by holding down **[Alt]** while pressing **[F10]**. Use the MAP command to create a root drive letter G: that points to your ##ADMIN directory. Record the MAP command you used on Student Answer Sheet 8.

❷ Use the LISTDIR G: /S > PRN command to document your revised directory structure. Attach your printout to Student Answer Sheet 8.

❸ Highlight the newly created REPORTS directory and the renamed FORMS directory. Use TLIST *[path]* > PRN commands to obtain printouts of the trustee assignments for the following directories: BUDGETS, GRADUATE, REPORTS, SYS:SOFTWARE.CTS, and MENUS. Record the TLIST commands on Student Answer Sheet 8. Attach the printouts to Student Answer Sheet 8.

❹ Use the NDIR *[path]* > PRN command to obtain a printout showing all files in your BUDGETS subdirectory. Record the NDIR command you used on Student Answer Sheet 8. Attach the printout to Student Answer Sheet 8.

❺ Change to drive G: and use the LISTDIR /R /E > PRN command to obtain a printout of your directories and subdirectories, along with the Inherited Rights Mask for each. Attach the printout to Student Answer Sheet 8.

❻ Log in as Virg Kent and Julie Miller and use the WHOAMI /R > PRN and LISTDIR /E /S > PRN commands to obtain printouts of their trustee assignments and effective rights, respectively. Attach the printouts to Student Answer Sheet 8.

Turn in Materials Write the assignment and step number on your printouts for Assignments 8-7, 8-8, 8-9, and 8-11 and attach them in the correct sequence to Student Answer Sheet 8. Also remember to attach a copy of your trustee directory security worksheets for Assignment 8-2. If instructed, turn in the materials to your instructor on or before the scheduled due date.

Student Name: _____ Date: _____

Assignment 8-1: **Start FILER**

❶ Record the contents of your file server window below.

File Servers

❷ Record the contents of your volume window below.

Volumes

❸ Record the contents of your directories window below.

Directories

❹ Record the current path name.

Assignment 8-2: **Assign Trustees**

❶ Attach a copy of the trustee directory security worksheets you used to make the trustee assignments.

Assignment 8-3: **Create a Directory Structure with FILER**

❶ Record the path to your GRADUATE directory.

Assignment 8-4: **Use FILER to Copy Files**

❶ In the space below, record the filenames to be copied from the SYS:SOFTWARE\SP directory.

Assignment 8-5: **Rename Files and Directories**

❶ Record your old and new filenames below.

Old Filename	New Filename

❷ In the space below, record each option you used from FILER to rename the STCFORMS directory to FORMS.

Assignment 8-6: **Set File Attributes**

❶ In the table below, record all file attributes shown in the Other Attributes window and their functions.

Other Attributes	Function

❷ In the table below, record the contents of your File Attributes window after inserting the new attributes.

File Attributes

❸ In the table below, record the contents of your File Attributes window after inserting the new attributes.

File Attributes

Assignment 8-7:   **Set Directory Attributes**

❶   Record the attributes you plan to use below.

❷   In the table below, record all directory attributes and their use in the Other Attributes window.

Other Directory Attributes	Functional Purpose

❸   Attach the printout of your Directory Contents screen.

Assignment 8-8:   **Viewing Hidden Directories**

❶   In the table below, record all possible directory search attributes.

Directory Search Attributes

❷   Attach the printout showing the MENUS directory.

Assignment 8-9:   **List Users with Effective Rights in a Directory
(Requires NetWare 3.11 or Higher)**

❶   Record the path to your Graduate placement system.

❷   Attach the printout showing all users with effective rights.

❸   In the table below, record each user, his or her rights, and how these rights were obtained.

Username	Rights	How Obtained

Assignment 8-10: **Change the Inherited Rights Mask**
(Requires NetWare 3.11 or Higher)

❶ Record any message here.

❷ In the space below, describe your results when attempting to delete all rights from the IRM.

Assignment 8-11: **Check Your Work**

❶ Record the MAP command you used to map drive G: to your ##ADMIN directory.

❷ Attach the printout obtained from the LISTDIR G: /S > PRN command.

❸ In the space below, record the TLIST commands you used to document your trustee assignments for the given directories.

Attach the printouts obtained from the TLIST command.

❹ In the space below, record the NDIR command you used to document the file in your BUDGETS directory. Attach the printout obtained from the NDIR command.

❺ Attach the printout obtained from the LISTDIR /R /E > PRN command.

❻ Attach the printouts obtained from the following commands for both Virg Kent and Julie Miller.
   LISTDIR /R /E > PRN
   WHOAMI /R > PRN

WORKING WITH FILE SYSTEM UTILITIES

In this chapter you will:

- Use the GRANT command to assign trustee rights

- Use the ALLOW command to set the IRM for a directory

- Use the REVOKE command to remove a trustee right

- Use the REMOVE command to remove a trustee from a directory

- Use the RIGHTS command to list a user's effective rights

- Use the DSPACE utility to limit disk space

- Use the SALVAGE utility to recover a deleted file

- Use the NBACKUP utility to back up and restore files

- Use the SECURITY command to view possible file server security violations

- Use the BINDFIX command to check or repair bindery problems

In addition to the menu utilities such as SYSCON, FILER, and SESSION, NetWare contains a number of command line utilities that can aid the network administrator. Many of the functions of the menu utilities can also be performed through command line utilities. While the menu utilities are interactive and easy to use, the command line utilities often can be more quickly executed and lend themselves to running from DOS batch files or menus. For example, it is more efficient to type the command RIGHTS DATA:BUSINESS than to start FILER, select the Directory Contents option, and then use the View/Set Directory Information option to see your effective rights. In this chapter, you will see how command line utilities can be used to manage trustee rights as well as document existing trustee assignments and view your effective rights.

Previous versions of NetWare contained an option to limit a user's disk space. In addition to this capability, NetWare 3.1x has the option to limit the amount of disk space consumed by a directory structure. This option is important if you have divided your disk by allocating a limited amount of capacity for each workgroup or application. When an application or workgroup exceeds the allocated space it can affect other users or applications. As you'll learn in this chapter, the DSPACE menu utility in NetWare 3.11 and above can be used to limit the amount of disk space consumed by a user or directory structure. In the project at the end of this chapter you will use the DSPACE utility to set the disk space allocations you defined for your directory structure for Superior Technical College.

NetWare 3.1x has a sophisticated system of recovering deleted files. When a file is deleted the directory that originally stored it keeps track of it. As the NetWare operating system needs more space, it will remove the oldest deleted files first and reuse the space. Depending on the amount of free disk storage on your file server, quite a long time can elapse before a file's space is reused. The SALVAGE utility may be used to recover deleted files any time before their space is reused. When a directory is deleted, the files that formerly occupied that directory are stored in a hidden directory called DELETED.SAV, located at the root of each volume.

Although most network administrators use a third-party backup system to make daily backups of the entire data system onto tape cartridges, you should know how to use the NBACKUP utility to make special backups of either data or system files such as the NetWare binderies. In this chapter you will see how to use NBACKUP to back up your data directories and restore selected files.

THE PC SOLUTIONS CASE

On her way to work, Leslie thought of several tasks she wanted to accomplish. Before she left work the day before, she used USERDEF to create a template and new usernames for the Help Desk staff. Now one of her first jobs was to give the Help Desk members access rights to the file system they need to use. Leslie also wanted to set up the disk usage restrictions for each of the directories according to the limits she defined when she designed the directory structure in Chapter 2. In addition, the previous night's thunderstorm made Leslie nervous; before she leaves work today she must back up the PC Solutions directory structure and NetWare bindery files so that she could restore her work on another machine if her current file server became disabled.

ASSIGNING TRUSTEE RIGHTS WITH THE GRANT COMMAND

The LISTDIR /S command in Figure 9-1 shows the HELPDESK directory structure Leslie created using the FILER utility. Nancy will be responsible for the Northeast (NE) and Southeast (SE) directories. Howell will be responsible for the Midwest (MW), West (WEST), and Canada (CA) directories. Nancy and Howell, along with the users in the Sales group, need to be able to read information from all the regional subdirectories. In addition, Nancy wants Mary Read to be able to work with files in the HELPDESK\WORK subdirectory as well as the Northeast (NE) and Southeast (SE) regional subdirectories.

Given the directory structure she created, Leslie considered possible ways of assigning the Sales and Help Desk workgroups the necessary rights. One method is to assign to both groups Read and File Scan rights to each of the regional subdirectories. This method is very straightforward, but it would entail making two trustee assignments for each subdirectory. In addition, if another regional subdirectory is added in the future, Leslie would need to remember to assign both groups the rights to that subdirectory as well.

FIGURE 9-1: The LISTDIR command showing Leslie's HELPDESK directory structure

```
F:\>LISTDIR HELPDESK /S

The sub-directory structure of VOYAGER_311/DATA:HELPDESK
Directory
---------------------------------------------------------------
->NE
->WORK
->SE
->MW
->WEST
->CA
->99HOWDAV
->99NANYIN
8 sub-directories found

F:\>
```

After considering the alternatives, Leslie decided to give both the Sales and Help Desk groups Read and File Scan rights to the HELPDESK directory; this allows them to inherit these rights to all the regional subdirectories. With this plan Leslie needed to make only two trustee assignments for the HELPDESK directory: one for the Sales group and one for the Help Desk group. However, as you will see, she will want to use an Inherited Rights Mask (IRM) to block the Read and File Scan rights for these groups from flowing into the Help Desk users' home directories.

Leslie could use the FILER utility to make these trustee assignments, but she decided it will be faster and more efficient to use the

GRANT command. The NetWare 3.11 Utilities manual shows the syntax of the GRANT command:

GRANT rightslist... (FOR path) TO
(User ¦ Group)

The RIGHTSLIST option can be the first letter of one or more of the trustee rights (Supervisory, Read, Write, Create, Erase, Modify, File Scan, or Access Control) separated by spaces. Other options for the RIGHTSLIST parameter are "ALL" for all rights or "N" for no rights. The PATH parameter can be the complete path, including volume name, directory, and subdirectory, or it may be a relative path from the current directory location. The USER ¦ GROUP parameter is the name of the user or group to receive the trustee rights to the specified directory path.

FIGURE 9-2: Leslie's screen after she used the GRANT command

```
F:\>GRANT R F FOR DATA:HELPDESK TO SALES

VOYAGER_311/DATA:HELPDESK
HELPDESK                            Rights set to [ R    F ]

F:\>GRANT R F W C E M FOR HELPDESK TO 99MARREA

VOYAGER_311/DATA:HELPDESK
HELPDESK                            Rights set to [ RWCEMF ]

F:\>GRANT ALL FOR HELPDESK\NE TO 99NANYIN

VOYAGER_311/DATA:HELPDESK\NE
NE                                 Rights set to [ RWCEMFA]

F:\>GRANT ALL FOR HELPDESK\SE TO 99NANYIN

VOYAGER_311/DATA:HELPDESK\SE
SE                                 Rights set to [ RWCEMFA]

F:\>
```

FIGURE 9-3: Leslie's screen after she changed to the HELPDESK directory and used the TLIST command

```
F:\>CD HELPDESK

F:\HELPDESK>TLIST

VOYAGER_311\DATA:HELPDESK
User trustees:
  99MARREA                            [ RWCEMF ]
  ----
Group trustees:
  SALES                               [ R    F ]
  HELPDESK                            [ R    F ]

F:\HELPDESK>
```

To assign the defined rights, Leslie used the GRANT commands shown in Figure 9-2. In our example, then, "GRANT R F FOR DATA: HELPDESK TO SALES" translates to "Grant the Read and File Scan rights for the HELPDESK directory to the Sales group members." "GRANT R F W C E M FOR \HELPDESK TO 99MARREA" translates to "Grant Read, File Scan, Write, Create, Erase, and Modify rights for the HELPDESK directory to Mary Read." This grant command will allow Mary to work in all regional subdirectories. "GRANT ALL FOR \HELPDESK \NE TO 99NANYIN" and "GRANT R F W C E M FOR \HELPDESK\SE TO 99NANYIN" commands give Nancy control of Northeast and Southeast regions. Leslie then entered GRANT commands to give Howell Davis control of the Midwest, West, and Canada regional subdirectories.

USING THE REVOKE AND TLIST COMMANDS

The TLIST command can be used to view the trustees of a specific directory or subdirectory. To view the trustees, Leslie changed the default DOS prompt to the HELPDESK directory and then used the TLIST command shown in Figure 9-3 to view all trustee assignments to the HELPDESK

FIGURE 9-4: Leslie's screen showing the output of the TLIST *. * command

```
VOYAGER_311\DATA:HELPDESK\NE
User trustees:
   99NANYIN                                   [ RWCEMFA]
No group trustees.

VOYAGER_311\DATA:HELPDESK\WORK
No user trustees.
Group trustees:
   HELPDESK                                   [ RWCEMF ]

VOYAGER_311\DATA:HELPDESK\SE
User trustees:
   99NANYIN                                   [ RWCEMFA]
No group trustees.

VOYAGER_311\DATA:HELPDESK\MW
User trustees:
   99HOWDAV                                   [ RWCEMFA]
No group trustees.

VOYAGER_311\DATA:HELPDESK\WEST
User trustees:
   99HOWDAV                                   [ RWCEMF ]
Press any key to continue ('C' for continue).
```

FIGURE 9-5: Leslie's screen showing the REVOKE commands used to remove the Access Control right

```
F:\HELPDESK>REVOKE A FOR NE FROM 99NANYIN
VOYAGER_311/DATA:HELPDESK\NE
Trustee's access rights set to [ RWCEMF ]

Rights for 1 directories were changed for 99NANYIN.


F:\HELPDESK>REVOKE A FOR SE FROM 99NANYIN
VOYAGER_311/DATA:HELPDESK\SE
Trustee's access rights set to [ RWCEMF ]

Rights for 1 directories were changed for 99NANYIN.


F:\HELPDESK>REVOKE A FOR WEST FROM 99HOWDAV
VOYAGER_311/DATA:HELPDESK\WEST
Trustee's access rights set to [ RWCEMF ]

Rights for 1 directories were changed for 99HOWDAV.


F:\HELPDESK>
```

FIGURE 9-6: Leslie's screen after she changed Mary Read's trustee assignment

```
F:\HELPDESK>REVOKE W C E M A FOR MW FROM 99MARREA
No trustee for the specified directory.

F:\HELPDESK>GRANT R F FOR MW TO 99MARREA

VOYAGER_311/DATA:HELPDESK\MW
MW                          Rights set to [ R     F ]


F:\HELPDESK>GRANT R F FOR WEST TO 99MARREA

VOYAGER_311/DATA:HELPDESK\WEST
WEST                        Rights set to [ R     F ]


F:\HELPDESK>GRANT R F FOR CA TO 99MARREA

VOYAGER_311/DATA:HELPDESK\CA
CA                          Rights set to [ R     F ]


F:\HELPDESK>
```

directory. To view the trustee assignments in each of the subdirectories, she used the TLIST *.* command, the output of which is shown in Figure 9-4.

With the exception of their home directories, Leslie did not want users to have the Access Control right to the shared directories they use. Having access control potentially allows users to assign rights to other users. Leslie knew that it's hard enough to keep track of who has rights where without other users being able to change the trustee rights she assigned. To remove Nancy and Howell's Access Control right in the HELPDESK regional subdirectories, Leslie used the REVOKE command, shown in Figure 9-5. Notice that the syntax of the REVOKE command is similar to that of the GRANT command. For instance, "REVOKE A FOR NE FROM 99NANYIN" translates to "Revoke the Access Control right for the Northeast regional subdirectory from Nancy Yin."

Leslie wanted Mary to have only Read and File Scan rights to the Midwest, West, and Canada regional subdirectories. As it stood, Mary would inherit the R F W C E M rights she was assigned in the HELPDESK parent directory. The first command in Figure 9-6 shows Leslie's attempt to use the REVOKE command to remove the W C E M A rights from the Midwest subdirectory. Notice that the REVOKE command failed because it can *only* be used in the directory in which the trustee assignment was made; it cannot be used to revoke inherited rights to subdirectories. To change the rights in a subdirectory, Leslie had to reassign them using the GRANT command, as shown in the rest of the commands in Figure 9-6.

FIGURE 9-7: Leslie's screen after she removed Howell as a trustee of the Canada regional subdirectory and gave control to Mary and Nancy

```
F:\HELPDESK>REMOVE 99HOWDAV FROM CA
VOYAGER_311/DATA:HELPDESK\CA
User "99HOWDAV" no longer a trustee to the specified directory.

Trustee "99HOWDAV" removed from 1 directories.


F:\HELPDESK>GRANT R F W C E M FOR CA TO 99NANYIN

VOYAGER_311/DATA:HELPDESK\CA
CA                            Rights set to [ RWCEMF ]


F:\HELPDESK>REMOVE 99MARREA FROM CA
VOYAGER_311/DATA:HELPDESK\CA
User "99MARREA" no longer a trustee to the specified directory.

Trustee "99MARREA" removed from 1 directories.


F:\HELPDESK>
```

FIGURE 9-8: Leslie's screen after she logged in as 99MARREA and used the WHOAMI /R command to display all trustee assignments for 99MARREA

```
F:\>WHOAMI /R
You are user 99MARREA attached to server VOYAGER_311, connection 1.
Server VOYAGER_311 is running NetWare v3.11 (100 user).
Login time: Friday  July 2, 1993  2:03 pm
[        ]  SYS:
[ R    F ]  SYS:LOGIN
[ R    F ]  SYS:PUBLIC
[   C    ]  SYS:MAIL
[ RWCEMF ]  SYS:MAIL/E000004
[ R    F ]  SYS:SOFTWARE
[        ]  DATA:
[ RWCEMF ]  DATA:FORMS
[ RWCEMF ]  DATA:BUSINESS
[SRWCEMFA]  DATA:SUPPORT
[SRWCEMFA]  DATA:SALES
[ RWCEMF ]  DATA:HELPDESK
[ R    F ]  DATA:HELPDESK/MW
[ R    F ]  DATA:HELPDESK/WEST


F:\>
```

FIGURE 9-9: Leslie's screen after she used the LISTDIR /S /E command to display 99MARREA's effective rights in HELPDESK subdirectories

```
F:\>LISTDIR DATA:HELPDESK /S /E

The sub-directory structure of VOYAGER_311/DATA:HELPDESK
Effective     Directory
--------------------------------------------------------
[ RWCEMF ]   ->NE
[ RWCEMF ]   ->WORK
[ RWCEMF ]   ->SE
[ R    F ]   ->MW
[ R    F ]   ->WEST
[ RWCEMF ]   ->CA
[ RWCEMF ]   ->99HOWDAV
[ RWCEMF ]   ->99NANYIN
8 sub-directories found

F:\>
```

USING THE REMOVE COMMAND

During her break, Leslie learned that Mary and Nancy, instead of Howell, will be responsible for handling the correspondence for the Canada region. To remove Howell as a trustee from the Canada region and assign the responsibility to Nancy, Leslie used the REMOVE and GRANT commands, as shown in the first two commands of Figure 9-7.

To give Mary the extra rights to help Nancy in the Canada subdirectory, Leslie removed her Read and File Scan trustee assignment, as shown in the third command in Figure 9-7. Mary will now inherit all the rights she was given to the HELPDESK parent directory. As you can see, in this case the REMOVE command actually increased a user's effective rights.

CHECKING EFFECTIVE RIGHTS

In her NetWare class, Leslie learned how to check trustee assignments and effective rights to the directory structure by using the WHOAMI and LISTDIR commands. Leslie wanted to check and document user's trustee assignments and effective rights in the HELPDESK directory structure. She started by logging in as 99MARREA and then used the WHOAMI /R command, as shown in Figure 9-8, to view all trustee assignments. Leslie next used the LISTDIR /S /E command shown in Figure 9-9 to list the effective rights for the user. Figure 9-9 illustrates how trustee rights are inherited into subdirectories. (To route the output of these commands to the printer Leslie would need to use the DOS > PRN statement at the end of each command.)

```
F:\>RIGHTS HELPDESK\MW
VOYAGER_311\DATA:HELPDESK\MW
Your Effective Rights for this directory are [ R     F ]
 * May Read from File.                      (R)
   May Scan for Files.                      (F)
* Has no effect on directory.

    Entries in Directory May Inherit [ R     F ] rights.

F:\>RIGHTS HELPDESK\CA
VOYAGER_311\DATA:HELPDESK\CA
Your Effective Rights for this directory are [ RWCEMF ]
 * May Read from File.                      (R)
 * May Write to File.                       (W)
   May Create Subdirectories and Files.     (C)
   May Erase Directory.                     (E)
   May Modify Directory.                    (M)
   May Scan for Files.                      (F)
* Has no effect on directory.

    Entries in Directory May Inherit [ RWCEMF ] rights.

F:\>
```

FIGURE 9-11: Leslie's screen after she entered the command HELP ALLOW

```
 File  Edit  Search  Options                         Help=F1
█ALLOW                                              21/27661

 ┌─ALLOW [path [TO INHERIT] [rightslist]]─┐

   Format          ▼Parameters. Supports wildcard characters.

   Purpose         Shows, sets, or modifies the Inherited
                   Rights Mask of a directory or file.

   How to use      Type ALLOW [path [rightslist]] <Enter>

                   ▼Examples

   Notes           To set or modify the Inherited Rights
                   Mask, you need the Access Control right.

   [path]          Directory path or file whose Rights Mask you
                   want to view, set, or modify.

   [rightslist]    One or more of the following:

 2:NetWare v3.11:
```

FIGURE 9-12: Using ALLOW commands to set the IRMs for Howell and Nancy

```
F:\>ALLOW DATA:HELPDESK\99HOWDAV TO INHERIT N
    Directories:
        99HOWDAV                [S      ]

F:\>CD DATA:HELPDESK

F:\HELPDESK>ALLOW 99NANYIN TO INHERIT N
    Directories:
        99NANYIN                [S      ]

F:\HELPDESK>
```

The RIGHTS command can also be used to view the effective rights of the current user in the default directory or in a subdirectory, as shown in Figure 9-10. The Read and Write rights marked with asterisks indicate that these rights affect only the files in the directory and have no effect on the directory itself because a directory cannot contain data that could be read or written.

USING THE ALLOW COMMAND TO CHANGE THE IRM OF A DIRECTORY

Looking at Mary's effective rights shown in Figure 9-9, Leslie noticed that Mary is inheriting all rights into Howell's and Nancy's home directories. Leslie planned to prevent this by setting the IRM on their home directories to block all inherited rights. The IRM can be changed using the FILER utility, but Leslie felt it would be faster to use the ALLOW command. To obtain the syntax of the ALLOW command, Leslie used the HELP ALLOW command. The help screen shown in Figure 9-11 appeared. To block all rights from being inherited into Howell's and Nancy's home directories, Leslie used the ALLOW commands shown in Figure 9-12. For instance, "ALLOW DATA:HELPDESK\99HOWDAV TO INHERIT N" translates to "Allow the directory 99HOWDAV to inherit no rights." The second ALLOW command illustrates how the path can be specified relative to the current default directory. By first using the CD command to change to the HELPDESK directory, Leslie only needed to type the name of the subdirectory whose IRM was being changed.

Leslie logged in again with Mary Read's username, then used the LIST-DIR /S /E command, as shown in

FIGURE 9-13: Leslie's screen showing Mary Read's rights after Leslie set IRMs for Howell and Nancy

```
F:\>LISTDIR DATA:HELPDESK /S /E

The sub-directory structure of VOYAGER_311/DATA:HELPDESK
Effective    Directory
-------------------------------------------------------
[ RWCEMF ]  ->NE
[ RWCEMF ]  ->WORK
[ RWCEMF ]  ->SE
[ R    F ]  ->MW
[ R    F ]  ->WEST
[ RWCEMF ]  ->CA
6 sub-directories found

F:\>
```

Figure 9-13. Because Howell's and Nancy's home directories do not show up, Leslie knows that the IRM has blocked any rights from being passed to their home directories. Because Mary is an experienced computer user, Leslie planned to give her the job of copying files from Help Desk staff diskettes into the regional subdirectories.

RESTRICTING DISK SPACE

When Leslie designed the directory structure described in Chapter 2, she created a storage requirements table containing her planned amount of disk space for each storage area (see Figure 2-4).

Leslie planned to use the DSPACE utility to place these limitations on the directories she created. Let's follow Leslie's steps as she used the DSPACE utility to place the planned space limitation on the BUDGETS directory.

1. To start the DSPACE utility, Leslie typed "DSPACE" and pressed [Enter]. The DSPACE menu shown in Figure 9-14 appeared.

FIGURE 9-14: The DSPACE Main Menu

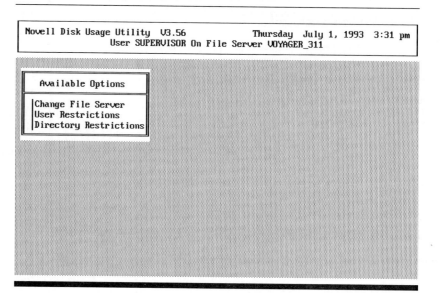

```
Novell Disk Usage Utility  V3.56            Thursday  July 1, 1993  3:31 pm
                 User SUPERVISOR On File Server VOYAGER_311

  Available Options

  Change File Server
  User Restrictions
  Directory Restrictions
```

2. Leslie highlighted the Directory Restrictions option and pressed [Enter]. DSPACE then asked for the path to the desired directory.

3. After Leslie entered the path to the BUDGETS directory, DSPACE displayed the Directory Disk Space Limitation Information screen.

4. Leslie filled out the Directory Disk Space Limitation Information screen as shown in Figure 9-15 and pressed [Esc] to save the space restrictions. DSPACE then returned to the Available Options menu.

FIGURE 9-15: Leslie's Directory Disk Space Limitation Information screen showing the 10MB limitation for the BUDGETS subdirectory

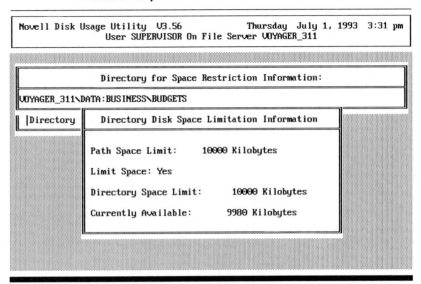

```
Novell Disk Usage Utility  V3.56            Thursday  July 1, 1993  3:31 pm
                    User SUPERVISOR On File Server VOYAGER_311

          ┌──────────────────────────────────────────────────────┐
          │        Directory for Space Restriction Information:    │
          ├──────────────────────────────────────────────────────┤
  VOYAGER_311\DATA:BUSINESS\BUDGETS
          ┌─────────┬────────────────────────────────────────────┐
          │Directory│   Directory Disk Space Limitation Information│
                    │
                    │  Path Space Limit:      10000 Kilobytes      │
                    │                                              │
                    │  Limit Space: Yes                            │
                    │                                              │
                    │  Directory Space Limit:    10000 Kilobytes   │
                    │                                              │
                    │  Currently Available:       9980 Kilobytes   │
                    └──────────────────────────────────────────────┘
```

Leslie then repeated this process to set disk space limitations on her other storage areas, as defined in her storage requirements table.

USING THE SALVAGE UTILITY

While trying to clean up a directory on her workstation's fixed disk, Leslie inadvertently erased all the files in the DATA:FORMS directory. Fortunately, NetWare keeps track of deleted files and allows recovery by using the SALVAGE utility. Let's follow Leslie's steps to use the SALVAGE utility to recover the files from the DATA:FORMS directory.

1. From the DATA:FORMS directory Leslie typed "SALVAGE" and pressed [Enter]. The SALVAGE Main Menu, shown in Figure 9-16, appeared. The first option can be used to recover files that are placed in the DELETED.SAV directory when their original directory structure is deleted. This option must be used to salvage files from a deleted directory. The second option can be used to change directories, and the third option is used to set special SALVAGE sort options such as sort by deletion date, file size, filename, or owner.

FIGURE 9-16: The SALVAGE utility Main Menu

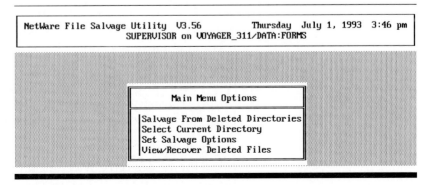

```
NetWare File Salvage Utility  V3.56         Thursday  July 1, 1993  3:46 pm
              SUPERVISOR on VOYAGER_311/DATA:FORMS

                        ┌─────────────────────────────┐
                        │       Main Menu Options      │
                        ├─────────────────────────────┤
                        │Salvage From Deleted Directories│
                        │Select Current Directory      │
                        │Set Salvage Options           │
                        │View/Recover Deleted Files    │
                        └─────────────────────────────┘
```

2. To recover her deleted files from the current FORMS directory, Leslie highlighted the fourth option, View/Recover Deleted Files, and pressed [Enter]. SALVAGE next asked her to enter a File Name Pattern to match. If she wanted a certain file or group of files she could enter the file's name or global identifier. To see all files she pressed [Enter]. The Salvageable File window shown in Figure 9-17 appeared.

FIGURE 9-17: Salvageable files in the FORMS directory

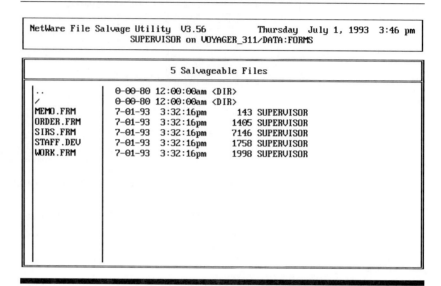

3. She used the arrow keys along with the F5 key to mark all the files and pressed [Enter]. She then pressed [Enter] again to confirm that she wanted to recover all the marked files. The SALVAGE utility then restored the files and removed them from the Salvageable Files window.

4. Leslie then pressed [Esc] until she exited the SALVAGE utility.

Leslie next used the NDIR command to verify that all files, along with their attributes, have been salvaged. To prevent any future problems, Leslie decided to use the FLAG *.* DI command to place the Delete-Inhibit attribute on the files in the FORMS directory.

BACKING UP FILES WITH NBACKUP

Leslie invested a lot of time in setting up the network file system and security. Even though she enjoyed the work, she would hate to have to do it again. Because she was still waiting for the new tape drive system to arrive, Leslie decided to use the NBACKUP command to save her existing bindery files and directory structure, along with the trustee assignments, to diskette. Because she did not have a lot of files in her directories at this time, Leslie thought the backup should fit on just a few high-density diskettes. Let's follow Leslie's steps as she used the NBACKUP utility to back up her bindery and data directories.

1. She first typed "NBACKUP" and pressed [Enter]. When NBACKUP asked for the desired device, she highlighted DOS Devices and pressed [Enter]. The NBACKUP Main Menu, shown in Figure 9-18, appeared.

2. Leslie highlighted Backup Options and pressed [Enter]. After giving a warning about backing up Macintosh files, the Backup Menu shown in Figure 9-19 appeared.

FIGURE 9-19: NBACKUP Backup Menu

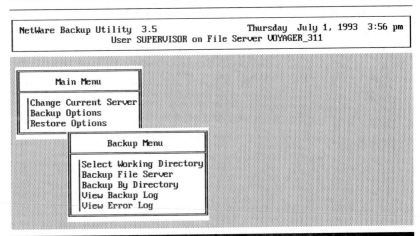

3. She next highlighted Select Working Directory and pressed [Enter]. NBACKUP asked for the path to the working directory. It is necessary to identify the location of the working directory before backing up files. The working directory, used to store the backup log and error logs, must be a directory on a nonremovable drive.

4. Because Leslie planned to place the working directory on her local hard drive, she typed "C:\BACKUP" and pressed [Enter]. NBACKUP asked if the drive is removable. She highlighted No and pressed [Enter]. The Backup Menu shown in Figure 9-19 appeared again.

5. Because she obviously did not want to back up the entire file server onto diskettes, Leslie selected the Backup By Directory option. The Backup Options screen appeared.

6. Leslie completed the Backup Options screen, as shown in Figure 9-20 on the following page.

FIGURE 9-20: Leslie's Backup Options window

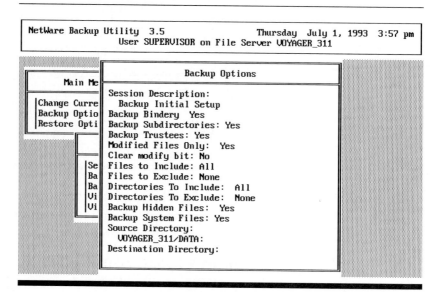

```
NetWare Backup Utility  3.5                    Thursday  July 1, 1993  3:57 pm
                     User SUPERVISOR on File Server VOYAGER_311

         ┌─── Main Me ──────────── Backup Options ──────────────┐
         │                │ Session Description:                │
         │ Change Curre   │   Backup Initial Setup              │
         │ Backup Optio   │ Backup Bindery  Yes                 │
         │ Restore Opti   │ Backup Subdirectories: Yes          │
         │                │ Backup Trustees: Yes                │
         │                │ Modified Files Only:  Yes           │
         │                │ Clear modify bit: No                │
         │          │Se│  │ Files to Include: All               │
         │          │Ba│  │ Files to Exclude: None              │
         │          │Ba│  │ Directories To Include:  All        │
         │          │Vi│  │ Directories To Exclude:  None       │
         │          │Vi│  │ Backup Hidden Files:  Yes           │
         │                │ Backup System Files: Yes            │
         │                │ Source Directory:                   │
         │                │   VOYAGER_311/DATA:                 │
         │                │ Destination Directory:              │
         └────────────────┴─────────────────────────────────────┘
```

When she came to the Directories To Include option, she pressed [Enter] to open the Directories To Include window. She then used the Ins key to add the DATA: volume to the window, as shown in Figure 9-21. Since she did not want to back up the GLSYSTEM software, she used the Directories To Exclude option, then pressed [Ins], then entered the DATA:BUSINESS\GLSYSTEM path.

FIGURE 9-21: Leslie's screen as she inserted directories to include in the backup

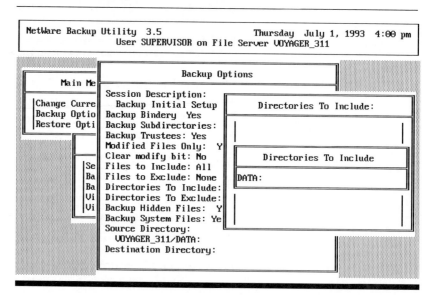

```
NetWare Backup Utility  3.5                    Thursday  July 1, 1993  4:00 pm
                     User SUPERVISOR on File Server VOYAGER_311

         ┌─── Main Me ──────────── Backup Options ──────────────┐
         │                │ Session Description:                │
         │ Change Curre   │   Backup Initial Setup              │
         │ Backup Optio   │ Backup Bindery  Yes    ┌─ Directories To Include: ─┐
         │ Restore Opti   │ Backup Subdirectories: │                           │
         │                │ Backup Trustees: Yes   │                           │
         │                │ Modified Files Only:  Y │                           │
         │                │ Clear modify bit: No   ├─ Directories To Include ──┤
         │          │Se│  │ Files to Include: All  │ DATA:                     │
         │          │Ba│  │ Files to Exclude: None │                           │
         │          │Ba│  │ Directories To Include:│                           │
         │          │Vi│  │ Directories To Exclude:│                           │
         │          │Vi│  │ Backup Hidden Files:  Y │                           │
         │                │ Backup System Files: Ye └───────────────────────────┘
         │                │ Source Directory:                   │
         │                │   VOYAGER_311/DATA:                 │
         │                │ Destination Directory:              │
         └────────────────┴─────────────────────────────────────┘
```

At the Source Directory parameter on the bottom of the Backup Options screen she entered the name of the volume that contained the data directories specified in the Directories To Include window. To specify drive A: as the destination for the backup, Leslie highlighted the Destination Directory field, then pressed [Enter]. She then entered A: as the destination drive.

7. After filling out the Backup Options screen, Leslie pressed [Esc] and saved the backup information. NBACKUP then gave her the choice of starting the backup now or later. She highlighted Now and pressed [Enter]. NBACKUP then asked her to insert her first diskette. During the backup process, NBACKUP displayed the status screen shown in Figure 9-22.

FIGURE 9-22: Leslie's NBACKUP status screen

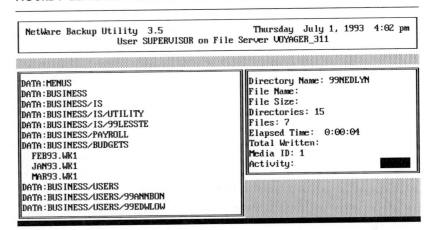

8. When the backup was completed Leslie pressed [Enter] to return to the Backup Menu screen. She then highlighted View Error Log and pressed [Enter]. After she selected her backup session, NBACKUP displayed the error log for this backup session, as shown in Figure 9-23.

FIGURE 9-23: Leslie's NBACKUP error log

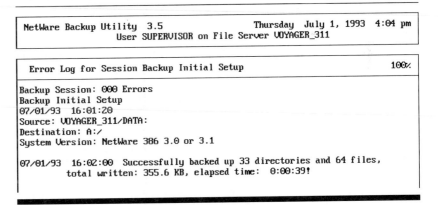

RESTORING A DIRECTORY STRUCTURE

To test the backup, Leslie decided to completely remove the HELP-DESK directory structure and then restore it from her backup diskettes. If it failed she could rebuild the directory structure and copy the files back from the Help Desk staff's diskettes. To remove the SERVICE directory structure Leslie did the following: She started FILER and selected the DATA volume. Next she highlighted the Directory Contents option and pressed [Enter]. To remove the HELPDESK directory structure, Leslie highlighted the HELPDESK directory and pressed [Del]. Next she selected the Delete Entire Subdirectory Structure option and pressed [Enter]. FILER then asked her to confirm the deletion. She highlighted YES and pressed [Enter]. The HELPDESK directory structure was removed.

Let's follow Leslie as she used the NBACKUP utility to restore the HELPDESK directory structure, files, and trustee rights.

1. She first started NBACKUP and selected the DOS Devices option. The NBACKUP Main Menu appeared.

2. Next she highlighted Restore Options and pressed [Enter]. After responding to the warnings about Non-DOS directory information, the Restore Menu shown in Figure 9-24 appeared.

FIGURE 9-24: Leslie's Restore Menu from the NBACKUP program

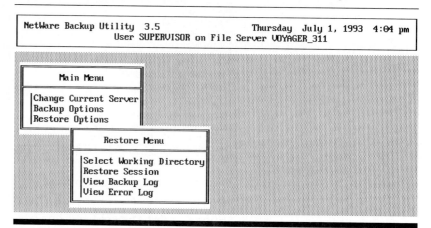

3. Leslie highlighted the Restore Session option and pressed [Enter]. After responding to more warnings about Non-DOS directory information, she was asked to enter the name of the working directory. After she typed "C:\BACKUP" and pressed [Enter], the Restore Session screen shown in Figure 9-25 was displayed. This screen displays all restore sessions stored in the specified work directory.

FIGURE 9-25: Leslie's Restore Session window from the NBACKUP program

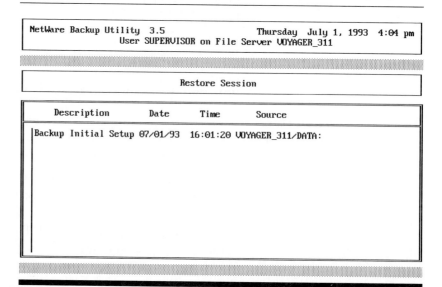

4. She highlighted the Backup Initial Setup session and pressed [Enter]. NBACKUP displayed the Restore Option window shown in Figure 9-26.

FIGURE 9-26: Leslie's Restore Option window

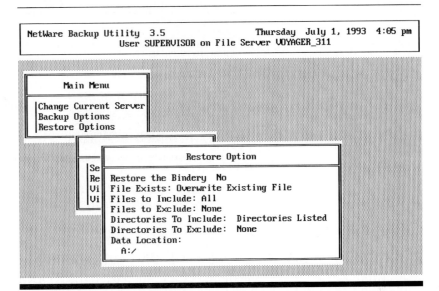

5. Leslie left the default options, highlighted the Directories To Include option, and pressed [Enter].

6. She used the Ins key and entered the path to the HELPDESK directory, as shown in Figure 9-27. She then pressed [Esc] to close the Directories To Include window. Next she used the Data Location field to specify drive A: as the location of the backup data.

FIGURE 9-27: Leslie's Directories To Include screen after she inserted the HELPDESK directory path

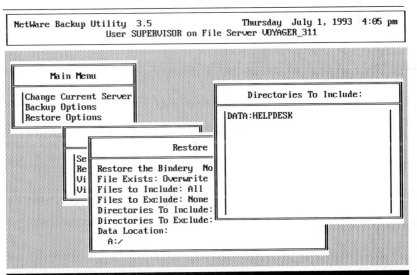

7. She then pressed [Esc] to save the RESTORE information and pressed [Enter] to start the restore process. After displaying a running status screen, NBACKUP responded with the encouraging words, "Directory restore completed," as shown in Figure 9-28 on the following page.

FIGURE 9-28: Leslie's Restore status screen

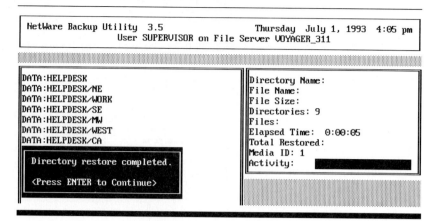

```
NetWare Backup Utility  3.5              Thursday  July 1, 1993  4:05 pm
                  User SUPERVISOR on File Server VOYAGER_311

DATA:HELPDESK                           Directory Name:
DATA:HELPDESK/NE                        File Name:
DATA:HELPDESK/WORK                      File Size:
DATA:HELPDESK/SE                        Directories: 9
DATA:HELPDESK/MW                        Files:
DATA:HELPDESK/WEST                      Elapsed Time:  0:00:05
DATA:HELPDESK/CA                        Total Restored:
   ┌────────────────────────────┐      Media ID: 1
   │ Directory restore completed.│     Activity:
   │                            │
   │ <Press ENTER to Continue>  │
   └────────────────────────────┘
```

8. Leslie pressed [Enter] to return to the Restore Menu, and then used the Esc key to exit the NBACKUP utility.

To verify that the directories and their trustees were restored properly, Leslie used the CD command to change to the HELPDESK directory and then used the NDIR and TLIST *.* commands to view the files and trustee assignments. She concluded that the backup and restore processes worked fine.

SETTING UP TIME AND STATION RESTRICTIONS

Because of the extra security needs for the PAYROLL system, Leslie has assured Ann that the payroll information will be accessible only from Ann's workstation during normal work hours. To determine Ann's station address, Leslie logged in from Ann's computer and used the USER-LIST /E > PRN command to document Ann's network and node address.

To set up time and station restrictions, Leslie started the SYSCON utility and selected the User Information option. She then highlighted Ann's username, 99ANNBON, and pressed [Enter] to display the User Information menu. Leslie then highlighted Time Restrictions and pressed [Enter]. SYSCON displayed the Allowed Login Times For User 99ANNBON screen. The screen was filled with asterisks (*), each of which represents a half-hour time period during which the user can access the system. To remove the asterisks, Leslie pressed the F5 key and used the arrow keys to highlight the times outside the normal 8:00 to 5:00 workday, then pressed [Del]. The screen showing the updated Allowed Login Times For User 99ANNBON is shown in Figure 9-29. Pressing the Esc key saved the login times and returned Leslie to the User Information menu.

FIGURE 9-29: Leslie's screen showing Ann's time restrictions from SYSCON

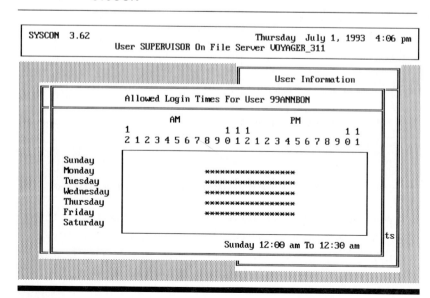

```
SYSCON  3.62                            Thursday  July 1, 1993  4:06 pm
              User SUPERVISOR On File Server VOYAGER_311

                                        ┌─ User Information ─┐

   ┌─ Allowed Login Times For User 99ANNBON ─┐

              AM                    PM
       1             1 1 1                   1 1
       2 1 2 3 4 5 6 7 8 9 0 1 2 1 2 3 4 5 6 7 8 9 0 1

  Sunday
  Monday                    *******************
  Tuesday                   *******************
  Wednesday                 *******************
  Thursday                  *******************
  Friday                    *******************
  Saturday

             Sunday 12:00 am To 12:30 am
```

FIGURE 9-30: Leslie's SYSCON screen as she inserted Ann's station restrictions

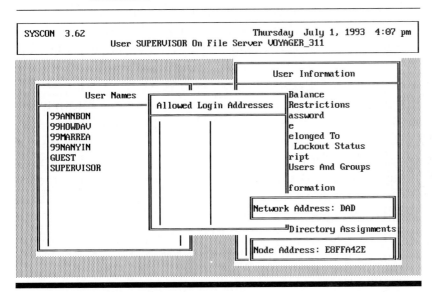

```
SYSCON  3.62                        Thursday  July 1, 1993  4:07 pm
                  User SUPERVISOR On File Server VOYAGER_311


                                            User Information

              User Names                 Balance
                          Allowed Login Addresses  Restrictions
         99ANNBON                         assword
         99HOWDAV                         e
         99MARREA                         elonged To
         99NANYIN                          Lockout Status
         GUEST                            ript
         SUPERVISOR                       Users And Groups

                                          formation

                                   Network Address: DAD

                                           Directory Assignments

                                   Node Address: E8FFA42E
```

FIGURE 9-31: Leslie's screen after she ran the SECURITY command from the SYS:SYSTEM directory

```
SECURITY EVALUATION UTILITY, Version 2.23

User 99MARREA (Full Name: Mary Read)
  Has password expiration interval greater than 60 days


User 99ANNBON (Full Name: Ann Bonny)
  Has password expiration interval greater than 60 days


User 99NANYIN (Full Name: Nancy Yin)
  Has password expiration interval greater than 60 days


User 99HOWDAV (Full Name: Howell Davis)
  Has password expiration interval greater than 60 days
  Has no password assigned


Group SALES
  No Full Name specified


Press any key to continue ... ('C' for continuous)
```

To restrict Ann's username to logging in from her assigned workstation, Leslie highlighted the Station Restrictions option and pressed [Enter]. SYSCON displayed the Allowed Login Address window. Leslie used the Ins key to enter the network and node addresses, as shown in Figure 9-30. She then used the Esc key to save the login addresses and exit the SYSCON utility.

CHECKING FILE SERVER SECURITY

In her NetWare class, Leslie learned that the supervisor can use the SECURITY command to check the file server bindery for such security violations as no password assigned, user accounts with supervisor equivalence, trustee assignments to the root of a volume, user accounts with no personal LOGIN script, users with rights to the SYS:SYSTEM directory, users who have more than Read and File Scan rights to SYS:PUBLIC and SYS:LOGIN, or users who have rights other than Write and Create to the SYS:MAIL directory. Figure 9-31 shows the output Leslie received on her first screen when she ran SECURITY. Since SECURITY is a supervisor-only command, the SECURITY.EXE program is stored in the SYS:SYSTEM directory.

USING THE BINDFIX COMMAND In her NetWare class Leslie learned that the bindery files NET$OBJ.SYS, NET$PROP.SYS, and NET$VAL.SYS contain information on all users and other objects such as print queues and printer that are created on the file server. Occasionally these files can become corrupted due to incomplete updating caused by software or hardware problems. When this happens it may not be possible to complete certain functions such as creating a new user or group, changing a user's password, or modifying user account restrictions.

BINDFIX is a supervisor-only program that is stored in the SYS:SYSTEM directory and can be used to correct most bindery problems or synchronize the bindery with directory trustee rights and user mail subdirectories. Before attempting to fix the bindery files, the BINDFIX program renames the original bindery files to NET$OBJ.OLD, NET$PROP.OLD, and NET$VAL.OLD.

If the bindery fix is unsuccessful, the supervisor can return to the original bindery files by using the BINDREST program. Leslie's NetWare instructor explained that the .OLD bindery files can also be useful to keep as backups of the bindery. These files can be copied onto a diskette and stored in a safe place. In the event of a loss of the bindery files, the .OLD files can be copied back into the SYS:SYSTEM directory and the BINDREST program used to restore the users and other objects. Because trustee assignments are kept with the directory names, it is important to back up trustee assignments in addition to the bindery files. It is also important to back up the SYS:MAIL directory because it might contain files, such as the user's LOGIN script. If the SYS volume is lost, it will be necessary to restore the SYS:MAIL directories in addition to the bindery and trustee assignments.

Since she has done a lot of bindery maintenance, Leslie decided to use the BINDFIX program to check the integrity of the bindery files and create a set of .OLD files for her to copy onto a backup diskette. Figure 9-32 shows the output Leslie received after running the BINDFIX program. She then used the NDIR *.OLD command to determine the size of the old bindery files in the SYS:SYSTEM directory. The output of the NDIR command, shown in Figure 9-33, showed that all the old bindery files will easily fit on one diskette.

Now that her users are created and the file system seems operational and secure, Leslie is ready to tackle the next major hurdle, setting up printing, which she will do in Chapter 10.

FIGURE 9-32: Leslie's screen after she ran the BINDFIX command

```
F:\SYSTEM>BINDFIX
Rebuilding Bindery.  Please Wait.
Checking object's property lists.
Checking properties to see if they are in an object property list.
Checking objects for back-link property.
Checking set consistency and compacting sets.
Checking Properties for proper order.
Checking user objects for standard properties.
Checking group objects for standard properties.
Checking links between users and groups for consistency.
Delete mail directories of users that no longer exist? (y/n): Y
Checking for mail directories of users that no longer exist.
Checking for users that do not have mail directories.
Delete trustee rights for users that no longer exist? (y/n): Y
Checking volume SYS.  Please wait.
Checking volume DATA.  Please wait.

Bindery check successfully completed.
Please delete the files NET$OBJ.OLD, NET$PROP.OLD, and NET$VAL.OLD after you
have verified the reconstructed bindery.

F:\SYSTEM>
```

FIGURE 9-33: Leslie's SYS:SYSTEM directory listing showing the .OLD bindery files

```
F:\SYSTEM>NDIR *.OLD
VOYAGER_311/SYS:SYSTEM

Files:              Size    Last Updated      Flags           Owner
------------------- ------- --------------- --------------- ----------
NET$OBJ     OLD      1,280  7-01-93  4:13p [Rw-------------] SUPERVISO
NET$PROP    OLD      4,046  7-01-93  4:13p [Rw-------------] SUPERVISO
NET$VAL     OLD     15,194  7-01-93  4:13p [Rw-------------] SUPERVISO

      20,520 bytes in   3 files
      24,576 bytes in   6 blocks

F:\SYSTEM>
```

In this chapter the following NetWare commands were used to perform the functions described below.

GRANT *rightslist* **FOR** *[path]* **TO** *[user | group]*

In this chapter the GRANT command was used to make trustee assignments to directories.

- ■ *rightslist:* The first letter of each trustee right you want assigned, separated by spaces.

- ■ **FOR** *[path]*: The path to the directory or file where you want the trustee assignment made. If no path is specified, the rights listed in RIGHTSLIST are granted to the user or group for the current directory.

- ■ **TO** *[user | group]*: The username or group name receiving the trustee assignment.

REVOKE *rightslist* **FOR** *[path]* **FROM** *[user | group]*

The REVOKE command is used to remove specific trustee rights from a user or group in a directory or file that previously had been assigned. If no path is specified, the rights listed in the RIGHTSLIST for the user or group are revoked from the current directory. The REVOKE command can be used only to revoke rights from an existing trustee in the same directory path that the trustee was granted. The parameters for the REVOKE command are the same as for the GRANT command.

REMOVE *[user | group] name* *[[FROM] path]*

The REMOVE command may be used to remove a user's or group's trustee assignment from a directory or file. If a path is not specified, the user trustee assignment for the current directory is removed. Removing a trustee assignment may allow the trustee to inherit rights into the directory from which the trustee assignment was removed. In some cases, this could increase a user's effective rights in the directory.

- ■ *[user | group] name*: The name of the user or group to be removed as a trustee of this directory or file.

- ■ **[FROM]**: Optional parameter.

- ■ *[path]*: The path to the directory or file from which the user's trustee right is to be removed. If no path is specified, the user's trustee assignment will be removed from the current directory.

ALLOW *[path* **[TO INHERIT]** *[rightslist]]*

In this chapter the ALLOW command was used to modify the Inherited Rights Mask (IRM) of Howell Davis and Nancy Yin's home directories to prevent users from inheriting rights into these directories from trustee assignments made in a parent directory.

- *[path]:* The path to the directory or file containing the IRM to modify. If no path is specified, the current directory's IRM will be changed. A user must have the Access Control right in a directory to modify the IRM.

- **[TO INHERIT]:** Optional parameter.

- *[rightslist]:* The first letter of each trustee right you want the directory to be able to inherit. Specifying "N" indicates that users will not be allowed to inherit any rights to the directory. Specifying "ALL" indicates a user can inherit any effective rights he or she has in the parent directory.

DSPACE Menu Utility

The DSPACE utility may be used to restrict the storage space of a user on a volume or the disk space used by a directory structure. This utility appears in NetWare 2.2 and above. In NetWare 3.1x, this utility may be used to restrict the amount of disk spaced used by a specific directory and its subdirectories. In this chapter the DSPACE utility was used to set the disk space limitations Leslie defined on her storage requirements table, created in Chapter 2.

SALVAGE Menu Utility

The SALVAGE menu utility may be used to restore deleted files. When a file is deleted from a directory, the server keeps the deleted file in the directory until its space is needed. The space of the oldest files is used first. In this chapter, Leslie used the SALVAGE utility to restore deleted files from the DATA:FORMS directory by first changing to the DATA:FORMS directory and then running the SALVAGE utility. Next she selected the View/Recover Deleted Files option and chose the file pattern to view. The * option displays all deleted files. To view only certain files, a search pattern such as *.WK1 could be entered. Leslie used the F5 key to mark files to be restored. After all files were marked, she pressed the Enter key to restore the marked files.

If the directory that contained the files is deleted, the Salvage From Deleted Directories option of the SALVAGE utility can be used to view and restore these files.

NBACKUP Menu Utility

The NBACKUP utility may be used to back up and restore data and bindery files on the file server. A working directory on a fixed drive must be selected to contain the backup and error logs. When using the backup option, you may select to back up either the entire file server or selected directories. In this chapter Leslie used the NBACKUP utility to make a backup of her bindery files and the DATA volume. By using the directories to include and directories to exclude options, she was able to specify what file to back up or skip. In addition, the backup options allowed her to specify backing up the trustee rights along with hidden or system files. The backup may be done now, or a later date and time can be selected.

The Restore options menu was used to restore the HELPDESK directory structure from the backup diskette. When using the restore option, you need to select a backup session to restore, along with the names of the directories to include or exclude.

SECURITY Command

SECURITY is a supervisor-only command that is stored in the SYS: SYSTEM directory. It searches the bindery files (NET$OBJ.SYS, NET$PROG.SYS, and NET$VAL.SYS) and displays a list of possible security violations. This list includes users, groups, and other objects such as print queues and print servers that have one or more of the following security problems:

- **No password assigned**

- **Insecure password:** An insecure password is the same as the username, is less than five characters, or is not required to be changed at least every 60 days.

- **Supervisor equivalence**

- **Root directory rights:** If rights are granted to the root of a volume, they would be inherited to all directories unless reassigned or blocked by an IRM.

- **LOGIN scripts:** LOGIN scripts are kept in a user's SYS:MAIL directory. Because everyone has Create rights in the SYS:MAIL directory, an intruder could create a LOGIN script and copy it to any user who does not already have one.

- **Excessive rights:** Users who have more rights in the standard directories than those shown below.

SYS:SYSTEM	( )
SYS:PUBLIC	(R F)
SYS:LOGIN	(R F)
SYS:MAIL	(W C)

BINDFIX Command

BINDFIX is a supervisor-only command that is also stored in the SYS:SYSTEM directory. When problems or error messages are encountered when attempts are made to add new users or change user account restrictions, the BINDFIX program can be run to correct bindery file problems. All users must be logged out of the file server before the supervisor can use the BINDFIX command. A backup of the bindery files NET$OBJ.OLD, NET$PROP.OLD, and NET$VAL.OLD is created during this process. If problems exist in the corrected bindery files, the BINDREST program can be used to restore the .OLD files as the current bindery. BINDFIX can correct the following problems:

- A username cannot be deleted or modified.

- A user's password cannot be changed.

- A user's rights cannot be modified.

- The error "Unknown server" occurs during print spooling.

- Error messages referring to the bindery are displayed at the console.

The .OLD bindery files can be copied to diskettes to act as a backup of the bindery in the event the server bindery files are lost. It is recommended the BINDFIX program be run occasionally to check for problems or to back up the .OLD bindery files.

BINDREST Command   BINDREST is a supervisor-only program that is stored in the SYS: SYSTEM directory. It is used to restore the .OLD bindery files to be the current bindery. You can use BINDREST to restore a backup of the .OLD files by copying the .OLD bindery files to the SYS:SYSTEM directory and then running BINDFIX. All users should be logged out of the server before the BINDREST program is run.

1. *True or false*: NetWare 2.x and above contains an option to limit a user's disk space use in a volume.

2. *True or false*: You must have NetWare 3.1x to limit the amount of disk space a specific directory structure can use.

3. The _____ utility is used to set up disk space restrictions.

4. The _____ utility may be used to recover deleted files any time before their space is reused.

5. Write a GRANT command to give the user 99MARREA Read, File Scan, Create, Write, Erase, and Access Control rights to the DATA: HELPDESK directory.

6. Write a GRANT command that would reduce 99MARREA's rights to Read and File Scan in the DATA:HELPDESK\WEST directory.

7. Write a command that would remove 99MARREA's Access Control right from the DATA:HELPDESK directory.

8. Write the command that would prevent 99MARREA from inheriting the Erase and Access Control rights into the DATA: HELPDESK\WORK subdirectory.

9. What command is used to remove 99MARREA as a trustee of the DATA:HELPDESK directory?

10. Assume you are logged in as 99MARREA. What command would you execute to see your effective rights in all directories and subdirectories of the DATA volume?

11. Write the command Mary would execute to see trustee assignments throughout the file system.

12. Write a command the supervisor could use to see all trustee assignments in the DATA:HELPDESK directory.

13. *True or false*: Any user can back up the bindery files using the NBACKUP utility.

14. *True or false*: When using NBACKUP, the working directory is where the backup data will be written.

15. *True or false*: In NetWare 3.11, when an entire directory is deleted using the FILER utility, the files that were in the directory and subdirectories cannot be salvaged.

16. *True or false*: The SALVAGE utility contains an option to view files sorted by owner.

17. *True or false*: The Restore Options menu contains an option to restore only the hidden files.

18. *True or false*: The Restore Options menu contains an option to exclude certain directories from the restore process.

19. The_____ command, found in the_____ directory can be used to find users who have supervisor equivalency.

20. If you receive an error message while creating a new user, you should change to the _____ directory and use the _____ command to fix the problem.

21. The _____ command will restore the OLD bindery files to the current bindery.

SUPERIOR TECHNICAL COLLEGE PROJECT 9

Now it's time to create a POLICY directory structure and assign rights, as well as use the DSPACE utility to set disk space allocations for your Superior Technical College network. With the exception of Assignment 9-11, all the assignments below can be done by logging into your file server using your assigned username.

Assignment 9-1: **Assign Trustee Rights with the GRANT Command**

❶ Build the following directory structure at the beginning of your Superior Technical College directory.

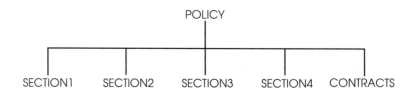

Use the LISTDIR /S > PRN command to obtain a printout of your directory structure. Highlight the POLICY directory and section subdirectories. Attach the printout to Student Answer Sheet 9.

❷ All staff should be able to read any section of the policy files. Ruth Olsen will be responsible for maintaining Section 1 and Section 2 files, and Clara Villa will be responsible for maintaining Section 4 and Section 5 files. In addition to helping Ruth maintain Sections 1 and 2 of the policy files, Virg Kent will maintain the staff CONTRACTS subdirectory. No other users except Lee Olsen should have Read and File Scan access to the CONTRACT subdirectory. Now use the GRANT command to give Virg all rights except Supervisory to the POLICY directory. Record the GRANT command you used on Student Answer Sheet 9.

❸ Use the GRANT command to give your ##EVERYONE group Read and File Scan rights to the POLICY directory. Record the GRANT command you used on Student Answer Sheet 9.

❹ Use GRANT commands to give Clara and Ruth rights to maintain their POLICY sections. Record the GRANT commands you used on Student Answer Sheet 9.

Assignment 9-2:   **Use the REVOKE and TLIST Commands**

❶ You do not want Virg to be able to assign rights to other users in the POLICY directory. Use the REVOKE command to remove this right from Virg. Record the command you used on Student Answer Sheet 9.

❷ You want Virg to have only Read and File Scan rights to SECTION3 and SECTION4 subdirectories. Use the appropriate command to accomplish this assignment. Record the command you used on Student Answer Sheet 9.

❸ Use the TLIST > PRN and TLIST *.* > PRN commands to document all trustee assignments in the POLICY directory structure. Attach your printouts to Student Answer Sheet 9.

Assignment 9-3:   **Use the REMOVE Command**
The responsibility for maintaining SECTION3 of the policy documents has been given to Ruth and Virg.

❶ Use the appropriate NetWare command to remove Clara's trustee assignment and give the rights to maintain files in the SECTION3 subdirectory to Ruth and Virg. Record the command(s) you used under Assignment 9-3 of Student Answer Sheet 9.

❷ Use the TLIST SECTION3 > PRN command to document trustee assignments to the SECTION3 subdirectory. Attach your printout to Student Answer Sheet 9.

Assignment 9-4:   **Check Trustee Assignments and Effective Rights**

❶ Log in as each of the following users and use the WHOAMI /R > PRN command to obtain a hardcopy of each user's trustee assignments. After printing the user's trustee assignments, change to the POLICY directory and use the LISTDIR /E /S > PRN command to obtain a hard copy of these users' effective rights: Virg Kent, Ruth Olsen, and Clara Villa. Attach your printouts to Student Answer Sheet 9.

Assignment 9-5: **Use the ALLOW Command**

❶ You need to prevent users from obtaining rights to the CONTRACTS subdirectory. Use the ALLOW command to restrict all rights from flowing down into this directory. Record the command you use on Student Answer Sheet 9.

❷ Log in as each of the following users, change to the POLICY directory, and use the RIGHTS command to view Virg Kent's and Ruth Olsen's effective rights. Record the rights each has to the CONTRACTS subdirectory on Student Answer Sheet 9.

❸ Log in using your username, and use the GRANT command to assign Virg all rights except Access Control to the CONTRACTS directory. Record the GRANT command you used on Student Answer Sheet 9.

❹ Log in as Virg Kent and Ruth Olsen, respectively. Change to the POLICY directory and use the LISTDIR /S /E > PRN command to obtain printouts of each user's effective rights. Attach the printouts to Student Answer Sheet 9.

❺ While still logged in as one of the above users, insert your student work diskette in a drive and use the NCOPY command to copy files from the POLICY directory of your student work diskette to the following section subdirectories. Record the NCOPY commands you use under Assignment 9-5 of Student Answer Sheet 9.

■ All files with the extension .1 into the SECTION1 subdirectory.

■ All files with the extension .2 into the SECTION2 subdirectory.

■ All files with the extension .3 into the SECTION3 subdirectory.

❻ Use the FLAG command to flag all files Sharable and Delete Inhibit. Record the FLAG command you used on Student Answer Sheet 9.

❼ Use the NDIR POLICY /SUB > PRN command to obtain a printout showing all files in the POLICY directory structure. Attach the printout to Student Answer Sheet 9.

Assignment 9-6: **Restrict Disk Space**

❶ Set the disk space limitation for the POLICY directory to 40 kilobytes. Select the Directory Restrictions option. Enter the path to your POLICY directory and press **[Enter]**. Enter **40** for the Kilobytes in the Directory Space Limit field. Press **[Esc]** to save the space restriction. Use DSPACE to enter the space restrictions you defined on your Storage Requirements Table from the Superior Technical College Project in Chapter 2. Exit DSPACE. Change to the POLICY directory and use the CHKDIR command; record the information on Student Answer Sheet 9.

Assignment 9-7: **Use the SALVAGE Utility**

❶ Change to your shared FORMS directory. Use the DEL *.* command to delete all files from the FORMS directory. Use the NDIR *.* > PRN command to obtain a printout showing an empty FORMS directory. Write "Form files deleted" on the printout and attach it to Student Answer Sheet 9.

❷ Use the SALVAGE utility to recover all files back to the FORMS directory. Use the FLAG command to flag all the files in the FORMS directory to be Delete-Inhibit. Record the FLAG command you used on Student Answer Sheet 9.

❸ Use the NDIR *.* > PRN command to obtain a printout listing all files in the FORMS directory. Write "Form files restored" on the printout and attach it to Student Answer Sheet 9.

Assignment 9-8: **Back Up Files with NBACKUP**

Now you'll use the NBACKUP utility to make a backup of all your Superior Technical College files and trustee assignments onto diskettes. Select your local workstation's fixed disk to store the work directory. If your local workstation does not have a fixed disk drive, your instructor will provide an area on the file server that you may use for your working directory. Be sure to have a couple of freshly formatted diskettes to contain your backup files, then do the steps below.

❶ Start NBACKUP and select the DOS devices option. Select Backup Options and press [Enter]. Highlight the Select Working Directory option and press [Enter]. Enter the path to your working directory (for example, C:\BACKUP). Select the Backup By Directory option. Fill in the Backup Options screen as shown below.

```
Session Description: Your name and date
Backup Bindery: No
Backup Subdirectories: Yes
Backup Trustees: Yes
Modified Files Only: No
Clear Modify Bit: Yes
Files to Include: All
Files to Exclude: None
Directories To Include:
    your volume:##ADMIN
Directories To Exclude: None
Backup Hidden Files: Yes
Backup System Files: Yes
Source Directory:
    your file server name\your volume:
```

Print the screen. Attach the screen printout to Student Answer Sheet 9.

❷ Press **[Esc]** and save the Backup Options screen. Select Start the Backup Now. View the Backup Error Log and print the screen. Attach the screen printout to Student Answer Sheet 9.

❸ After the backup has been completed, copy the files BACK$ERR and BACK$LOG onto one of your diskettes. These files are necessary to restore a session.

Assignment 9-9: **Restore a Directory Structure**

❶ Use FILER to delete your POLICY directory structure. Use the LISTDIR /S > PRN command to document that the directory structure is no longer with us. Write "POLICY structure deleted" on the printout and attach it to Student Answer Sheet 9.

❷ Use the NBACKUP restore session utility to restore the POLICY directory structure and files. Change to the POLICY directory and use the NDIR /SUB > PRN command to document that the directory structure and files have been restored. Write on the printout "POLICY directory restored" and attach it to Student Answer Sheet 9.

Assignment 9-10: **Assign Time and Station Restrictions**
In this assignment you are to use SYSCON to assign time and station restrictions to Ode Wiggert's user account.

❶ Log in using your workgroup manager username. Use the USERLIST /E command to obtain the network and node address of your workstation. Record the address information on Student Answer Sheet 9.

❷ Start SYSCON. Select User Information. Select your Ode Wiggert username. Select Time Restrictions. Use the F5 and arrow keys to highlight and delete all asterisks outside normal working hours (8:00 a.m. to 5:00 p.m.). Print your screen. Attach the screen printout to Student Answer Sheet 9.

❸ Press **[Esc]** to save the login times screen and return to the User Information menu. Select the Station Restrictions option. Press **[Ins]** and enter the network address from your USERLIST command. Enter **No** when asked if the user can log in from any station. Enter the node address of the workstation from your USERLIST command. Print your screen showing the allowed login addresses. Attach the screen printout to Student Answer Sheet 9.

❹ Press **[Esc]** to save the login addresses. Hold down **[Alt]** and press **[F10]** to exit SYSCON.

Assignment 9-11: **Use the SECURITY Command**

❶ Log in using the supervisor-equivalent name supplied by your instructor. Use the SECURITY ¦ MORE command to obtain a list of all security violations. Record security violations you wish to fix under Assignment 9-11 of Student Answer Sheet 9.

Turn in Materials Assemble and identify each of the printouts you obtained in Assignments 9-1 through 9-5 and 9-7 through 9-11. Attach the printouts to your Student Answer Sheet and, if requested, turn them into the instructor on or before the scheduled due date.

Student Name: _____ Date: _____

Assignment 9-1: **Assign Trustee Rights with the GRANT Command**

❶ Attach your printout from LISTDIR command.

❷ Record the GRANT command you used to give Virg all rights except Supervisory to POLICY.

❸ Record the GRANT command you used to give ##EVERYONE Read and File Scan rights to POLICY.

❹ Record the GRANT commands you used to give Clara and Ruth rights in their POLICY sections.

Assignment 9-2: **Use the REVOKE and TLIST Commands**

❶ In the space below, record the REVOKE command used to remove Access Control right from Virg to the POLICY directory.

❷ In the space below, record the commands used to give Virg Read and File Scan rights to SECTION3 and SECTION4 subdirectories.

❸ Attach your printouts from the TLIST commands.

Assignment 9-3: **Use the REMOVE Command**

❶ In the space below, record the REMOVE command(s) you used.

❷ Attach your printout from the TLIST command.

Assignment 9-4: **Check Trustee Assignments and Effective Rights**

❶ Attach WHOAMI and LISTDIR printouts from Virg Kent, Ruth Olsen, and Clara Villa.

Assignment 9-5: Use the ALLOW Command

❶ In the space below, record the ALLOW command for the CONTRACTS subdirectory.

❷ Record results from using the RIGHTS command in the table below.

User	Rights in CONTRACTS
Virg Kent	
Ruth Olsen	

❸ In the space below, record the GRANT command to give Virg rights to the CONTRACTS directory.

❹ Attach the LISTDIR /S /E printout of POLICY directory for Virg Kent and the LISTDIR /S /E printout of POLICY directory for Ruth Olsen.

❺ In the space below, record the NCOPY commands you used to copy policy files into the appropriate subdirectories.

❻ In the space below, record the FLAG command you used to make all policy files Sharable and Delete Inhibit.

❼ Attach the NDIR printout showing all policy files.

Assignment 9-6: **Restrict Disk Space**

❶ Record CHKDIR information in the table below.

Maximum	In Use	Available

Assignment 9-7: **Use the SALVAGE Utility**

❶ Attach the "Form files deleted" printout.

❷ In the space below, record the FLAG command you used to flag all files Delete Inhibit.

❸ Attach the "Form files restored" printout.

Assignment 9-8: **Back Up Files with NBACKUP**

❶ Attach the Backup Options screen printout.

❷ Attach the Backup Error Log screen printout.

Assignment 9-9: **Restore a Directory Structure**

❶ Attach the "POLICY structure deleted" printout.

❷ Attach the "POLICY structure restored" printout.

Assignment 9-10: **Assign Time and Station Restrictions**

❶ Record the USERLIST /E information for your workstation below.

Network Address	Node Address

❷ Attach the SYSCON screen printout showing time restrictions for Ode.

❸ Attach the SYSCON printout showing station restrictions for Ode.

Assignment 9-11: **Use the SECURITY Command**

❶ In the space below, record security violations for your users.

In this chapter you will:

• Use PCONSOLE to create and

configure print queues

• Use PCONSOLE to place a job in a print

queue and view print job information

• Use PCONSOLE to create and

configure a print server

• Learn how to load a print server

• Use RPRINTER to set up a remote printer

• Use the CAPTURE command to direct

application output to a print queue

• Use the NPRINT command to place a

text file in a print queue

• Use the PRINTDEF utility to define print forms

NETWORK PRINTING

The ability to share printers is an important advantage of network use. NetWare has a sophisticated network printing environment that has many features found in the mainframe computer world. The printing environment consists of three major components: the print queue, the print server, and the workstation.

The **print queue** is the holding area for print jobs until they are ready to print and the printer is available. Print queues are actually subdirectories in the SYS:SYSTEM directory and are assigned random, eight-digit hexadecimal names. As a result, only the supervisor can create and delete print queues. Print queues may be assigned users and operators. When a print queue is created, the group EVERYONE is assigned as the default user, and SUPERVISOR is the default operator. Print queue users have the right to place jobs in the print queue and manage their own print jobs. The print queue operator can add, delete, or resequence print queue jobs as well as assign other operators and users.

The **print server** is the logical component that sends jobs that are ready to print from the print queue, one at a time, to a physical printer. A print server does not store print job information; it only directs and controls the actual printing operation. The print server must be configured to identify each printer and its location.

A print server can control a maximum of 16 printers. A maximum of five of these printers can be local printers attached to LPT1, LPT2, LPT3, COM1, and COM2 ports of the computer running the print server program. A print server can also be configured to control up to 16 remote printers attached to other computers on the network. Each printer defined on the print server must also be configured to identify which print queue(s) it will be getting jobs from, along with the priority to be assigned to each print queue being serviced by the printer.

NetWare contains several commands and menu utilities to set up and maintain the network printing environment. The **PCONSOLE menu utility** is used to create and maintain print queues and print servers. The **PRINTDEF menu utility** is used to maintain a printer database in the SYS:PUBLIC directory called NET$PRN.DAT. This database contains printer form definitions and ESC code sequences to set up special printer functions. The **PRINTCON menu utility** is used to create and maintain print jobs that can be copied into user SYS:MAIL subdirectories. These jobs can specify defaults for each printer job created, such as print queue, banner, number of copies, forms, and printer modes defined by the PRINTDEF program.

Print jobs originate at the workstation. Printed output from the workstation must be directed to the appropriate print queue. If an application is NetWare aware, jobs can be sent to the correct print queue directly from the program you are running. If an application is designed to print on local DOS printer ports (LPT1, LPT2, or LPT3) the output from the application must be redirected to the print queue via the network adapter. This is the job of the CAPTURE and NPRINT commands. CAPTURE will redirect output from an application or DOS that would normally be printed on a local printer port such as LPT1, LPT2, or LPT3 and send it instead to a specified print queue on a file server. The CAPTURE command contains a number of optional parameters that may be used to specify the file server and print queue, banner, forms, tabs, and printcon job. The NPRINT command will copy the contents of an ASCII text file to the specified print queue.

In this chapter you will follow Leslie as she plans the printing environment and then uses NetWare menu utilities and commands to establish network printing for PC Solutions. You will be able to apply this information to setting up your own printing environment in the Superior Technical College project at the end of the chapter. Because creating print queues and print servers requires supervisor equivalency, two sets of project assignments are included; which set you will complete will depend on whether you will be able to use a supervisor-equivalent username on your assigned file server.

THE PC
SOLUTIONS
CASE

DEFINING THE PRINTING ENVIRONMENT

After analyzing the printing needs of users in each workgroup, Leslie decided to set up a network printing environment. She planned to use the file server to run the print server (PSERVER.NLM) program and to share several of the printers currently attached to workstations by making them remote printers. One of the big advantages of putting the printers on the network is the users' ability to direct output to whichever printer they need to use. When Business Department users need to print letter-quality documents or presentation graphics, they can direct that output to one of the laser printers. When the Sales Department wants to print the monthly sales report, they can direct the output to the dot-matrix printer that holds standard forms. In addition, sending draft output to the dot-matrix printer rather than printing it on the laser can save some print supply costs during the year. Another nice feature is redundancy. For example, if one of the printers needs to be removed for servicing, users can easily redirect output to another printer.

Figure 10-1 on the following page shows Leslie's printer environment for PC Solutions. In the Business Department, Ned has a dot-matrix printer attached to his PC for local printing of spreadsheets. Ann has a high-speed, 24-pin dot-matrix printer attached to her computer for printing accounting reports and payroll checks. Ed recently received his own computer, but he will share Ann's high-speed dot-matrix printer for printing spreadsheets and reports.

FIGURE 10-1: Leslie's network printer table

Printer Number	Printer Type and Model	Location	Users	Operator
0	Dot matrix (Epson LQ-1070)	Business (Ann Bonny)	99ANNBON 99EDWLOW	SUPERVISOR 99ANNBON
1	Bubblejet (Canon BJC-820)	File server	99EDWLOW 99MARREA	SUPERVISOR 99MARREA
2	Laser (Panasonic KX-P4420)	Sales	Sales	SUPERVISOR 99GEOMOO
3	Dot matrix (Panasonic KX-P1624)	Sales (Invoices)	Sales	SUPERVISOR 99GEOMOO
4	Dot matrix (Panasonic KX-P1624)	Sales (Reports)	Sales	SUPERVISOR 99GEOMOO
5	Dot matrix (Citizen GSX-145)	Help Desk	Help Desk	SUPERVISOR 99HOWDAV
6	PostScript Laser (Data Products LZR-965)	Mary's computer	99MARREA 99EDWLOW 99RITDUN	SUPERVISOR 99MARREA

Because Ed also uses the spreadsheet program to prepare graphs for his presentations, he would like to be able to send these presentation graphics to a color printer. Mary Read also needs to share this color printing capability because she often helps put together presentations for Ben. To provide this capability to both Ed and Mary, Leslie decided to purchase a color bubblejet printer and attach it to the LPT1 of the file server. In her NetWare class, she learned that graphics printing is faster and more reliable if it is directed to the print server's local printer port rather than if directed to a remote printer attached to a workstation somewhere on the network.

For the Sales Department, Leslie purchased a second dot-matrix printer to be attached to a new workstation. Each salesperson now has a PC that can be used to enter orders or price quotations. The existing laser printer and dot-matrix printer will be defined as remote printers controlled by the print server. All Sales personnel will share the laser printer for printing flyers and price quotations. In addition, the old dot-matrix printer will be reserved for printing invoice forms, while the new dot-matrix printer is available for printing sales reports from the order entry system.

The printer switch box currently used by the Help Desk staff will be replaced; they will share their existing dot-matrix printer through the print server. Mary Read has a laser printer attached to her workstation for printing the catalog and other desktop publishing jobs. Leslie wants Ed Low and Rita Dunn to share this printer with Mary when it is not being used for printing desktop publishing jobs.

DEFINING PRINTER NAMES AND PRINT QUEUES

Leslie's next consideration was to define the print queues and associated printer names. In her NetWare class, she learned that keeping the names of printers and associated print queues similar is important to making sense out of the printing environment. Some of the other network administrators in Leslie's class described how they used the name of the printer or print queue to help document the location of the printer, the type of printer, and whether it was locally or remotely attached to the print server.

To document her printing setup and assign names to her print queues and printers, Leslie recorded the table shown in Figure 10-2. On the Sales laser and bubblejet printers, Leslie decided to define a high-priority print queue in addition to the normal print queue. The high-priority queue would give her a way of printing a "rush" job without having to rearrange the sequence of printing in the primary print queue.

FIGURE 10-2: Leslie's printer definition table

Printer definition form for print server 99PCS

Printer Number	Location	Local/Remote	Port	Printer Name*	Print Queue Priority and Name
0	Business	Remote	LPT1	BUSACC-R0	BUSACC-R0-Q1
1	File server	Local	LPT1	SRV-COLOR-L1	SRV-COLOR-L1-Q1
					SRV-COLOR-L1-Q1
2	Sales	Remote	LPT1	SAL-LASER-R2	SAL-LASER-R2-Q1
3	Sales	Remote	LPT1	SALINV-R3	SALINV-R3-Q1
4	Sales	Remote	LPT1	SALRPT-R4	SALRPT-R4-Q1
5	Help Desk	Remote	LPT1	HLP-R5	HLP-R5-Q1
6	Support	Remote	LPT1	SUP-PSCRIPT-R6	SUP-PSCRIPT-R6-Q1

* Printer/queue names:
First three letters represent department, the next three may represent user or function, followed by printer type, remote or local code, printer number, and print queue priority.
BUS — Business
SRV — File server
SAL — Sales
HLP — Help Desk
SUP — Support staff (Mary Read, Rita Dunn)

CREATING PRINT QUEUES WITH PCONSOLE

Leslie's first action was to use the PCONSOLE utility to create the print queues defined on her printer definition form. To create the print queues, Leslie logged in as supervisor, typed "PCONSOLE," and pressed [Enter].

Let's follow the steps Leslie took as she used the PCONSOLE menu utility to create the print queues defined on her printer definition form.

1. After she started PCONSOLE, the Available Options menu shown in Figure 10-3 on the following page appeared.

FIGURE 10-3: PCONSOLE Available Options menu

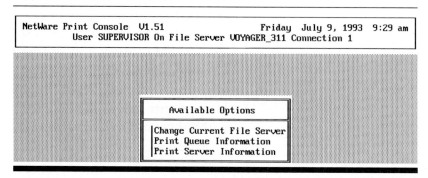

```
NetWare Print Console  V1.51                Friday  July 9, 1993   9:29 am
            User SUPERVISOR On File Server VOYAGER_311 Connection 1

                              Available Options
                        Change Current File Server
                        Print Queue Information
                        Print Server Information
```

2. Leslie highlighted the Print Queue Information option and pressed [Enter]. A window showing any existing print queues appeared.

3. To create a new print queue, she pressed [Ins], typed the name of the first print queue as shown in Figure 10-4, and pressed [Enter]. The new print queue name then appeared in the Print Queues window.

FIGURE 10-4: Leslie's PCONSOLE screen as she created the BUSACC-R0-Q1 print queue

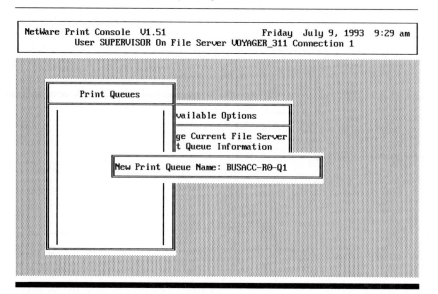

```
NetWare Print Console  V1.51                Friday  July 9, 1993   9:29 am
            User SUPERVISOR On File Server VOYAGER_311 Connection 1

         Print Queues
                                    vailable Options

                                  ge Current File Server
                                  t Queue Information

                        New Print Queue Name: BUSACC-R0-Q1
```

4. Leslie repeated step 3 until all print queues were created.

5. Leslie then pressed [Esc] to return to PCONSOLE's Available Options menu.

By default, the group EVERYONE is a user of each print queue and SUPERVISOR is the print queue operator. Leslie also wanted to make George Moon an operator of all Sales Department print queues. Because the SALINV-R3 printer has special forms mounted, Leslie did not want everyone to be able to use the SALINV-R3-Q1 print queue; only members of the Sales group running the order entry package should have access to this print queue.

Here are the steps Leslie followed as she modified the SALINV-R3-Q1 print queue to restrict access to the Sales Department:

1. First she selected Print Queue Information from the Available Options menu to see the available print queues displayed in the Print Queues window. Next she highlighted the SALINV-R3-Q1 print queue and pressed [Enter]. The Print Queue Information window shown in Figure 10-5 was displayed.

FIGURE 10-5: The Print Queue Information window

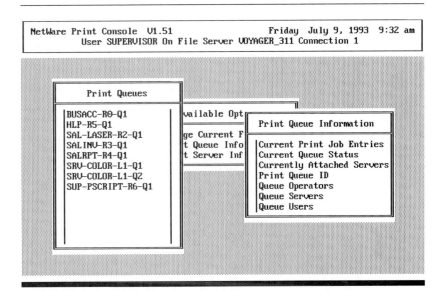

2. To add a print queue operator, Leslie highlighted Queue Operators and pressed [Enter]. A window showing the SUPERVISOR as the print queue operator was displayed, as shown on the right in Figure 10-6.

FIGURE 10-6: The Queue Operator Candidates and Queue Operators windows

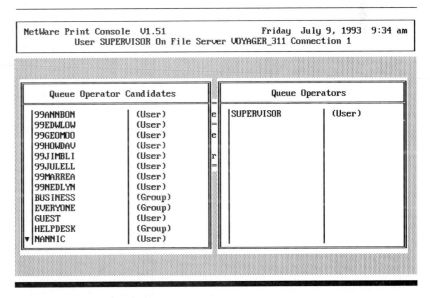

3. To add George Moon as an operator, Leslie pressed [Ins] and highlighted 99GEOMOO in the Queue Operator Candidates window. When she pressed [Enter], the username 99GEOMOO was added to the Queue Operators window.

4. Leslie then pressed [Esc] to return to the Print Queue Information window.

5. To change the print queue users, she highlighted the Queue Users option and pressed [Enter]. The Queue Users window, shown in Figure 10-7, was displayed.

FIGURE 10-7: The Queue Users window

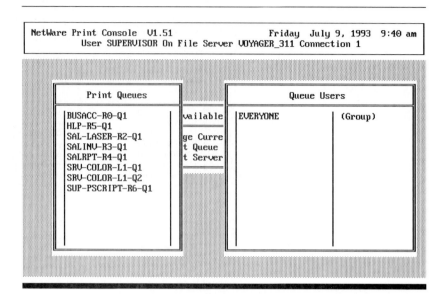

6. To remove the group EVERYONE as a user of this queue, Leslie highlighted the group EVERYONE and pressed [Del]. After confirming that she really wanted to delete this group, PCONSOLE displayed a blank Queue Users window.

7. In her NetWare class Leslie learned that when you remove the group EVERYONE as a print queue user, you must make the SUPERVISOR a queue user if you want to send output to this queue when logged in as SUPERVISOR. To add the Sales group and SUPERVISOR to the Queue Users window, she pressed [Ins] and then used the arrow keys along with the F5 key to select the SALES group and SUPERVISOR username. When she pressed [Enter], the selected group and user were added to the Queue Users screen, as shown in Figure 10-8.

FIGURE 10-8: Adding SALES and SUPERVISOR to the Queue Users window

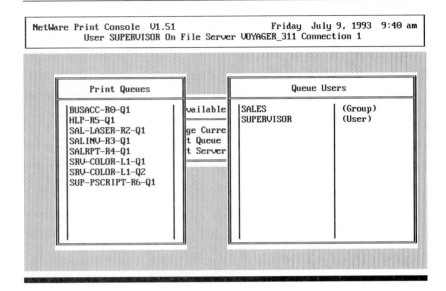

8. She then pressed the Esc key twice to return to the Print Queues window.

Leslie repeated this process to make 99GEOMOO an operator of all three print queues.

CREATING A PRINT SERVER DEFINITION

Once the print queues were created, Leslie addressed the next component of the NetWare printing environment: the print server. The print server uses a configuration file to define each printer and the print queues to be serviced by that printer. Leslie recalled that she can define up to 16 printers to be serviced by one print server.

Let's follow the steps Leslie took as she created a print server definition for her printers.

1. First she highlighted the Print Server Information option from PCONSOLE's Available Options menu and pressed [Enter]. The Print Servers window listing any existing print server definitions was displayed.

2. To create a new print server definition, Leslie pressed [Ins], typed "PCS_PRINTER," the name of her print server file, and pressed [Enter]. The new print server definition was highlighted in the Print Servers window, as shown in Figure 10-9 on the following page.

FIGURE 10-9: The Print Servers window

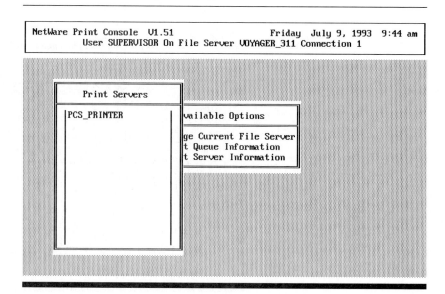

```
NetWare Print Console  V1.51                Friday  July 9, 1993  9:44 am
                User SUPERVISOR On File Server VOYAGER_311 Connection 1

         ┌─────────────────────┐
         │    Print Servers    │
         ├─────────────────────┤
         │PCS_PRINTER          │ vailable Options
         │                     ├─────────────────────┐
         │                     │ ge Current File Server│
         │                     │ t Queue Information   │
         │                     │ t Server Information  │
         │                     └─────────────────────┘
         │                     │
         │                     │
         │                     │
         └─────────────────────┘
```

To configure the newly created print server, Leslie did the following:

1. Because the new print server was highlighted, she pressed [Enter] to display the Print Server Information menu, shown in Figure 10-10.

FIGURE 10-10: The Print Server Information window

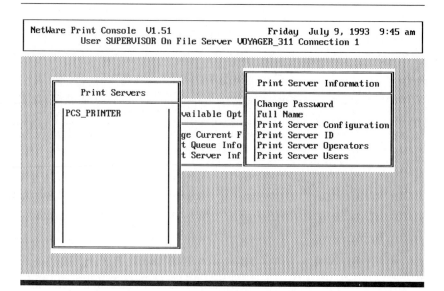

```
NetWare Print Console  V1.51                Friday  July 9, 1993  9:45 am
                User SUPERVISOR On File Server VOYAGER_311 Connection 1

                                      ┌─────────────────────────┐
                                      │ Print Server Information │
         ┌─────────────────────┐      ├─────────────────────────┤
         │    Print Servers    │      │Change Password          │
         ├─────────────────────┤      │Full Name                │
         │PCS_PRINTER          │vailable Opt│Print Server Configuration│
         │                     ├─────────│Print Server ID          │
         │                     │ge Current F│Print Server Operators   │
         │                     │t Queue Info│Print Server Users       │
         │                     │t Server Inf└─────────────────────────┘
         │                     │
         │                     │
         │                     │
         │                     │
         └─────────────────────┘
```

2. She then highlighted the Print Server Configuration option and pressed [Enter]. The Print Server Configuration menu help screen shown in Figure 10-11 was displayed.

FIGURE 10-11: The Print Server Configuration menu help screen

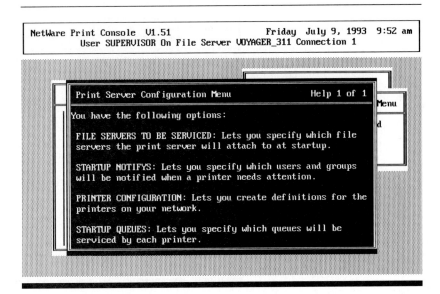

3. To enter her printer definitions, Leslie highlighted the Printer Configuration option and pressed [Enter]. The Configured Printers window shown in Figure 10-12 was displayed.

FIGURE 10-12: Leslie's Configured Printers window before she configured any printers

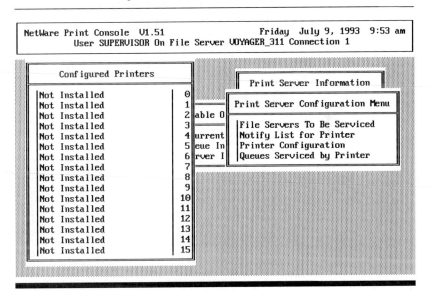

To set up the configuration of printer number 0 as Ann's accounting printer, BUSACC-R0, Leslie did the following:

1. She highlighted Not Installed 0 and pressed [Enter]. The Printer 0 configuration window shown in Figure 10-13 on the following page was displayed.

FIGURE 10-13: Leslie's Printer 0 configuration window

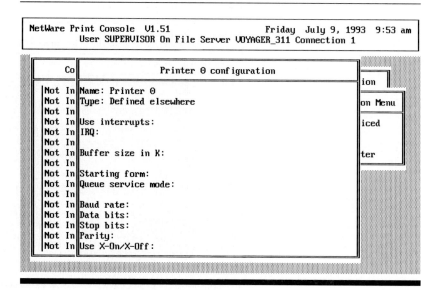

```
NetWare Print Console  V1.51                Friday  July 9, 1993  9:53 am
                    User SUPERVISOR On File Server VOYAGER_311 Connection 1

        Co                     Printer 0 configuration                        ion
   Not In Name: Printer 0
   Not In Type: Defined elsewhere                                          on Menu
   Not In
   Not In Use interrupts:                                                   iced
   Not In IRQ:
   Not In
   Not In Buffer size in K:                                                 ter
   Not In
   Not In Starting form:
   Not In Queue service mode:
   Not In
   Not In Baud rate:
   Not In Data bits:
   Not In Stop bits:
   Not In Parity:
   Not In Use X-On/X-Off:
```

2. She typed "BUSACC-R0" for the printer name and pressed [Enter]. Next, the Type: Defined elsewhere field was highlighted.

3. To define the printer type, Leslie pressed [Enter] and the Printer types window, shown in Figure 10-14, appeared.

FIGURE 10-14: Leslie's Printer types window for printer 0 configuration

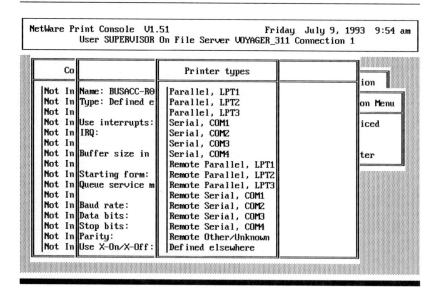

```
NetWare Print Console  V1.51                Friday  July 9, 1993  9:54 am
                    User SUPERVISOR On File Server VOYAGER_311 Connection 1

        Co                          Printer types                             ion
   Not In Name: BUSACC-R0    Parallel, LPT1
   Not In Type: Defined e    Parallel, LPT2                                on Menu
   Not In                    Parallel, LPT3
   Not In Use interrupts:    Serial, COM1                                   iced
   Not In IRQ:               Serial, COM2
   Not In                    Serial, COM3
   Not In Buffer size in     Serial, COM4                                   ter
   Not In                    Remote Parallel, LPT1
   Not In Starting form:     Remote Parallel, LPT2
   Not In Queue service m    Remote Parallel, LPT3
   Not In                    Remote Serial, COM1
   Not In Baud rate:         Remote Serial, COM2
   Not In Data bits:         Remote Serial, COM3
   Not In Stop bits:         Remote Serial, COM4
   Not In Parity:            Remote Other/Unknown
   Not In Use X-On/X-Off:    Defined elsewhere
```

4. To define this printer as a remotely attached printer on the LPT1 port of a workstation, she highlighted Remote, LPT1 and pressed [Enter]. The other entry fields in the Printer 0 configuration window were given default values, as shown in Figure 10-15.

FIGURE 10-15: Leslie's final Printer 0 default configuration

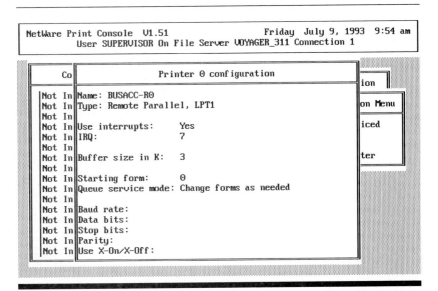

```
NetWare Print Console  V1.51              Friday  July 9, 1993  9:54 am
                 User SUPERVISOR On File Server VOYAGER_311 Connection 1

       ┌─────┬─────────────────────────────────────────┬──────┐
       │  Co │           Printer 0 configuration         │  ion │
       ├─────┤                                           ├──────┤
       │Not In│Name: BUSACC-R0                           │      │
       │Not In│Type: Remote Parallel, LPT1              │n Menu│
       │Not In│                                          │      │
       │Not In│Use interrupts:    Yes                    │ iced │
       │Not In│IRQ:               7                      │      │
       │Not In│                                          │      │
       │Not In│Buffer size in K:  3                      │ ter  │
       │Not In│                                          │      │
       │Not In│Starting form:     0                      │      │
       │Not In│Queue service mode: Change forms as needed│      │
       │Not In│                                          │      │
       │Not In│Baud rate:                                │      │
       │Not In│Data bits:                                │      │
       │Not In│Stop bits:                                │      │
       │Not In│Parity:                                   │      │
       │Not In│Use X-On/X-Off:                           │      │
       └─────┴─────────────────────────────────────────┴──────┘
```

5. She left the default entries unchanged and pressed [Esc] to save the printer 0 configuration. The Configured Printers window shown in Figure 10-16 was displayed, showing the newly defined BUSACC-R0 printer.

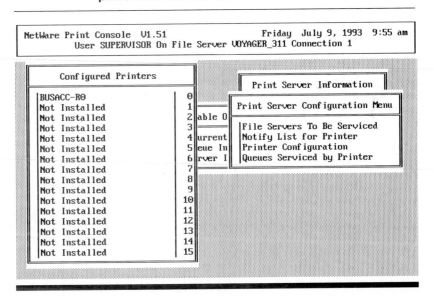

```
NetWare Print Console  V1.51              Friday  July 9, 1993  9:55 am
                 User SUPERVISOR On File Server VOYAGER_311 Connection 1

  ┌──────────────────────────┐      ┌──────────────────────────────┐
  │   Configured Printers     │      │   Print Server Information    │
  ├──────────────────────────┤      ├──────────────────────────────┤
  │BUSACC-R0              0   │      │ Print Server Configuration Menu│
  │Not Installed         1   │      ├──────────────────────────────┤
  │Not Installed         2   │able 0│ File Servers To Be Serviced   │
  │Not Installed         3   │══════│ Notify List for Printer       │
  │Not Installed         4   │urrent│ Printer Configuration         │
  │Not Installed         5   │eue In│ Queues Serviced by Printer    │
  │Not Installed         6   │rver I│                              │
  │Not Installed         7   │      └──────────────────────────────┘
  │Not Installed         8   │
  │Not Installed         9   │
  │Not Installed        10   │
  │Not Installed        11   │
  │Not Installed        12   │
  │Not Installed        13   │
  │Not Installed        14   │
  │Not Installed        15   │
  └──────────────────────────┘
```

Leslie then repeated this process to set up the configurations for the other printers defined on her printer definition form.

After configuring her printers, Leslie pressed [Esc] until she returned to the Print Server Configuration Menu. Her next job was to define from which print queue(s) each printer will get its print jobs.

Let's follow the steps Leslie took as she connected the SRV-COLOR-L1 printer to the appropriate print queues.

1. She highlighted the Queues Serviced by Printer option and pressed [Enter]. The Defined Printers window, shown in Figure 10-17, was displayed.

FIGURE 10-17: Leslie's Defined Printers window, used for assigning print queues to each printer

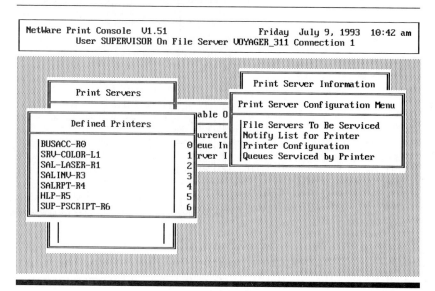

2. Next she highlighted SRV-COLOR-L1 printer and pressed [Enter]. A window appeared, showing any print queues assigned to this printer.

3. To add a print queue to this window, she pressed [Ins]. A window listing all available print queues was displayed.

4. To add the first print queue to be serviced, Leslie highlighted print queue SRV-COLOR-L1-Q1 and pressed [Enter]. PCONSOLE then asked for the queue priority, as shown in Figure 10-18.

FIGURE 10-18: Leslie's screen after she selected SRV-COLOR-L1-Q1 print queue

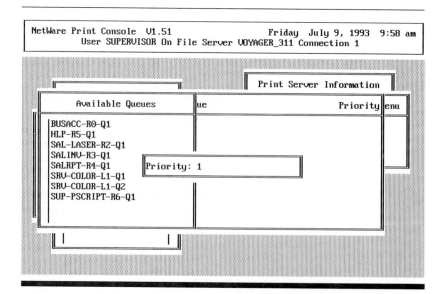

5. She pressed [Enter] to accept priority 1; the print queue was added to the File Server Queue window.

6. To add the second print queue to the list, Leslie pressed [Ins] and selected the next queue, SRV-COLOR-L1-Q2. When asked for queue priority, she changed the 1 to a 2. Figure 10-19 shows the new item added to the File Server Queue window as priority Q2.

FIGURE 10-19: Leslie's screen after she added SRV-COLOR-L1-Q2 to the print queue and giving it priority 2

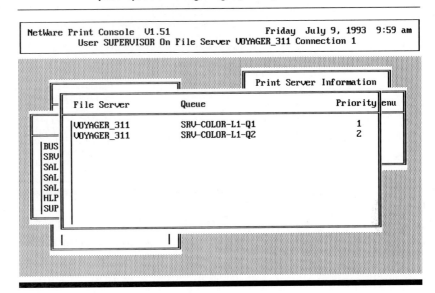

7. She then pressed [Esc] to return to the Defined Printers window.

Leslie then repeated this process to define the print queue for each of the other printers. When she finished configuring the print server, she pressed [Esc] until she returned to the Print Server Information screen.

At this point Leslie could assign a password for the print server or modify the print server operators or users. Just as with a print queue, the default print server operator is the SUPERVISOR and the default users are EVERYONE. The print server operator can perform such printer control tasks as pausing a printer, rewinding a printer to a previous page, restarting a printer, or changing forms. Because Ann Bonny will be responsible for changing forms on the accounting printer, Leslie would like to make Ann and Mary Read print server operators. To do this, Leslie selected the Queue Operators option of the Print Queue Information menu and then pressed [Ins] to display a list for users and groups. She then used the arrow keys along with the F5 key to mark Mary Read's and Ann Bonny's usernames. When she pressed [Enter], Ann and Mary were added to the list of operators. She then pressed [Esc] to return to PCONSOLE's Available Options Menu.

LOADING THE PRINT SERVER

Leslie planned to load the print server on her file server. The file server currently displays the Information for Server screen, as shown in Figure 10-20. Leslie followed these steps as she loaded the print server module on the file server:

FIGURE 10-20: Leslie's Information for Server screen

```
                Information For Server VOYAGER_311

 File Server Up Time:    0 Days  1 Hour  15 Minutes 29 Seconds
 Utilization:                    2     | Packet Receive Buffers:    10
 Original Cache Buffers:       701     | Directory Cache Buffers:   22
 Total Cache Buffers:          345     | Service Processes:          2
 Dirty Cache Buffers:            0     | Connections In Use:         1
 Current Disk Requests:          0     | Open Files:                 9


                     Available Options

               ┌─────────────────────────────┐
               │Connection Information        │
               │Disk Information              │
               │LAN Information               │
               │System Module Information     │
               │Lock File Server Console      │
               │File Open / Lock Activity     │
               │Resource Utilization          │
               │Exit                          │
               └─────────────────────────────┘
```

1. To change from the monitor screen to the console command screen, Leslie could do one of two procedures. She could hold down the Ctrl key while pressing [Esc] to obtain a list of modules and then select the System Console option, as shown in Figure 10-21, or she could hold down the Alt key and press [Esc] until the System Console screen shown in Figure 10-22 was displayed. The Ctrl and Esc key sequence, often called the "hot key," rotates the console from one module to the next. The colon at the bottom of the console screen is the console prompt, which indicates NetWare is ready to accept a command.

FIGURE 10-21: Leslie's Console Screen after she held down (Ctrl) while pressing (Esc)

```
Current Screens

     1. System Console
     2. Monitor Screen

Select screen to view:
```

FIGURE 10-22: Leslie's System Console screen

```
:CONFIG
File server name: VOYAGER_311
IPX internal network number: 00000001

Standard Microsystems Star/EtherCard PLUS Server Driver   v3.01
(920319)
     Hardware setting: I/O Port 300h to 31Fh, Memory CC000h to
CFFFFh, Interrupt
 Ah
     Node address: 0000C0AC9D56
     Frame type: ETHERNET_802.3
     No board name defined
     LAN protocol: IPX network 00000DAD
```

2. To load the print server software, Leslie typed ":LOAD PSERVER PCS_PRINTER" and pressed [Enter]. The PSERVER module "self-loaded" several other modules. After the PSERVER module successfully loaded, the Novell NetWare Print Server screen, shown in Figure 10-23, was displayed.

FIGURE 10-23: Leslie's Print Server screen after she loaded PSERVER

```
0: BUSACC-R0              4: SALRPT-R4
   Not connected             Not connected


1: SRV-COLOR-L1           5: HLP-R5
   Waiting for job           Not connected


2: SAL-LASER-R1           6: SUP-PSCRIPT-R6
   Not connected             Not connected


3: SALINV-R3              7: Not installed
   Not connected
```

If a typing error is made when the name of the print server definition file PCS_PRINTER is entered, the system will ask for a password and then exit the PSERVER program. This is similar to the security process NetWare goes through when a user attempts to log in using an invalid username.

ATTACHING A REMOTE PRINTER WITH RPRINTER

To allow a printer attached to a local workstation to serve as a network remote printer, a special Terminate and Stay Resident (TSR) program called RPRINTER must be loaded. A **TSR program** stays in the computer memory after it is run and continues to perform its function; in a sense, it becomes part of DOS. When the RPRINTER program is first loaded, it asks for the print server name and the printer number to which it is defined. This printer number must match the number assigned for this printer during the configuration process. The print server will now take output from the print queue assigned to that printer and send it to the RPRINTER program. The RPRINTER program "listens" for output from the print server and prints the data it receives on the workstation's attached printer. RPRINTER also sends printer status messages such as "Printer out of paper" or "Printer offline" to the print server. Once it is loaded, RPRINTER will continue to operate, whether or not the user is logged in on the workstation.

Leslie followed these steps to load the RPRINTER program on Ann's computer:

1. First Leslie went to Ann's computer and logged in as GUEST. Leslie could have logged in as any user, including 99ANNBON, who has rights to use the SYS:PUBLIC directory.

2. After logging in, Leslie typed "RPRINTER" and pressed [Enter]. RPRINTER displayed a window showing the PCS_PRINTER print server, as shown in Figure 10-24.

FIGURE 10-24: Leslie's screen after she started RPRINTER on Ann Bonny's computer

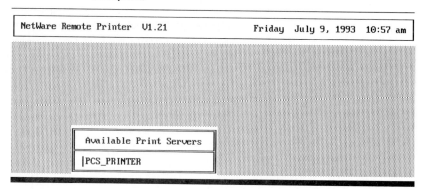

3. Leslie pressed [Enter] to select the PCS_PRINTER print server. RPRINTER next displayed a list of all available printer numbers, as shown in Figure 10-25.

FIGURE 10-25: RPRINTER's Printer Names and Numbers screen

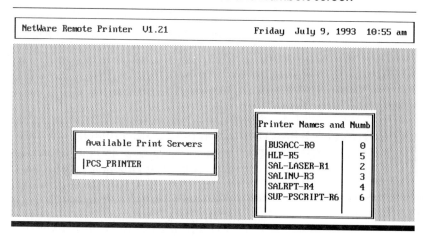

4. Referring to her printer definition form, Leslie highlighted printer 0, then pressed [Enter].

5. RPRINTER responded by displaying the message shown in Figure 10-26.

FIGURE 10-26: Leslie's screen showing RPRINTER is loaded on Ann's computer

```
**** Remote Printer "BUSACC-R0" (Printer 0) installed *****




















F:\>
```

Once RPRINTER was loaded on Ann's computer, the PSERVER screen on the file server changed to show the status of printer BUSACC-R0 changed from "Not Connected" to "Waiting for Job."

In the future, Leslie plans to copy the necessary RPRINTER files IBM$RUN.OVL, RPRINTER.EXE, RPRINTER.HLP, RPRINT$$.EXE, SYS$HELP.DAT, SYS$MSG.DAT, and SYS$ERR.DAT in the SYS:LOGIN directory. She then can have RPRINTER load directly by placing the command RPRINTER PCS_PRINTER 0 in the network startup batch file on Ann's computer, as shown below. This will load the RPRINTER program automatically each time Ann boots her computer.

```
STARTNET.BAT
    LSL
    SMCPLUS
    IPXODI
    NETX
    F:
    RPRINTER PCS_PRINTER 0
    LOGIN
```

CHANGING PRINT QUEUE STATUS TO DEFER PRINTING

Leslie had been meaning to print two rather large documentation files, one called ORDERS.DOC from the sales orders system, the other called GL.DOC from the accounting general ledger system. Because these print jobs take a long time to print, she put off printing them. Leslie recalled from her NetWare class that she could use PCONSOLE to defer printing until a specified time. Because Ed wants to start reading these files soon, Leslie decided to place the GL.DOC documentation file on the Accounting dot-matrix print queue, BUSACC-R0-Q1, and print it during her lunch hour. This approach will allow her to use the BUSACC-R0 printer to output some smaller jobs that she wants to distribute to Ned and Mary before lunch.

To prevent the print server from starting to print the job as soon as she puts it in the queue, Leslie needed to change the print queue status. Leslie followed these steps as she used PCONSOLE to change the status of the BUSACC-R0-Q1 print queue to prevent jobs from being printed immediately:

1. She first highlighted Print Queue Information from the Available Topics menu and pressed [Enter]. A window was displayed showing all her print queues.

2. She next highlighted BUSACC-R0-Q1 and pressed [Enter]. The Print Queue Information menu was displayed.

3. To prevent print jobs from starting, Leslie highlighted the Current Queue Status option and pressed [Enter]. The Current Queue Status window shown in Figure 10-27 was displayed.

FIGURE 10-27: Leslie's PCONSOLE screen after she selected the Current Queue Status option

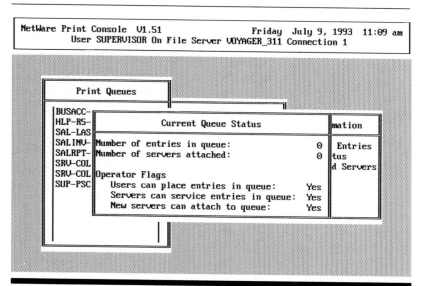

4. She highlighted the Servers can service entries in queue: Yes option and changed the "Yes" to "No."

5. She pressed [Esc] to save the new status and returned to the Print Queue Information menu.

USING PCONSOLE TO PLACE JOBS IN THE PRINT QUEUE

Since the print server will not start printing jobs from this print queue, Leslie was ready to place the large print job GL.DOC in the BUSACC-R0-Q1 queue. The documentation file was already in printable DOS ASCII format, so no application program was necessary; it was just a matter of putting it in the print queue by using PCONSOLE or the NPRINTER command. Leslie was already in PCONSOLE, so she decided to use this utility to place the GL.DOC file in the print queue. Let's follow her steps.

1. First she highlighted Current Print Job Entries from the Print Queue Information menu and pressed [Enter]. The Current Print Jobs window, shown in Figure 10-28, was displayed.

FIGURE 10-28: Leslie's Current Print Jobs window for the BUSACC-R0-Q1 print queue

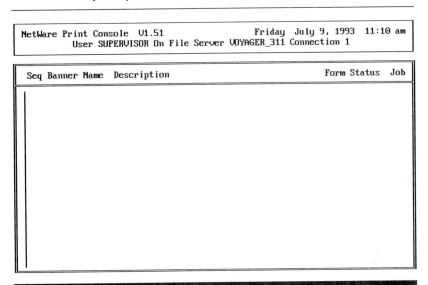

2. To place the job on the print queue, Leslie pressed [Ins], typed the path to the DATA:BUSINESS\GLSYSTEM directory, and pressed [Enter]. The Available Files window listing the names of all files in this directory, as shown in Figure 10-29, was displayed.

FIGURE 10-29: Leslie's Current Print Jobs window after she pressed (Ins) to add the GL.DOC print job

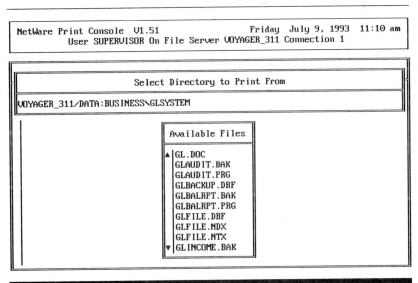

3. She highlighted the GL.DOC file and pressed [Enter]. The Print Job Configurations window was displayed, with the option (Pconsole Defaults) highlighted.

4. Leslie pressed [Enter] to select the PCONSOLE defaults. The New Print Job to be Submitted window, shown in Figure 10-30, was displayed.

FIGURE 10-30: The New Print Job to be Submitted window

```
┌─────────────────────────────────────────────────────────────────────────┐
│ NetWare Print Console  V1.51                    Friday  July 9, 1993  11:13 am │
│          User SUPERVISOR On File Server VOYAGER_311 Connection 1          │
└─────────────────────────────────────────────────────────────────────────┘

┌─────────────────────────────────────────────────────────────────────────┐
│                    New Print Job to be Submitted                         │
├─────────────────────────────────────────────────────────────────────────┤
│ Print job:                          File size:                           │
│ Client:             SUPERVISOR[1]                                        │
│ Description:        GL.DOC                                               │
│ Status:                                                                  │
│                                                                          │
│ User Hold:          No              Job Entry Date:                       │
│ Operator Hold:      No              Job Entry Time:                       │
│ Service Sequence:                                                        │
│                                                                          │
│ Number of copies:   1               Form:              0                  │
│ File contents:      Byte stream     Print banner:      Yes                │
│ Tab size:                           Name:              SUPERVISOR         │
│ Suppress form feed: No              Banner name:       GL.DOC             │
│ Notify when done:   No                                                   │
│                                     Defer printing:    No                 │
│ Target server:      (Any Server)    Target date:                         │
│                                     Target time:                         │
└─────────────────────────────────────────────────────────────────────────┘
```

5. She entered "GL.DOC" in the Description field and pressed [Enter].

6. Because this is a text file, she decided to change the File Contents field from "Byte stream" to "Text." The byte stream option should normally be used when output is sent to a printer that contains special control codes. Because this is an ASCII text file, the only codes should be tab codes. The text option will convert any tab codes it finds to eight spaces.

7. To make this job print at a later time, Leslie highlighted the Defer Printing: No field and changed "No" to "Yes." She then highlighted the Target time field and pressed [Enter]. When asked for the time to start printing, Leslie typed "12:30 pm" and pressed [Enter].

8. She then pressed [Esc] to save the changes shown in Figure 10-31. The new print job was displayed in the Current Print Jobs window. This print job was released for printing during Leslie's lunch hour.

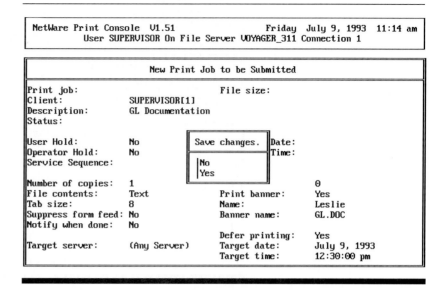

```
NetWare Print Console   V1.51                    Friday  July 9, 1993  11:14 am
                 User SUPERVISOR On File Server VOYAGER_311 Connection 1

┌──────────────────────────────────────────────────────────────────────────┐
│                       New Print Job to be Submitted                        │
│Print job:                           File size:                             │
│Client:              SUPERVISOR[1]                                          │
│Description:         GL Documentation                                       │
│Status:                                                                     │
│                              ┌──────────────┐                              │
│User Hold:           No       │Save changes. │Date:                         │
│Operator Hold:       No       │              │Time:                         │
│Service Sequence:             │ No           │                              │
│                              │ Yes          │                              │
│                              └──────────────┘                              │
│Number of copies:    1                                           0          │
│File contents:       Text              Print banner:    Yes                 │
│Tab size:            8                 Name:            Leslie               │
│Suppress form feed:  No                Banner name:     GL.DOC               │
│Notify when done:    No                                                     │
│                                       Defer printing:  Yes                  │
│Target server:       (Any Server)      Target date:     July 9, 1993         │
│                                       Target time:     12:30:00 pm          │
└──────────────────────────────────────────────────────────────────────────┘
```

Leslie then added the print jobs for Mary and Ned.

CHANGING PRINT JOB PARAMETERS

After she added the print job for Ned, Leslie remembered that Ned wanted his printout before noon if possible. Because Mary's print job is rather large, Leslie decided to change the sequence of print jobs to allow Ned's to print first. In her NetWare class, Leslie learned that print jobs can be modified or deleted from the Current Print Jobs window by highlighting the job and pressing either [Enter] or [Del]. Any user has the ability to modify or delete jobs that he or she has placed in the print queue.

Leslie called up and changed the print sequence of the print jobs on the BUSACC-R0-Q1 print queue following these steps:

1. From the Current Print Jobs window, shown in Figure 10-32 on the following page, Leslie highlighted the Accounting Report job and pressed [Enter]. The Print Queue Entry Information shown in Figure 10-33 on the following page was displayed.

FIGURE 10-32: Leslie's Current Print Jobs window before she changed
the print job sequence

```
NetWare Print Console  V1.51                   Friday  July 9, 1993  11:18 am
              User SUPERVISOR On File Server VOYAGER_311 Connection 1

┌──────────────────────────────────────────────────────────────────────────┐
│ Seq Banner Name  Description                         Form Status   Job     │
│                                                                            │
│   1 Leslie       GL Documentation                      0 Waiting   384     │
│   2 SUPERVISOR   Catalog File                          0 Ready     960     │
│   3 SUPERVISOR   Accounting Report                     0 Ready     672     │
│                                                                            │
│                                                                            │
│                                                                            │
│                                                                            │
│                                                                            │
│                                                                            │
│                                                                            │
│                                                                            │
└──────────────────────────────────────────────────────────────────────────┘
```

FIGURE 10-33: The Print Queue Entry Information window

```
NetWare Print Console  V1.51                   Friday  July 9, 1993  11:19 am
              User SUPERVISOR On File Server VOYAGER_311 Connection 1

┌──────────────────────────────────────────────────────────────────────────┐
│                     Print Queue Entry Information                          │
│ Print job:        672                File size:          4021              │
│ Client:           SUPERVISOR[1]                                            │
│ Description:      Accounting Report                                        │
│ Status:          Ready To Be Serviced, Waiting For Print Server           │
│                                                                            │
│ User Hold:        No                 Job Entry Date:     July 9, 1993      │
│ Operator Hold:    No                 Job Entry Time:     11:16:26 am       │
│ Service Sequence: 3                                                        │
│                                                                            │
│ Number of copies: 1                  Form:               0                 │
│ File contents:    Byte stream        Print banner:       No                │
│ Tab size:                            Name:                                 │
│ Suppress form feed: No               Banner name:                          │
│ Notify when done:  No                                                      │
│                                      Defer printing:     No                │
│ Target server:    (Any Server)       Target date:                         │
│                                      Target time:                          │
└──────────────────────────────────────────────────────────────────────────┘
```

2. To change the sequence, she highlighted the Service Sequence: 2 field, pressed [Enter], changed the 2 to 1, and pressed [Enter].

3. To have a banner printed on the Accounting Report job, Leslie highlighted the Banner name option and changed "No" to "Yes." She then entered the name and banner fields, as shown in Figure 10-34.

```
NetWare Print Console  V1.51                  Friday  July 9, 1993  11:20 am
              User SUPERVISOR On File Server VOYAGER_311 Connection 1

┌──────────────────────────────────────────────────────────────────────────┐
│                       Print Queue Entry Information                        │
├──────────────────────────────────────────────────────────────────────────┤
│Print job:         672            File size:        4021                    │
│Client:            SUPERVISOR[1]                                            │
│Description:       Accounting Report                                        │
│Status:            Ready To Be Serviced, Waiting For Print Server           │
│                                                                            │
│User Hold:         No             Job Entry Date:   July 9, 1993            │
│Operator Hold:     No             Job Entry Time:   11:16:26 am             │
│Service Sequence:  1                                                        │
│                                                                            │
│Number of copies:  1              Form:             0                       │
│File contents:     Byte stream    Print banner:     Yes                     │
│Tab size:                         Name:             Ned Lynch               │
│Suppress form feed: No            Banner name:      Accounts Rpt            │
│Notify when done:  No                                                       │
│                                  Defer printing:   No                      │
│Target server:     (Any Server)   Target date:                             │
│                                  Target time:                             │
└──────────────────────────────────────────────────────────────────────────┘
```

4. To save the changes and return to the Print Job screen, Leslie pressed
[Esc]. The jobs were displayed in their new sequence, as shown in
Figure 10-35.

FIGURE 10-35: The revised print queue

```
NetWare Print Console  V1.51                  Friday  July 9, 1993  11:20 am
              User SUPERVISOR On File Server VOYAGER_311 Connection 1

┌──────────────────────────────────────────────────────────────────────────┐
│ Seq Banner Name  Description                          Form Status   Job    │
├──────────────────────────────────────────────────────────────────────────┤
│   1 Ned Lynch    Accounting Report                      0 Ready     672    │
│   2 Leslie       GL Documentation                       0 Waiting   384    │
│   3 SUPERVISOR   Catalog File                           0 Ready     960    │
│                                                                            │
│                                                                            │
│                                                                            │
│                                                                            │
│                                                                            │
│                                                                            │
│                                                                            │
│                                                                            │
│                                                                            │
│                                                                            │
│                                                                            │
└──────────────────────────────────────────────────────────────────────────┘
```

5. She then pressed [Esc] to return to the Print Queue Information menu.

To allow the print server to service the jobs in the print queue, Leslie
then used the Current Queue Status option to change the Servers can
service entries in queue: No to "Yes." The print queue jobs flagged as
ready will now be printed on printer number 0 by the print server.

USING NPRINT TO SEND OUTPUT TO A PRINTER

After returning from lunch, Leslie was pleased to find that the GL.DOC file had printed. Next she wanted to look at the README.DOC file that came with the general ledger system. Rather than going through all the steps in PCONSOLE to place the job on the print queue, Leslie recalled that the NPRINT command line utility will copy a DOS text file directly into the selected print queue. To use the NPRINT command to copy the README.DOC file from the DATA:BUSINESS\GLSYSTEM directory into the BUSACC-R0-Q1 print queue, Leslie typed the NPRINT command, as shown in Figure 10-36. The NB parameter specified that no banner was to be printed. Within a couple of minutes, the README.DOC file started to print on Ann's printer.

Figure 10-36: Leslie's use of the NPRINT command to send the README.DOC file to BUSACC-RO printer

```
F:\>NPRINT DATA:BUSINESS\GLSYSTEM\README.DOC  Q=BUSACC-R0-Q1  NB
Queuing data to Server VOYAGER_311, Queue BUSACC-R0-Q1.
VOYAGER_311\DATA:BUSINESS\GLSYSTEM
      Queuing file README.DOC

F:\>
```

DEFINING FORMS WITH PRINTDEF

Leslie planned to use the Business Department's dot matrix to print standard reports on $8\frac{1}{2} \times 11$" paper, wide reports on 11×14" paper, and payroll checks. This plan means that paper must be changed before certain jobs are printed from the print queue. To be sure the right paper is mounted in the printer for each job, she planned to establish three form types: standard, wide, and checks. In her NetWare class, Leslie learned that the PRINTDEF utility can be used to define form types and set up escape code sequences for special printer functions. PRINTDEF maintains a printer database file called NET$PRN.DAT in the SYS:PUBLIC directory. NetWare uses this file to contain the form definitions as well as the escape code sequences used by any printers on the network.

Leslie used the PRINTDEF utility to define her form for the Accounting printer as follows:

1. When she typed "PRINTDEF" at the DOS prompt, the PrintDef Options menu shown in Figure 10-37 was displayed.

FIGURE 10-37: The PrintDef Options menu

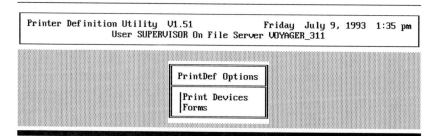

2. She highlighted the Forms option and pressed [Enter]. The Forms window was displayed.

3. To add a new form, Leslie pressed [Ins] to display the Form Definition window.

4. Next she typed the name of the first form, the form number, and the length and width of the form in lines and characters. The Length and Width fields are used for documentation purposes only.

5. To save the form definition, she pressed [Esc]. The new form's name and number appeared in the Forms window.

6. She then repeated steps 3 through 5 to add her remaining forms, as shown in Figure 10-38.

FIGURE 10-38: Leslie's screen after she created Forms number 0 and 1

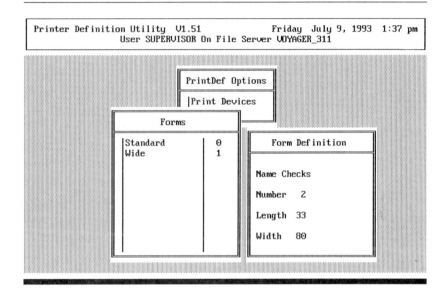

7. After all print forms were defined, Leslie pressed [Esc] to exit to the PRINTDEF utility. The Exit Options menu, shown in Figure 10-39, was displayed.

FIGURE 10-39: The Exit Options menu

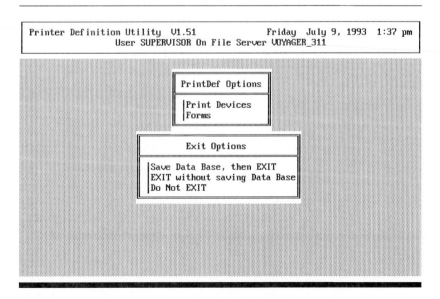

8. To save the form definitions in her database file, NET$PRN.DAT, Leslie selected the Save Data Base, then EXIT option and pressed [Enter]. The database was saved, and the PRINTDEF program exited to the DOS prompt.

USING THE CAPTURE AND ENDCAP COMMANDS

Leslie wanted to be able to direct output from her workstation to either the BUSACC-R0 or SALRPT-LASER-R2 printers. She could do this by using the CAPTURE command to redirect output from the LPT ports to the corresponding print queues. While the NPRINT command can send an ASCII text file to the selected print queue, the CAPTURE command will intercept output coming from an application to a DOS printer and redirect it as it is being printed to the selected print queue. When the application is done printing, the print job is made available for printing by the print server. In her NetWare class, Leslie learned there are three ways for a print job to be considered ready for printing. The first way is for the application to end (called Automatic Endcap). The second method is for the workstation to issue an ENDCAP command or log out. The third method is for a specified amount of time to elapse with no printing activity; after this time lapse the job is considered complete and ready for printing.

Leslie decided to direct the output going to the DOS LPT1 port to the Sales laser printer, and output going to the LPT2 port to the Business dot-matrix printer. Output from the word processor is preformatted by the application and always ejects the last page upon completion. Because the laser printer is located in another office, Leslie would like a banner containing her name and the job name to be printed on the printout.

FIGURE 10-40: Leslie's screen after she ran the CAPTURE commands

```
F:\>CAPTURE Q=SAL-LASER-R2-Q1  TI=5  NT  NAM=Leslie  NFF
Device LPT1: re-routed to queue SAL-LASER-R2-Q1 on server VOYAGER_311.

F:\>CAPTURE L=2  Q=BUSACC-R0-Q1  NB  F=1
Device LPT2: re-routed to queue BUSACC-R0-Q1 on server VOYAGER_311.

F:\>CAPTURE SH

LPT1:  Capturing data to server VOYAGER_311 queue SAL-LASER-R2-Q1.
       User will not be notified after the files are printed.
       Capture Defaults:Enabled       Automatic Endcap:Enabled
       Banner :LST:                    Form Feed       :No
       Copies :1                       Tabs            :No conversion
       Form   :0                       Timeout Count :5 seconds

LPT2:  Capturing data to server VOYAGER_311 queue BUSACC-R0-Q1.
       User will not be notified after the files are printed.
       Capture Defaults:Enabled       Automatic Endcap:Enabled
       Banner :(None)                  Form Feed       :Yes
       Copies :1                       Tabs            :Converted to 8 spaces
       Form   :1                       Timeout Count :Disabled

LPT3:  Capturing Is Not Currently Active.

F:\>
```

Leslie used the first CAPTURE command shown in Figure 10-40 to route output from LPT1 to the SAL-LASER-R2-Q1 print queue. The TI=5 parameter sets a time out of five seconds. If no output is received from the workstation for five seconds, the print job will be closed and made available for printing. The NT parameter in the CAPTURE command stands for "No Tabs" and tells NetWare not to expand any tab codes into spaces. This is also called byte stream mode; it is important for this job because the word processor has already formatted the output for the laser printer. In Leslie's NetWare class she learned that if you do not include this option, "junk" may print on the laser printer. The NAM= parameter places her name on the top half of the banner page. The NFF parameter stands for "No Form Feeds" and prevents the print server from sending a form feed code to the printer at the conclusion of the print job. If Leslie did not include this option here, an extra blank piece of paper would be printed after each word processor print job.

The second CAPTURE command in Figure 10-40 shows the parameters entered to direct output from the LPT2 port to the BUSACC-R0-Q1 print queue. The L=2 parameter is necessary in this command since the default is to direct output from the LPT1 port. The NB parameter will prevent the banner page from being printed on the dot-matrix printer. The F=1 option selects wide forms for this printer. Print jobs with forms F=1 will be held in the print queue until the print server operator issues a command to print them. Because Leslie's database program does not send a form feed command at the end of a printout, Leslie omitted the NFF option used in the previous command. By default, a form feed will be sent to the printer after each job. Because she may send text files that contain tab codes to this printer, she also omitted the NT option. Output sent to LPT2 will have any tab codes expanded into spaces during printing.

FIGURE 10-41: Leslie's screen after she used ENDCAP commands to return LPT ports to the local workstation

```
F:\>ENDCAP
Device LPT1: set to local mode.

F:\>ENDCAP ALL
LPT1:, LPT2:, and LPT3: set to local mode.

F:\>
F:\>
```

To view the capture status of all ports Leslie used the SH (for SHow) parameter of the CAPTURE command, shown as the third command in Figure 10-40. To return output to the DOS printer ports, she used END-CAP commands, as shown in Figure 10-41. The syntax of the ENDCAP command is

ENDCAP (LPT*n* **⌐ ALL)**

Notice that the first ENDCAP command in Figure 10-41 released only the LPT1 port. Because no printer port was specified, the END-CAP command defaulted to LPT1. The ENDCAP ALL command as used on the second ENDCAP command returned all ports to the local printer.

Setting up printing is a big job, but Leslie felt confident that her environment will meet the immediate printing needs of her users. To automate the use of the CAPTURE command for each user, she planned to include a default CAPTURE command in the LOGIN scripts. She will then provide options to allow the users to select a printer for the menu system that she will design in Chapter 11.

PCONSOLE Utility The PCONSOLE utility, illustrated in Figure 10-42, is a major tool necessary to set up network printing.

FIGURE 10-42: The PCONSOLE Menu

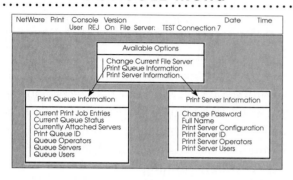

The PCONSOLE utility allows you to create and manage print queues, define print servers and printers, control printer functions such as changing forms, and assign operators and users for both print queues and print servers.

Print Queue Information

Selecting the Print Queue Information option will display a window of existing print queues on the selected file server. A supervisor-equivalent user can create or delete print queues from this window. New print queues can be added by pressing the Ins key and entering the name of the new print queue. Print queues can be deleted by highlighting the print queue name and pressing the Del key. To access the Print Queue Information menu for a specific print queue, highlight the desired print queue name and press [Enter].

■ **Current Print Job Entries**: This option allows you to view, modify, insert, resequence, or delete jobs in the selected print queue.

■ **Current Queue Status**: This option allows you to view such status information as number of entries in the queue and number of servers attached. In addition, it can be used to determine whether users can place jobs in the queue, whether servers can print jobs in the queue, and whether new servers can attach to the queue.

■ **Currently Attached Servers**: This option displays a window showing any print servers that are currently ready to print jobs from this queue.

■ **Print Queue ID**: This option displays the eight-digit hexadecimal print queue ID. This is the name of the subdirectory of SYS:SYSTEM used to store the print jobs.

■ **Queue Operators**: This option displays a window of users who will be able to manage jobs on this print queue. Use the Ins key to add another print queue operator; use [Del] to remove a user from the print queue operator list.

■ **Queue Servers**: This option displays a window of print servers that will be allowed to print jobs from this print queue. Press [Ins] to attach another print server to this queue.

- **Queue Users:** This option displays a window of users or groups that are allowed to place jobs on this print queue. Use [Ins] to add another print queue operator; use [Del] to remove a user from the print queue users' list.

Print Server Information

A print server is a logical process that can control up to 16 printers. Each printer must be defined as either local or remote, and the port it is connected to must be specified. Selecting the Print Server Information option displays a list of currently defined print servers. A supervisor-equivalent user can create, configure, or delete print server definitions. To access the Print Server Information menu for a specific print server, highlight the desired print server name and press [Enter].

- **Change Password**: This option allows you to set or change a password for the print server. Once a password is set, it must be entered correctly before this print server definition can be run.

- **Full Name**: This option allows you to define a longer name for your print server.

- **Print Server Configuration**: This option allows you to configure the print server by providing you with the following functions:

  File Servers to Be Serviced: Defaults to your current file server
  Notify List for Printer: Displays a list of users who will be sent a message if a printer needs attention. A separate notify list can be established for each printer.
  Printer Configuration: Allows you to define up to 16 printers as local or remote. A maximum of five printers may be defined as locally attached to the print server.
  Queues Serviced by Printer: Uses the option to define print queue(s) from which each of the printers will get jobs.

PSERVER *printserver_name*

The print server program PSERVER.NLM can be run as a NetWare Loadable Module (NLM) on a NetWare 3.1x file server, PSERVER.EXE can be run on a dedicated workstation, or PSERVER.VAP can be loaded as a Value-Added Process (VAP) on a NetWare 2.x file server or router. *Printserver_name* is the name of the print server definition file as defined using PCONSOLE. If the *printserver_name* is entered incorrectly, NetWare will ask for a password to help prevent someone from violating security.

RPRINTER *[printserver_name printer_number]*

RPRINTER is a TSR program that may be loaded on a workstation that has a printer controlled by a print server. You must supply the name of the print server and the number of the remote printer defined as this workstation's physical printer. This can be done interactively by typing "RPRINTER" with no parameters or by supply the printer server name and number. For example, the command RPRINTER PCS_PRINTER 1 will attach the workstation's physical printer to printer definition 1 of the currently running print server named PCS_PRINTER. If you enter "RPRINTER" with no options, you will be able to select the print server and printer number from the screen.

To run RPRINTER, you may either log in as any user and enter the RPRINTER command or you may copy the RPRINTER files to a local disk and run RPRINTER from a batch file after loading IPX and NETX.

PRINTDEF Utility   The PRINTDEF utility, shown in Figure 10-43, can be used to define printer forms and customize printer setup modes. Forms and printer configuration modes are stored in a database called NET$PRN.DAT in the SYS:PUBLIC directory.

FIGURE 10-43: The PRINTDEF Menu

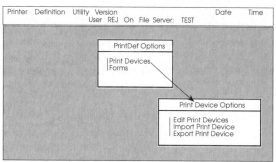

The Print Devices option can be used to edit, import, or export printer definitions into the printer database (SYS:PUBLIC\NET$PRN.DAT). A printer definition consists of functions and modes. A **function** is an escape code sequence that is defined in the printer to perform a specific operation such as condensed print or landscape (sideways orientation). A **mode** is one or more functions used to customize a print job. For example, if you wanted a job to be printed landscape in condensed print, you would create a mode consisting of the landscape and condensed functions.

The Edit Print Devices option allows you to define or modify printer functions and modes. The Import Print Device option allows you to copy Printer Definition Files (PDFs), supplied by Novell for popular printers, into your printer database. This option saves you from having to define all your own functions and modes. The Export Print Device option allows you to copy a modified set of printer functions and modes to a PDF file. The set can then be imported into another file server.

The Forms option allows you to create, delete, or modify print form definitions. Print forms can be used to prevent jobs from printing on the wrong type of paper. Forms number 0 is the default form type used by the CAPTURE and NPRINT commands.

PRINTCON Utility The PRINTCON utility, illustrated in Figure 10-44, can be used to define printer jobs to be used by CAPTURE and NPRINT commands.

FIGURE 10-44: The PRINTCON Menu

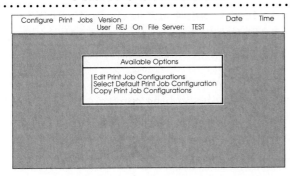

A print job can consist of the following information:

```
Number of copies
File contents: Text or Byte Stream
   Tab size may be defined on text jobs.
Suppress form feed: Yes or No
Notify when done: Yes or No
   If Yes, the user who sent the job will be sent
   a message when the job is printed.
Form name: (from PRINTDEF database)
Print banner: Yes or No
   If Yes, banner and file name may be specified.
Local Printer: LPT1, 2, or 3. LPT1 is default.
Auto endcap: Yes or No
   If Yes, the job will be printed when the
   application ends.
   If No, the job will be printed when the
   ENDCAP command is issued.
Enable timeout: Yes or No
  If Yes, the job will be printed when no output
  is received for the specified time.
File Server: The file server containing the
  print queue to be used.
Print Queue: Name of the print queue the job is
  to be placed in.
Print Server: The print server attached to the
  above print queue.
Device: The printer device type from the
PRINTDEF database.
Mode: The printer setup mode for this job from
  the PRINTDEF database.
```

The Select Default Print Job Configuration option allows the user or supervisor to select a PRINTCON job as the default job to be used with the CAPTURE or NPRINT commands.

PRINTCON jobs exist for each user in that user's subdirectory of the SYS:MAIL directory. The Copy Print Job Configurations option can be used only by a supervisor-equivalent user to copy a print job from one user to another. Before copying PRINTCON jobs, it is necessary to exit from the PRINTCON utility and save the PRINTCON database. To delete all PRINTCON jobs for a user, you must go to the user's mail subdirectory and delete the PRINTCON.DAT file.

NPRINT *path [option...]* The NPRINT command will send the contents of an ASCII formatted file to the specified print queue. If no options are specified, the default PRINTCON job for that user will be used. Options include:

■ **NOTI**fy or **NoNOTI**fy: Whether or not a message will be displayed on your workstation when the job is printed.

■ **Server=fileserver:** Replace fileserver with the name of the file server containing the print queue.

■ **Queue=queuename:** Replace queuename with the name of the desired print queue.

■ **J**ob=jobname: Replace jobname with the defined printcon name. Must exist in your SYS:MAIL subdirectory.

■ Form=formsnumber: Replace formsnumber with a number of a forms defined by the PRINTDEF utility.

■ Copies=*n*

■ **T**ab or **N**o **T**ab: **T**ab for Text output (Default); **NT** for Byte Stream output

■ **NAM**e=name: Specify what is to appear on the upper half of banner page.

■ **B**anner=name: Specify what is to appear on the lower half of banner page.

■ No **B**anner: No banner page to be printed.

■ Form **F**eed: Eject page of paper upon completion of printing the job.

■ **NFF:** Do not eject page after printing the job.

CAPTURE *[options...]* The CAPTURE command directs output from the workstation's printer port(s) to a print queue on a file server. Options are the same as NPRINT except for the following additions:

■ **TI**meout=*n*: Indicates that the job will be printed after no output has been received from the application for the indicated number of seconds.

- **Autoendcap:** Indicates that the job will be printed after the application exits.

- **L=LPT port:** Output from the indicated LPT port will be sent to the specified print queue. LPT1 is the default print port.

- **CR**eate=path: Directs output to the specified file.

Printing Environment The printing environment is summarized in Figure 10-45.

FIGURE 10-45: The printing environment

Set Up Queue and Print Server

Run PCONSOLE

1. Create print queue and assign print queue operators and users.

2. Create printer server and assign password, print server operators, and users.

3. Specify which file server the printer server should service (if other than default).

4. Service queues from multiple file servers (optional).

5. Define printers.

6. Add notification (optional).

7. Assign queues to printers.

Run Print Server Software

Dedicated workstation

1. Modify SHELL.CFG
   SPX CONNECTIONS = 60

2. Run PSERVER.EXE

File Server

1. Load PSERVER.NLM

2. MODIFY AUTOEXEC.NCF

Run RPRINTER

for printer attached to workstations

Customize Printing (Optional)

1. Decide whether to use PRINTDEF and PRINTCON

2. Define print device defintion files (PRINTDEF).

3. Define the forms your printer will accept (PRINTDEF).

4. Set up print job configurations (PRINTCON).

1. A _____ is a holding area for print jobs until they are printed.

2. When a print queue is created, _____ is assigned as the default user, and _____ is assigned as the default operator.

3. The _____ is the logical component that controls the printing of jobs for up to _____ printers.

4. What ports are available for attaching local printers to a print server?

5. The _____ utility is used to create print queues.

6. The _____ utility is used to create print servers.

7. The _____ utility is used to attach a local printer on a workstation to a printer number defined as remote on the print server.

8. List where the print server program can be run and what the name of the PSERVER extension is for each location.

9. The _____ utility is used to define forms.

10. The _____ utility is used to set up a default print configuration job for a user.

11. A _____ is a single ESC code sequence to set up a specific printer configuration.

12. Which option of the Print Queue Information menu is used to prevent print servers from servicing jobs in a print queue? _____

13. If the PSERVER program asks for a password when none was assigned, what is probably the problem?

14. Write a command to connect a workstation's local printer to printer number 2 of print server PCS_PRINTER.

15. Write the command to send the text file DATA:SALES\ ORDERS\README.DOC to the print queue SALRPT-R4 so that it prints a banner containing your name, ejects a blank page after printing, and uses form type 1.

16. Write the command to redirect the output of the word processor program to print queue SAL-LASER-R2 with a timeout of 10 seconds, a banner containing your name, which does not eject a blank page, and uses byte stream output.

17. Write a command to redirect output from port LPT2 to print queue SRVCOLOR-L1 with no banner, no paper eject, forms number 1, and byte stream output.

18. Write a command to return the output from LPT2 to the local printer.

19. Write a command to return the output of all printer ports to the local workstation.

20. What option of the CAPTURE command would cause all output to be held until the application ended?

21. Write the CAPTURE command to send output to print queue SUP_PSCRIPTR6 on file server PCS_HOST using printjob CONDSLAND.

22. If you enter the CAPTURE command without any options, what must happen for your jobs to be printed?

SUPERIOR TECHNICAL COLLEGE PROJECT 10

In these assignments you will set up and work with the network printing environment for your Superior Technical College system. The assignment steps in Section 1 require that you have access to a supervisor-equivalent username. If you do not have supervisor-equivalent access, your instructor will have set up the necessary components for you to work with and you should do only the assignments in Section 2. Whether you do Section 1 or Section 2, use Student Answer Sheet 10 for your responses.

Section 1:   Supervisor Equivalency Required

Assignment 10-1:   Define Your Printing Environment

❶ Using the information from Chapter 1, document your printing environment by filling out the printer definition form in Assignment 10-1 of Student Answer Sheet 10. When you name the print queues, be sure to prefix each queue name with your assigned student number. Virg Kent's printer should have a second print queue to allow for high-priority print jobs. In addition, because this printer is used to print graphic output for presentations and the catalog, it needs to be attached to a local print server.

Assignment 10-2:   Create Print Queues with PCONSOLE

❶ Create the print queues you defined on your printer definition form. Be sure each print queue name is prefixed with your assigned student number. Make your username, SUPERVISOR, and Virg Kent the only users of the high-priority print queue. Make your username and Virg Kent operators of all print queues. Record the print queue ID for each print queue on Student Answer Sheet 10.

Assignment 10-3:   Create a Print Server Definition

❶ Create a print server definition prefixed by your assigned student number. Configure each printer and assign print queue(s) as defined on your printer definition form. Record the requested information for each printer on Student Answer Sheet 10.

Assignment 10-4:   Use PCONSOLE to Change Print Queue Status

❶ Use PCONSOLE to change the print queue status of your dot-matrix print queue to prevent print servers from servicing jobs from the queue. Record the options you used to do so on Student Answer Sheet 10.

❷ Print the screen showing your print queue status. Attach the printout to Student Answer Sheet 10.

Assignment 10-5:   Use PCONSOLE to Place Jobs on a Print Queue

❶ Place the GRADUATE.DOC file from your graduate system on the dot-matrix print queue. Use default PCONSOLE values. Make the file deferred to print 30 minutes from the time you entered it. Place the TEST.DOC file from the testing application directory on the dot-matrix print queue. Use default PCONSOLE values. Make the file deferred to print the same time as the GRADUATE.DOC file. Print the screen showing the print job entries in your dot-matrix print queue. Attach the printout to Student Answer Sheet 10.

Assignment 10-6:   Change Print Job Parameters

❶ Rearrange the print jobs so that the TEST.DOC is printed first. Remove the banner from the GRADUATE.DOC print job. Print the screen showing the print job entries in your dot-matrix print queue. Attach the printout to Student Answer Sheet 10.

Assignment 10-7: **Use NPRINT**

❶ Use the NPRINT command to place the README file from the GRADUATE software directory on the dot-matrix print queue. Record the NPRINT command and parameters used on Student Answer Sheet 10.

Assignment 10-8: **Use CAPTURE**

❶ Enter a CAPTURE command to direct output from LPT1 to the dot-matrix print queue with a timeout factor of 10 seconds, a form feed, and text. The top half of the banner should contain your name, and the bottom half of the banner should say "Assignment 10-8." Record the CAPTURE command and parameters on Student Answer Sheet 10.

❷ Enter a CAPTURE command to direct output from LPT2 to the laser print queue with a timeout factor of 10 seconds, no form feed, and no banner. Record the CAPTURE command and parameters on Student Answer Sheet 10.

Assignment 10-9: **Test Your CAPTURE Commands**

❶ Use the SHow parameter of the CAPTURE command. Record the results of the SHow parameter on Student Answer Sheet 10.

❷ Use the MAP command to see whether you have a search drive to the SYS:SOFTWARE.CTS\WP directory. If you do not have a search drive to this directory, use the MAP command at this time to create one. Record the command you used on Student Answer Sheet 10.

❸ Type **WP** and press [**Enter**]. Create a text file describing today's weather. Include temperature, wind speed and direction, cloud cover, and any precipitation. Use the F2 key to print the document. The CAPTURE command should redirect the output from LPT1 to your assigned print queue. Attach the printout to Student Answer Sheet 10.

❹ Use PCONSOLE to view the contents of your print queue. Change the job description to "Weather Report." Print the screen showing your weather report job information. Attach the printout to Student Answer Sheet 10.

❺ Exit PCONSOLE. Use the ENDCAP command to return LPT2 to local mode. Record the ENDCAP command you used on Student Answer Sheet 10.

Assignment 10-10: **Create Forms with PRINTDEF**

❶ Use the PRINTDEF utility to create your own standard and wide forms preceded by your assigned student number. Record the form numbers for your forms under Assignment 10-10 of Student Answer Sheet 10.

Assignment 10-11: **Test Your Printer Environment**

To do this assignment, your instructor will team you up with at least one other student. You will then use one of your computers as an external print server, and the other computer as a remote printer and workstation. Each student should take a turn performing the following process:

❶ Modify the NET.CFG file on the external print server to contain the command SPX CONNECTIONS=60. Run the PSERVER.EXE program on the external print server computer. Run RPRINTER on your other computer and attach to the available printer on your print server. Your output should be printed on one or both printers. Attach your printouts to Student Answer Sheet 10.

Turn in Materials   Assemble your Student Answer Sheet 10 and printouts from Assignments 10-4, 10-5, 10-6, 10-9, and 10-11. If requested, turn in these materials to your instructor on or before the due date.

Section 2:   **Supervisor Equivalency Not Required**

Assignment 10-1:   **Define Your Printing Environment**

❶ Using the information from Chapter 1, document your printing environment by filling out the printer definition form under Assignment 10-1 of Student Answer Sheet 10. When you name the print queues, be sure to prefix each queue name with your assigned student number. Virg Kent's printer should have a second print queue to allow for high-priority print jobs. In addition, because this printer is used to print graphic output for presentations and the catalog, it needs to be attached to a local print server.

Assignment 10-2:   **View Your Print Queues**

If you do not have access to a supervisor-equivalent name, your instructor will have created three print queues for you to use. These print queues are ##DOTMATRIX-Q1, ##LASER-Q1, and ##LASER_Q2, where the ## represents your assigned student number. The dot-matrix print queue is assigned to printer 0, which is the main printer for your file server. The laser print queues are assigned to a printer whose number corresponds to the last digit of your assigned student number.

❶ Use PCONSOLE to view each of your print queues and record the print queue ID for each print queue on Student Answer Sheet 10.

Assignment 10-3:   **Create a Print Server Definition**

❶ Your instructor will supply you with information to fill in the table under Assignment 10-3 of Student Answer Sheet 10.

Assignment 10-4:   **Use PCONSOLE to Change Print Queue Status**

❶ Use PCONSOLE to change the print queue status of your dot-matrix print queue to prevent print servers from servicing jobs from the queue. Record the options you use to do so on Student Answer Sheet 10.

❷ Print the screen showing your print queue status. Attach your printout to Student Answer Sheet 10.

Assignment 10-5:   **Use PCONSOLE to Place Jobs on a Print Queue**

❶ Place the GRADUATE.DOC file from your graduate system on the dot-matrix print queue. Use default PCONSOLE values. Make the file deferred to print 30 minutes from the time you entered it. Place the

TEST.DOC file from the testing application directory into the dot-matrix print queue. Use default PCONSOLE values. Make the file deferred to print the same time as the GRADUATE.DOC file. Print the screen showing the print job entries in your dot-matrix print queue. Attach your printout to Student Answer Sheet 10.

Assignment 10-6: **Change Print Job Parameters**

❶ Rearrange the print jobs so that TEST.DOC is printed first. Remove the banner from the GRADUATE.DOC print job. Print the screen showing the print job entries in your dot-matrix print queue. Attach the printout to Student Answer Sheet 10.

Assignment 10-7: **Use NPRINT**

❶ Use the NPRINT command to place the README file from the GRADUATE software directory on the dot-matrix print queue. Record the NPRINT command and parameters you used on Student Answer Sheet 10.

Assignment 10-8: **Use CAPTURE**

❶ Enter a CAPTURE command to direct output from LPT1 to the dot-matrix print queue with a timeout factor of 10 seconds, a form feed, and text. The top half of the banner should contain your name, and the bottom half of the banner should say "Assignment 10-8." Record the CAPTURE command and parameters on Student Answer Sheet 10.

❷ Enter a CAPTURE command to direct output from LPT2 to the laser print queue with a timeout factor of 10 seconds, no form feed, and no banner. Record the CAPTURE command and parameters on Student Answer Sheet 10.

Assignment 10-9: **Test Your CAPTURE Commands**

❶ Use the SHow parameter of the CAPTURE command. Record the results on Student Answer Sheet 10.

❷ Use the MAP command to see whether you have a search drive to the SYS:SOFTWARE.CTS\WP directory. If you do not have a search drive to this directory, use the MAP command at this time to create one. Record the MAP command you used on Student Answer Sheet 10.

❸ Type **WP** and press [**Enter**]. Create a text file describing today's weather. Include temperature, wind speed and direction, cloud cover, and any precipitation. Use the F2 key to print the document. The CAPTURE command should redirect the output from LPT1 to your assigned print queue. Attach the printout to Student Answer Sheet 10.

❹ Use PCONSOLE to view the contents of your print queue. Change the job description to "Weather Report." Print the screen showing your weather report job information. Attach the printout to Student Answer Sheet 10.

⑤   Exit PCONSOLE. Use the ENDCAP command to return LPT2 to local mode. Record the ENDCAP command you used on Student Answer Sheet 10.

Assignment 10-10:   **Create Forms with PRINTDEF**

❶   Use the PRINTDEF utility to view the forms in your file server's printer database. Record the forms and form number in the table under Assignment 10-10 of Student Answer Sheet 10.

Assignment 10-11:   **Test Your Printer Environment**

To do this assignment, your instructor will team you up with at least one other student. You will then use one of your computers as an external print server, and the other computer as a remote printer and workstation. Each student should take a turn performing the following process:

❶   Modify the NET.CFG file on the external print server to contain the command SPX CONNECTIONS=60. Run the PSERVER.EXE program on the external print server computer. Run RPRINTER on your other computer and attach to the available printer on your print server. Your output should be printed on one or both printers. Attach your printouts to Student Answer Sheet 10.

Turn in Materials   Assemble your Student Answer Sheet 10 and printouts from Assignments 10-4, 10-5, 10-6, 10-9, and 10-11. If requested, turn in these materials to your instructor on or before the due date.

Student Name: _____ Date: _____

Assignment 10-1: **Define Your Printing Environment**

❶ Complete your printer definition form below.

Printer definition form for print server _____

Printer Number	Location	Type/Model	Local or Remote	Printer Name	Print Queue Name and Priority

Assignment 10-2: **Create and View Print Queues with PCONSOLE**

❶ In the table below, record each print queue ID.

Print Queue Name	ID

Assignment 10-3: **Create a Print Server Definition**

❶ In the table below, record your printer information.

Name	Type and Port	Interrupt	Buffer Size	Starting Form	Service mode

Assignment 10-4: **Use PCONSOLE to Change Print Queue Status**

❶ Record the options you used to change the print queue status.

❷ Attach the printout showing the print queue status.

Assignment 10-5:   **Use PCONSOLE to Place Jobs on a Print Queue**

❶   Attach the printout showing the print job entries in your dot-matrix print queue.

Assignment 10-6:   **Change Print Job Parameters**

❶   Attach the printout showing the resequenced job entries in your dot-matrix print queue.

Assignment 10-7:   **Use NPRINT**

❶   Record the NPRINT command you used to send the README file from the GRADUATE software directory.

Assignment 10-8:   **Use CAPTURE**

❶   Record the CAPTURE command you used.

❷   Record the CAPTURE command you used.

Assignment 10-9:   **Test Your CAPTURE Commands**

❶   Record the output from your CAPTURE SH command.

❷   Record the MAP command you used.

❸   Attach the printout showing the job information for the weather report.

❹   Attach the printout showing the weather report change.

❺   Record the ENDCAP command you used.

Assignment 10-10:   **Create Forms with PRINTDEF**

❶   In the table, record the form number for each of your defined forms.

Form Name	Number

Assignment 10-11:   **Test Your Printer Environment**

❶   Attach your test printouts.

In this chapter you will:

NETWARE
MENUS

- Decide from which directory users will run the MENU program

- Define a common set of submenu options for your organization

- Design a menu for each workgroup in your organization

- Enter and test each workgroup menu

- Assign users the necessary rights to use the menu system

- Protect the menu files and make them available to multiple users

- Document your menu system

LOGIN scripts and menus are the major ways to create a user environment that will make the network system easy to use. Creating and testing the menus first can help the network administrator define any necessary drive mappings and other requirements that must be placed in the system or user LOGIN scripts. In addition, the users' personal LOGIN scripts may need to be modified to run the appropriate menu for each user. In this chapter you will create and test the menus first, then write the LOGIN scripts command that will set up the necessary environment and link each user to his or her appropriate menu.

The NetWare 2.x through 3.11 menu system consists of three components: the MENU.EXE program found in the SYS:PUBLIC directory, menu command files that contain menu options along with associated commands, and temporary files created by the MENU.EXE program.

The MENU.EXE program controls the display and execution of menu options and remains in memory during the execution of the menu commands. The memory used by the MENU.EXE program must be taken into account in determining if a workstation has enough available memory to run a desired application. In addition, it is important not to load Terminate and Stay Resident (TSR) programs from a menu command file. Because TSR programs load after MENU.EXE, a large "hole" will be left in memory when the MENU program exits.

Menu command files are standard DOS text files that have a default extension of MNU. A menu command file consists of menu titles, options, and commands, as shown in the skeleton menu below:

```
%Menu Title,12,40,0
option 1
    command line
option 2
    command line 1
    ..
    command line n
option 3
    %Submenu
option 4
    command line
%Submenu Title,1,80,0
option 1
    command line
option 2
    command line
```

Menu titles are preceded by a percent sign (%), menu options are aligned on the left-hand margin, and commands are indented by a Tab key or at least five spaces preceding the command statement. A menu title line consists of the name of the menu, the location of the center of the menu box given in row and column coordinates (12 and 40 in our example), and an optional color palette number (0-4). If no color palette is given, default color palette zero is assumed.

When no location is given, the middle of the screen, row 24 and column 40, is used as the default location for the menu. If the specified location of the center of the menu is in an area of the screen that would cut off part of the menu title or options, the menu window is positioned as far as possible in that direction without truncating any information. For example, the title line "%MAIN MENU,24,80" would locate the menu titled MAIN MENU in the lower right of the screen with the right side of the menu box along the right-most edge of the screen at position 80.

A menu command file can consist of multiple submenus. The first title line is considered the main menu; subsequent title lines define submenus. All options following a title line are considered part of that menu's window. A menu option can refer to a submenu by specifying the name of the submenu indented in a command line, as shown following option 3 in the skeleton menu outlined above.

Menu options are displayed within the menu box in alphabetical order rather than in the sequence in which they are entered. Any statement aligned along the left margin of the menu file that does not start with a percent sign is considered an option and is displayed in the menu box with the previously defined title.

A command line may be a DOS executable statement, the title of another menu preceded by a percent sign, or a request for user input preceded by an @ symbol. Command lines are indented by using the tab key or at least five spaces preceding the command statement. Command lines may contain an @ symbol followed by a number (#) and a message in quotation marks to allow a user to enter input into the command line. Up to nine @# variables can be used in a menu file. An example of using the @ symbol input is given in the PC Solutions case.

Commands within a menu option must always return to the directory containing the menu temporary files before you exit. This is necessary for the menu program to redisplay the menu and continue operating.

To use a menu, you must have a search drive mapped to the SYS:PUBLIC directory, rights necessary to create and delete the temporary files in your current directory, and access to the desired MNU command file. The MNU command file may be located in your current directory or located in a separate directory that may either be specified when the MENU program is run or accessed through a search drive mapped to that directory.

For example, NetWare contains a sample menu called MAIN.MNU in the SYS:PUBLIC directory. To use this menu from your home directory on drive H: you could use any one of the following procedures:

```
H:\>MENU SYS:PUBLIC\MAIN
```
(Provides the specific path to MAIN.MNU file)
```
H:\>MENU MAIN
```
(Uses the search drive to find the MAIN.MNU file)
```
H:\>COPY MAIN.MNU H:
H:\>MENU MAIN
```
(Uses the MAIN.MNU file from the current directory)

THE PC SOLUTIONS CASE

When Leslie designed her directory structure in Chapter 2, she decided to store menu command files in the DATA:MENUS directory. In her NetWare class, Leslie learned that the menu system creates temporary files in the directory in which the MENU.EXE program is started. Therefore, to run the menus from the DATA:MENUS directory, users will need to have Read, File Scan, Create, Write, and Erase rights in this directory.

PLANNING THE LOCATION OF MENU FILES

Because each option of a menu must always return to the DATA:MENUS directory to find its temporary files, Leslie planned to map drive pointer M: to the DATA:MENUS directory for all users. Each menu option can then end with commands to change to the MENUS directory on the M: drive. An advantage to running the MENU program from the DATA:MENUS directory is that the temporary files created and deleted by the MENU program will be immediately purged because of the purge attribute set on this directory in Chapter 8.

Another alternative would be to run the MENU program from each user's own home directory. Although this method would eliminate the need to give users extra rights in the DATA:MENUS directory, it would require all users to have a home directory as well as a search drive mapped to the DATA:MENUS directory.

To allow multiple users to access the same menu options simultaneously, Leslie planned to flag the menu command files as Sharable. To protect the menu files in the DATA:MENUS directory from being accidentally erased or changed, she planned to flag them as Read Only.

PLANNING MENU OPTIONS

As a result of her analysis, Leslie decided to create a standard menu system for all users, as shown in Figure 11-1. Each menu will have the submenus Applications, Printing, Network Functions, and DOS Functions. The Applications and Printing menus will be tailored for each workgroup, as shown in Figure 11-2. Because the Payroll option will be used only by Ann Bonny, Leslie plans to create a special application menu for her.

FIGURE 11-1: Leslie's menu design

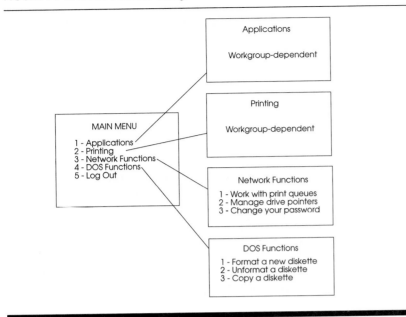

FIGURE 11-2: Leslie's workgroup applications

```
BUSINESS workgroup:

    PAYROLL
        Only on Ann's menu
        Change to PAYROLL directory and run PAYMAN
    GENERAL LEDGER
        Change to GLSYSTEM and run GLMENU
    BUDGETS
        Change to BUDGETS directory and run SP
    WORD PROCESSING
        Change to H: drive and run WP

SALES workgroup:

    ORDERS
        Change to ORDERS directory and run ORDMENU
    WORD PROCESSING
        Change to H: and run WP

HELPDESK workgroup:

    WORD PROCESSING
        Change to the HELPDESK directory and run WP

SUPPORT workgroup:

    WORD PROCESSING
        Change to H: and run WP
    GRAPHICS
        Change to CATALOG directory and run GRA
```

CREATING THE BUSINESS DEPARTMENT MENU FILE

Leslie decided to create and test the menu file for the Business Department first. She can then modify the contents of the Applications and Printing submenus to create menu files that meet the needs of the other workgroups or individuals.

The contents of Leslie's main menu file for the Business Department is show in Figure 11-3 on the following page. The main menu, titled Business Department Menu, will be located in the center of the screen using color palette 0. Each option of the main menu activates a submenu. The numbers ahead of the menu options allow Leslie to control the sequence in which the options will be displayed. Notice that the name of the submenu to be activated is indented and preceded by a percent sign. The name of the submenu must exactly match the option and the title lines. Uppercase and lowercase, as well as the number of spaces used, are important. The exclamation mark preceding the LOGOUT command is necessary to allow the menu program to exit before the user logs out of the file server. If you do not include the exclamation mark, the menu program will crash after the user logs out.

Each submenu of the Business Department menu (Applications, Printing, and so on) will be displayed in the upper-right corner of the screen using color palette 1. In the DOS Functions submenu, the @1 "Enter drive letter to Format diskette in" command line will display a message box on the screen prompting the user to input the drive letter. The drive letter entered will then be stored in variable @1 and is substituted into the FORMAT @1 /V command to cause formatting of the diskette in the drive letter specified.

FIGURE 11-3: Leslie's Business Department menu

```
%Business Department Menu,12,40,0          ← Centers menu box on Line 12, Column 40
1 - Applications
       %Applications                        ← Calls the submenu titled "Applications"
                                              (title name must match exactly)
2 - Printing
       %Printing
3 - Network Functions
       %Network Functions
4 - DOS Functions
       %DOS Functions
5 - Log Out
       !LOGOUT                              ← Exclamation point will cause MENU
%Applications,1,80,1                          program to end before it logs out
1 - General Ledger
       G:
       CD \BUSINESS\GLSYSTEM                ← Changes to GLSYSTEM directory
       GLMENU
       M:                                   ← Returns to menu starting point (M: must be
2 - Budgets                                   root mapped to DATA:MENUS
       G:
       CD \BUSINESS\BUDGETS
       SP
       M:                                   ← Returns to menu starting point
3 - Word Processing
       H:                                   ← Goes to user's home directory
       WP
       M:                                   ← Returns to menu starting point
%Printing,1,80,1
1 - Send Output to Color Printer
       CAPTURE Q=SRV-COLOR-L1 TI=10 NB NT
2 - Send Output to Post Script Laser
       CAPTURE Q=SUP-PSCRIPT-R6-Q1 TI=10 NB NT        Options of all menus are
3 - Send Standard Output to the Business Dot Matrix   numbered to appear in
       CAPTURE Q=BUSACC-R1-Q1 TI=5 NB NT F=0          sequence shown
4 - Send Wide Output to the Business Dot Matrix
       CAPTURE Q=BUSACC-R1-Q1 TI=5 NB NT F=1
5 - Send output to local printer
       ENDCAP
%Network Functions,1,80,1
1 - Work with print queues
       PCONSOLE
2 - Manage drive pointers
       SESSON
3 - Change your password
       SETPASS
4 - Send a message                                    Asks for user input for message
       SEND "@"Enter a Message"" TO @"Enter Username"  ← and username. The
%DOS Functions,1,80,1                                   @"Message" will be replaced
1 - Format a new diskette
       @1 "Enter drive letter to Format diskette in"
       FORMAT @1                            ← Substitutes operator input for @1
2 - Unformat a diskette
       @1 "Enter drive letter where diskette to UNFORMAT is"
       UNFORMAT @1
3 - Copy a diskette
       DISKCOPY @"Source drive" @"Target drive"
```

ENTERING THE MAIN MENU

Leslie wanted to use the DOS EDIT program to enter the Business Department menu file. Since she planned to place all menu files in the MENUS directory, she changed her drive pointer to the MENUS directory before starting the EDIT program. When starting the EDIT program, Leslie entered the name of the Business menu command file following the EDIT command as follows:

EDIT BUSINESS.MNU

By default all menu files should use the extension .MNU. After she entered the main menu commands shown in Figure 11-3, Leslie held down the Alt key while pressing [F] to display the File menu. She then used the X option to save the menu command file and exit the EDIT program.

FIGURE 11-4: Leslie's screen after she tested the Business Department DOS Functions submenu

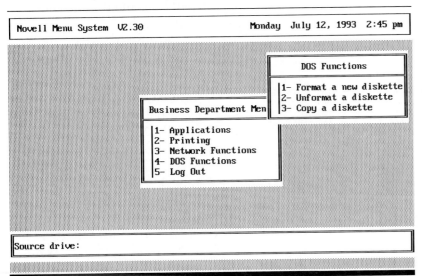

FIGURE 11-5: Leslie's NCOPY command to copy menu files for workgroups

```
G:\MENUS>NCOPY BUSINESS.MNU ANN.MNU
From VOYAGER_311/DATA:\MENUS
To   VOYAGER_311/DATA:\MENUS
     BUSINESS.MNU  to ANN.MNU

     1 file copied.

G:\MENUS>NCOPY BUSINESS.MNU SALES.MNU
From VOYAGER_311/DATA:\MENUS
To   VOYAGER_311/DATA:\MENUS
     BUSINESS.MNU  to SALES.MNU

     1 file copied.

G:\MENUS>NCOPY BUSINESS.MNU SUPPORT.MNU
From VOYAGER_311/DATA:\MENUS
To   VOYAGER_311/DATA:\MENUS
     BUSINESS.MNU  to SUPPORT.MNU

     1 file copied.

G:\MENUS>
```

TESTING THE BUSINESS DEPARTMENT MENU

To test the main menu file, Leslie typed the command MENU BUSINESS and pressed [Enter]. She then highlighted the DOS Functions option and pressed [Enter]. Next she highlighted the Format a New Diskette option and pressed [Enter]. The results of testing these options are shown in Figure 11-4.

CREATING OTHER WORKGROUP MENUS

After Leslie tested all the options of the Business Department menu, she was ready to create menus for each of the workgroups. First she used the NCOPY command to create other menu files for each workgroup, as shown in Figure 11-5.

Leslie next used the DOS EDIT command to edit each workgroup MNU file to change the main menu title and modify the application and printing submenus to meet the requirements of the other workgroups, as she defined in Figure 11-2.

After all menus were entered, Leslie used the MENU *menu_name* command to test each of the new menu options.

FIGURE 11-6: Leslie's screen after she used the GRANT and FLAG commands

```
G:\MENUS>GRANT R F W C E TO EVERYONE

VOYAGER_311/DATA:MENUS
MENUS                                   Rights set to [ RWCE F ]


G:\MENUS>FLAG *.MNU S RO
     BUSINESS.MNU               [ Ro S A - -- -- - - -- -- -- DI RI ]
     ANN.MNU                    [ Ro S A - -- -- - - -- -- -- DI RI ]
     SALES.MNU                  [ Ro S A - -- -- - - -- -- -- DI RI ]
     SUPPORT.MNU                [ Ro S A - -- -- - - -- -- -- DI RI ]
     HELPDESK.MNU               [ Ro S A - -- -- - - -- -- -- DI RI ]

G:\MENUS>
```

FIGURE 11-7: Leslie's screen after she documented her menu files

```
G:\MENUS>NDIR *.MNU
VOYAGER_311/DATA:MENUS

Files:              Size      Last Updated        Flags              Owner
--------  ------   --------   ---------------   ------------------   --------
ANN       MNU       1,135     7-12-93  2:44p  [RoSA-------------DR]  SUPERVISO
BUSINESS  MNU       1,135     7-12-93  2:44p  [RoSA-------------DR]  SUPERVISO
HELPDESK  MNU       1,135     7-12-93  2:44p  [RoSA-------------DR]  SUPERVISO
SALES     MNU       1,135     7-12-93  2:44p  [RoSA-------------DR]  SUPERVISO
SUPPORT   MNU       1,135     7-12-93  2:44p  [RoSA-------------DR]  SUPERVISO

        5,675 bytes in    5 files
       20,480 bytes in    5 blocks

G:\MENUS>TLIST

VOYAGER_311\DATA:MENUS
No user trustees.
Group trustees:
     EVERYONE                                  [ RWCE F ]

G:\MENUS>
```

FIGURE 11-8: The NPRINT commands Leslie used to print copies of her menu command files

```
G:\MENUS>NPRINT BUSINESS.MNU Q=BUSACC-R0-Q1 NB
Queuing data to Server VOYAGER_311, Queue BUSACC-R0-Q1.
VOYAGER_311\DATA:MENUS
     Queuing file BUSINESS.MNU

G:\MENUS>NPRINT SALES.MNU  Q=BUSACC-R0-Q1  NB
Queuing data to Server VOYAGER_311, Queue BUSACC-R0-Q1.
VOYAGER_311\DATA:MENUS
     Queuing file SALES.MNU

G:\MENUS>NPRINT SUPPORT.MNU Q=BUSACC-R0-Q1  NB
Queuing data to Server VOYAGER_311, Queue BUSACC-R0-Q1.
VOYAGER_311\DATA:MENUS
     Queuing file SUPPORT.MNU

G:\MENUS>NPRINT HELPDESK.MNU  Q=BUSACC-R0-Q1  NB
Queuing data to Server VOYAGER_311, Queue BUSACC-R0-Q1.
VOYAGER_311\DATA:MENUS
     Queuing file HELPDESK.MNU

G:\MENUS>
```

PROVIDING USER ACCESS AND PROTECTING THE MENU COMMAND FILES

To allow users to run the menu program from the MENUS directory, Leslie needed to give the group EVERYONE the necessary rights to the DATA:MENUS directory using the following GRANT command:

GRANT R F C E W FOR DATA:MENUS TO EVERYONE

Because her users will now have rights to change or erase files in the MENUS directory, Leslie wanted to protect the .MNU files from being accidentally modified or deleted. To provide for multiple users running the menu at the same time, she also needed to make the files Sharable. Leslie used the FLAG command FLAG *.MNU RO S to set the necessary file attributes. The results of Leslie's GRANT and FLAG commands are shown in Figure 11-6.

DOCUMENTING MENU COMMAND FILES

Once all menus were tested, Leslie used the NDIR > LPT1 and TLIST > PRN commands shown in Figure 11-7 to document all files, attributes, and trustee assignments in the MENUS directory. To obtain a hardcopy of each menu file, Leslie used the NPRINT commands shown in Figure 11-8 to place a copy of each menu file on the BUSACC-R0 print queue.

Leslie's next job is to establish the LOGIN script commands necessary to provide her users with the environment they need to use the network system and menus she created. In Chapter 12 you'll follow her steps as she completes the task and gets the PC Solutions network up and running.

MENU *menu_name*   The MENU program will read the contents of the specified menu command file and control the display and execution of the menu options. By default, the menu command file should have an extension of .MNU. If another extension is used, the complete filename, including the extension, must be specified after the MENU command.

Menu command files contain titles, options, and command lines. Titles are always aligned on the left margin and are preceded by a percent sign. Options are text lines aligned on the left margin and displayed in alphabetic sequence. Command lines immediately follow the option and are indented at least five spaces or one tab from the left margin. Command lines may be the title of a submenu preceded by a percent sign, a DOS internal or external command, or the name of an application program or batch file. You should always precede the name of the batch file with the word CALL to cause control to be passed back to the menu at the end of the batch file. An @ symbol may be used to allow the user to make an entry into the batch file to provide parameters for commands or application programs.

The *menu_name* can be located in the current directory or in a directory specified by a search drive. The MENU program creates temporary files in the directory from which it is run, and a menu option must always return to the menu starting directory after it has completed all operations.

1. List the three components of the NetWare menu system discussed in this chapter.

2. *True or false:* The MENU.EXE program is a Terminate and Stay Resident (TSR) program.

3. Write a menu title line that will position the menu named MAIN MENU in the lower-left part of the screen using color palette 2.

4. *True or false:* Menu options are displayed in the menu box in the order in which they are entered.

5. What rights are necessary in the directory from which the menu program is run?

6. *True or false:* Commands from a menu option must always return to the directory from which the menu was run.

7. Identify which of the following menu lines are incorrect.

```
%Main menu
Wordperfect
        WP
Printing
        %Printing
Logout
        LOGOUT
```

8. Write a menu command line that will ask the user for the drive letter to check when the command CHKDSK drive is used.

9. On a separate sheet of paper, write a simple menu command file with the title Study Menu that has the following three options. Option 2 should display a printer submenu that gives the user the choice of sending output to the laser print queue, dot-matrix print queue, or local printer. The menu program will be run from a root drive letter M:.

■ **Option 1:** Select Printer

■ **Option 2:** Start Test Program (Change to the G:\TEST directory and run STUDY)

■ **Option 3:** Logout

10. Describe an advantage of running the menu program from each user's home directory.

SUPERIOR TECHNICAL COLLEGE PROJECT 11

Now it's time to set up NetWare menus for the Superior Technical College users. In addition to applications, the users should be able to perform a minimum of the following functions. You may want to include other items in your menu.

- Send output to a laser, dot-matrix, or local printer. For each workgroup, the laser and dot-matrix printers should be the ones in closest proximity to the workgroup. If your workstation does not have a local printer, but uses the classroom network printer, the local printer option should direct output to the laboratory print queue.

- Change their passwords.

- Use the SESSION command to work with drive mappings.

- Use PCONSOLE to view jobs in a print queue.

- Use the CHKDSK command to check a disk in drive A, B, or C. This option should ask the user to enter the drive to be checked.

- Use the DISKCOPY command and be able to specify the source and target drives.

- Log out.

Assignment 11-1: **Plan Your Menu Design**

❶ Users in the Business Department need to be able to use the spreadsheet program to access the budget files and use the word processing program to create and edit documents. To run the spreadsheet program, first change to the BUSINESS directory and use the command CALL SP. Be sure to include commands to return to your menu starting point after this command. To run the word processing program, first change to the drive letter for the user's home directory and use the command WP. As with the spreadsheet option, be sure to include commands to return to your menu's starting point. On Student Answer Sheet 11, record the path from which users will run the menu system.

❷ Your username needs to be able to run the utility program and the word processor. To run the utility program, first change to the UTILITY directory and use the command CALL UTILMENU. Be sure to include the command to return to your menu starting point. To run the word processing program, first change to the user's home directory drive letter and then use the command WP. As with the UTILITY program option, be sure to include commands to return to the MENU directory after the WP command. On Student Answer Sheet 11, record the drive pointer and mapping to be used to return to the MENU directory.

❸ Instructional Service users need to be able to access the word processing program and testing system. When using the word processing program, Instructional Services users should start out in their own home directories. Review documentation files for information on how to run the testing system. In both options, be sure to include commands to return to the MENU directory after the application program is run. Record your commands on Student Answer Sheet 11.

❹ The users in the Student Services Department need to be able to access the graduate system and use the word processing and spreadsheet packages in their home directories. Review the documentation files to determine how to run the graduate system. Be sure to include commands to return to your MENU directory after each application is run. On Student Answer Sheet 11, record your commands.

❺ Virg Kent and Ruth Olsen need to be able to run spreadsheet, word processing, and graphics programs. To start the graphics software, first change to the catalog directory and then use the command GRA. In all options, be sure to include commands to return to your menu starting point after each application is run. Record your commands on Student Answer Sheet 11.

❻ Use the above specification to design a standard set of menu options to be used by all workgroups. On Student Answer Sheet 11, document the main menu for each workgroup, including all options and the commands necessary to run each option.

❼ On Student Answer Sheet 11, document the submenus that are common to all workgroups, including the options and the commands necessary to run each option.

Assignment 11-2: **Write the Menu File for the Business Department**

❶ Using the menu specifications for the Business Department, write the menu file for the Business Department on Student Answer Sheet 11.

Assignment 11-3: **Enter the Business Menu File**

❶ Change to your MENUS directory and use a word processing program or the DOS EDIT command to enter your menu file. Save the menu file and record the name of your Business Department menu on Student Answer Sheet 11.

Assignment 11-4: **Test the Business Menu File**
Use the MENU *menu_name* command to test your business menu. Test each application option to be sure all applications run and will return to the main menu.

❶ Select the Diskcopy option of the DOS Functions submenu and print the screen showing the input boxes asking for the source and target drives. Attach the screen printout to Student Answer Sheet 11.

❷ Select the Printer Option and print the screen showing all the printer options. Attach the screen printout to Student Answer Sheet 11.

Assignment 11-5: **Create and Test Workgroup Menus**

❶ Use the NCOPY command to copy the Business menu to each workgroup menu you defined in Assignment 11-1. Record the name of each workgroup menu file on Student Answer Sheet 11.

❷ Use the editor program to modify each workgroup menu to contain the application options you defined in Assignment 11-1. Be sure to include a comment at the beginning of each menu identifying the workgroup or user the menu is for. Use the MENU *menu_name* command to test the application options in each of the workgroup menus. Use the print screen key to obtain a printout showing the application menus for the Instructional Services and Student Services Departments. Attach the printouts to Student Answer Sheet 11.

Assignment 11-6: **Provide User Access and Protect the Menu Files**

❶ Change to the directory containing your menu files. Use the TLIST *path* > PRN command to determine if your users have rights to the directory containing your menus. If necessary, use the GRANT command to give your group ##EVERYONE the necessary access rights to the directory from which the menu program will be run. Attach the printout showing the trustee rights to Student Answer Sheet 11.

❷ Use the FLAG command to set attributes that will allow your menu files to be shared by multiple users and protected from being deleted. On Student Answer Sheet 11, record the FLAG command you used and the purpose of each attribute.

Assignment 11-7: **Document Menu Files**

❶ Use the NDIR *.MNU > PRN command to document all menu files. If you are using a network printer, use the command NPRINT *menu_name*.MNU Q=CLASSROOM to print the contents of each menu file. If using a local printer, use the DOS PRINT command to print a copy of each menu file. Record the commands you use on Student Answer Sheet 11.

❷ Attach your printouts to Student Answer Sheet 11. Label each printout with the appropriate menu name.

Turn in Materials Assemble your printouts for Assignments 11-4, 11-5, 11-6, and 11-7 and attach them to Student Answer Sheet 11. If requested, turn in all materials to your instructor on or before the scheduled due date.

Student Name: _____ Date: _____

Assignment 11-1: **Planning Your Menu Design**

❶ Record the path from which users will run the menu system.

❷ Record the drive pointer and mapping to be used to return to the above directory.

❸ Record your commands to return to the MENU directory.

❹ Record your commands to return to the MENU directory.

❺ Record your commands to return to your MENU directory.

❻ Document the main menu for each workgroup in the tables below.

BUSINESS Workgroup Menu	Menu Position Line: _____ Column: _____ Palette: _____
Option 1:	Commands:
Option 2:	Commands:
Option 3:	Commands:
Option 4:	Commands:
Option 5:	Commands:
Option 6:	Commands:

INSTRUCTIONAL Workgroup Menu	Menu Position Line: _____ Column: _____ Palette: _____
Option 1:	Commands:
Option 2:	Commands:
Option 3:	Commands:
Option 4:	Commands:
Option 5:	Commands:
Option 6:	Commands:

STUDENT SERVICES Workgroup Menu	Menu Position Line: _____ Column: _____ Palette: _____
Option 1:	Commands:
Option 2:	Commands:
Option 3:	Commands:
Option 4:	Commands:
Option 5:	Commands:
Option 6:	Commands:

SUPPORT SERVICES Workgroup Menu	Menu Position Line: _____ Column: _____ Palette: _____
Option 1:	Commands:
Option 2:	Commands:
Option 3:	Commands:
Option 4:	Commands:
Option 5:	Commands:
Option 6:	Commands:

Your Personal Menu	Menu Position Line: _____ Column: _____ Palette: _____
Option 1:	Commands:
Option 2:	Commands:
Option 3:	Commands:
Option 4:	Commands:
Option 5:	Commands:
Option 6:	Commands:

❼ Using the tables below, document each submenu that was used in the workgroup menus you defined in step 6.

Submenu Name	Menu Position Line: _____ Column: _____ Palette: _____
Option 1:	Commands:
Option 2:	Commands:
Option 3:	Commands:
Option 4:	Commands:
Option 5:	Commands:

Submenu Name	Menu Position Line: _____ Column: _____ Palette: _____
Option 1:	Commands:
Option 2:	Commands:
Option 3:	Commands:
Option 4:	Commands:
Option 5:	Commands:

Submenu Name	Menu Position Line: _____ Column: _____ Palette: _____
Option 1:	Commands:
Option 2:	Commands:
Option 3:	Commands:
Option 4:	Commands:
Option 5:	Commands:

Submenu Name	Menu Position Line: _____ Column: _____ Palette: _____
Option 1:	Commands:
Option 2:	Commands:
Option 3:	Commands:
Option 4:	Commands:
Option 5:	Commands:

Assignment 11-2: **Write the Menu File for the Business Department**

❶ Write the Business Department menu command on a separate sheet of paper and attach it to Student Answer Sheet 11.

Assignment 11-3: **Enter the Business Menu File**

❶ Record the name of your Business Department menu command file.

Assignment 11-4: **Test the Business Menu File**

❶ Attach the screen printout showing the input boxes from the Diskcopy option of the DOS Function menu.

❷ Attach the screen printout showing the printer submenu options.

Assignment 11-5: **Create and Test Workgroup Menus**

❶ Record the name of each workgroup's menu file below.

Workgroup	Menu Filename

❷ Attach the screen printouts showing the application menus for the Instructional Services and Student Services Departments.

Assignment 11-6: **Provide User Access and Protect the Menu Files**

❶ Attach the printout showing trustee rights to your MENUS directory. In the table below, record the FLAG command you used and document your reason for using each attribute.

FLAG command	Reason

Assignment 11-7: **Document Menu Files**

❶ In the space below, record the commands you used to print each menu file.

❷ Attach printouts from each menu file. Label each with the name of the menu.

In this chapter you will:

LOGIN SCRIPTS

- Describe the way the system, user, and default LOGIN scripts work together

- Use LOGIN script variables in the LOGIN scripts you write

- Design a system LOGIN script to meet the needs of your organization

- Enter and test the system LOGIN script

- Define user LOGIN script requirements

- Enter and test user LOGIN scripts

LOGIN scripts help to set up the processing environment for a user by establishing drive mappings, directing printer output to the default print queue, and executing the correct menu for each user. A LOGIN script is a file containing command statements that are executed by the LOGIN.EXE program when a user logs in. There are three types of LOGIN script files: the system LOGIN script file, user LOGIN script files, and the default LOGIN script. The **system LOGIN script** is stored in the SYS:PUBLIC\NET$LOG.DAT file. Whenever a user logs in, the login program (LOGIN.EXE) looks in the SYS:PUBLIC directory for this file. If the file exists, the LOGIN.EXE program will execute the LOGIN script statements stored in this file. **User LOGIN script** files are stored in each user's SYS:MAIL subdirectory in a file called LOGIN. The **default LOGIN script** is built into the LOGIN.EXE program and is executed when there is no user LOGIN script.

The SYSCON utility is used to maintain the system and user LOGIN script files. In Chapter 4 you used SYSCON to create a user LOGIN script that established drive pointers for your username. In addition, this LOGIN script contained additional statements to display a welcome message and remind you of a meeting date on Monday mornings. A list of LOGIN script commands with an example of each is provided in the Command Summary at the end of this chapter.

THE SYSTEM LOGIN SCRIPT

At a minimum, your system LOGIN script file should contain the commands shown in Figure 12-1. The INS option in the MAP commands for the search drives S1: and S2: will preserve the DOS path by inserting the search drive mappings prior to any DOS directory paths. If you leave off the INS parameter, existing DOS paths will be replaced by NetWare search drive pointers.

The COMSPEC=S2:COMMAND .COM statement will cause the workstation to go to the DOS directory on the file server to load the COMMAND.COM program after certain application programs are run. If all your workstations boot off hard drives, this statement is unnecessary because the system will be automatically set up to load COMMAND.COM off the local fixed drive. However, if some workstations boot off diskettes, this statement is required to avoid the message "Insert disk containing COMMAND.COM in drive d:."

FIGURE 12-1: Essential system LOGIN script commands

```
MAP S1:=SYS:PUBLIC

MAP S2:=SYS:PUBLIC\%MACHINE\%OS_VERSION

COMSPEC=S2:COMMAND.COM
```

THE USER LOGIN SCRIPT User LOGIN script statements are stored in a file called LOGIN that may be found in each user's SYS:MAIL subdirectory. A user's LOGIN script should contain commands that are unique to that user, and all users should have a user LOGIN script file, even if it contains just the EXIT command. If a user does not have a user LOGIN script, the LOGIN.EXE program will execute the default LOGIN script commands after the system LOGIN script, causing duplicate search drive mappings to the SYS:PUBLIC and DOS directories. Creating a user LOGIN script for all users prevents this from happening and protects the user from someone else creating a personal LOGIN script for them. Because everyone has Create rights to the SYS:MAIL directory, when no LOGIN file exists it is possible for another user to create a LOGIN file in a user's mail directory, causing possible security violations.

Whenever possible, it is best to put commands in the system LOGIN script rather than the individual user LOGIN scripts. This makes it easier for the network administrator to document and maintain LOGIN script commands and provides better control because a user has the right to modify his or her own LOGIN script.

THE DEFAULT LOGIN SCRIPT If no LOGIN file is found in a user's SYS:MAIL subdirectory, the LOGIN program will perform the following default LOGIN script commands:

WRITE "Good %GREETING_TIME, %LOGIN_NAME."
MAP DISPLAY OFF
MAP ERRORS OFF
MAP *1:=SYS:
MAP INS S1:=SYS:PUBLIC
MAP INS S2:=s1:IBM_PC\MSDOS\%OS_VERSION
MAP DISPLAY ON
MAP

LOGIN SCRIPT VARIABLES In Chapter 4 you used the GREETING_TIME and DAY_OF_WEEK variables in your user LOGIN script to display the greeting time and check for Monday. Figure 12-2 on the following page contains a list of other variables that may be used in your LOGIN scripts. When a percent sign is placed before the LOGIN script variable, the LOGIN script program will substitute the characters stored in that variable into the command before executing it.

Using LOGIN Script Variables Within Messages
Whenever you use a LOGIN script variable within quotation marks the variable should be preceded by a percent sign (%) and typed using UPPER-CASE. The percent sign tells the LOGIN script processor to substitute the value of the variable into the LOGIN script statement before executing it.

FIGURE 12-2: LOGIN script variables

Identifier Variable	Function
CONDITIONAL	
ACCESS_SERVER	Returns TRUE if access server is functional, otherwise FALSE
ERROR_LEVEL	An error number; 0=no errors
MEMBER OF "*group*"	Returns TRUE if member of group, otherwise FALSE
DATE	
DAY	Day number (01–31)
DAY_OF_WEEK	Day of week (Monday, Tuesday, etc.)
MONTH	Month number (01–12)
MONTH_NAME	Month name (January, June, etc.)
NDAY_OF_WEEK	Weekday number (1–7, Sunday=1)
SHORT_YEAR	Year in short format (88, 89, etc.)
YEAR	Year in full format (1988, 1989)
DOS EVIRONMENT	
< >	Use any DOS environment variable as a string
NETWORK	
NETWORK_ADDRESS	Network number of the cabling system (8 hexadecimal digits)
FILE_SERVER	Name of the file server
TIME	
AM_PM	Day or night (a.m. or p.m.)
GREETING_TIME	Morning, afternoon, or evening
HOUR	Hour of day or night (1–12)
HOUR24	Hour (00–23, midnight=00)
MINUTE	Minute (00–59)
SECOND	Second (00–59)
USER	
FULL_NAME	User's full name (from SYSCON files)
LOGIN_NAME	User's unique login name
USER_ID	Number assigned to each user
WORKSTATION	
MACHINE	The machine for which the shell was written (e.g., IBM PC)
OS	The workstation's operating system (e.g., MS DOS)
OS_VERSION	The version of the workstation's DOS
P_STATION	Station number or node address (12 hexadecimal digits)
SHELL_TYPE	The workstation's shell version
SMACHINE	Short machine name (e.g., IBM)
STATION	Connection number

Using LOGIN Script Variables Within IF Statements

When you work with IF statements, it is best to leave off the percent sign. In this case, the LOGIN script processor will look up the value of the variable during execution of the statement much the same way as when an IF statement is processed by any computer language.

Using LOGIN Script Variables to Map Home Drives

A common use for LOGIN script variables within drive mappings is to map user home directories. When LOGIN script variables are used to map home directories, the name of the user's home directory must be the same as the username stored in the LOGIN_NAME variable. The command MAP ROOT H:=DATA:USERS\%LOGIN_NAME in the system LOGIN script would then cause the LOGIN script processor to substitute the username for the path and attempt to map drive H: to that subdirectory. For example, when 99EDWLOW logs in the processor would execute the command MAP H:=DATA:USERS\99ED-WLOW.

By using the IF MEMBER OF *"group name"* THEN BEGIN statement, you can include statements that are executed only for certain workgroups. This statement, along with the use of the %LOGIN_NAME variable, can be useful to map drive pointers to user home directories based on workgroup. For example, the following statements could be used in a system LOGIN script to map users in the Business and Sales Departments to their respective home directories:

```
IF MEMBER OF "BUSINESS" THEN BEGIN
        MAP ROOT H:=DATA:BUSINESS\USERS\%LOGIN_NAME
END
IF MEMBER OF "SALES" THEN BEGIN
        MAP ROOT H:=DATA:SALES\%LOGIN_NAME
END
```

Using LOGIN Script Variables to Map a DOS Search Drive

To provide the ability to map a search drive to the correct DOS version used by a workstation, the %MACHINE, %OS, and %OS_VERSION variables may be used as shown below:

```
MAP INS S2:=SYS:PUBLIC\%MACHINE\%OS\%OS_VERSION
```

The default value for the %MACHINE variable is IBM_PC. This value may be changed by placing the command LONG_MACHINE_NAME=*name* in the SHELL.CFG or NET.CFG file. The default value for %OS is MSDOS. Again, this value may be changed in the NET.CFG file. The %OS_VERSION variable gets its value from the NETX shell program. For example, if NETX is run on DOS version 5.00, the value will be "V5.00." To use the above mapping in your system LOGIN script file, you need to create the directory structure for DOS shown in Figure 12-3.

LOGIN script variables are only available to the LOGIN script processor (LOGIN.EXE) and cannot be used in menus and batch files. If you wish to use one or more of the values found in the LOGIN script variables within a menu or batch file, you will need to

Figure 12-3: Sample DOS directory structure

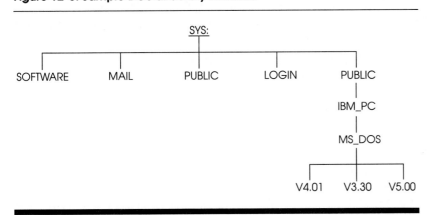

use the DOS SET statement to store the contents of that variable in the DOS environment space. For example, the following LOGIN script command would store the user's login name in the DOS environment space: DOS SET *username*="%LOGIN_NAME." Later you could use the following commands in a menu option to change to a word processing document storage area based on user login names:

1 - Word Processing
>   **G:**
>   **CD \WPDATA\%username%**

>   **WP**
M:

The percent signs around the username cause the system to get this value from DOS environment space.

In this chapter you will see how to create system and user LOGIN scripts given the processing specifications for each workgroup in the PC Solutions company. In the Superior Technical College project at the end of the chapter, you will apply these concepts to create both system and user LOGIN scripts. Because you may be sharing the file server with other students, you will need to create a special SCRIPTS directory where your system LOGIN script file will be stored. Whenever a user logs in who is a member of your ##EVERYONE group, the main LOGIN script program will run your commands in place of the actual system LOGIN script for that user. This approach will allow you to create your own unique LOGIN script to meet the needs of your system.

THE PC SOLUTIONS CASE

Once her menus for each workgroup were working, Leslie needed to establish the LOGIN script commands that will set up the drive mapping and other requirements necessary to allow the users to access the system through their menus.

DESIGNING THE SYSTEM LOGIN SCRIPT

Leslie started by laying out the design of the system LOGIN script. She used the LOGIN script worksheet provided with the NetWare installation manual to help her do the planning. First, she needed to include the required commands she learned in her NetWare class. Next, she needed to establish the drive mappings that will be used by all users. To do this Leslie refered to the drive mappings she defined in Chapter 4, as shown in the charts in Figure 12-4.

FIGURE 12-4: Leslie's drive pointer usage

Network Drive Policies

Drive Letter	Path	Description
F:	SYS:	Drive letter to access SYS volume
G:	DATA:	Root drive to access directories in the PC Solutions data area
H:	User home directory path	Root drive to user home directory
L:	Local workgroup directory	Root drive to common directory for the workgroup
M:	DATA:MENUS	Root drive to return to the MENUS directory

Search Drive Pointers

Pointer Number	Path	Description
S1:	SYS:PUBLIC	Required mapping
S2:	S1:IBM_PC\MSDOS\version	Mapping to correct DOS version
S3:	SYS:SOFTWARE\WP	Word processing package
S4:	SYS:SOFTWARE\DB	Database package
S5:	SYS:SOFTWARE\SP	Spreadsheet package

The LOGIN script statements to set up these mappings are on the LOGIN script worksheets shown in Figures 12-5 and 12-6 on the following two pages. Notice that the drive mappings for the user home directory and local workgroup directory depend on the workgroup to which a user belongs.

Next Leslie needed to look at the requirements for each workgroup. To help determine the department LOGIN script requirements, she referred to the menu specifications she developed in Chapter 11 and the printer environment she defined in Chapter 10. In addition to home, workgroup, and search drive mappings, each workgroup has default printer and special needs.

■ The Business workgroup users will need a default capture command to direct output to the BUSACC-R0-Q1 print queue.

■ The Sales workgroup will need a default capture command to direct output to the SAL-LASER-R2-Q1 print queue. In addition, Leslie planned to hold one-hour training sessions for the Sales Department users on the next several Wednesdays, starting at 8:30 a.m. She wants to put a note in the LOGIN script to remind the sales staff about this training.

■ After reading the documentation for the ORDERS system, Leslie learned that all users who are going to use the ORDERS system will need a root drive mapped to the ORDERS directory. Currently these users include all those in the Sales Department, plus Ed Low and Mary Read.

FIGURE 12-5: Leslie's system LOGIN script planning worksheet

Rem Preliminary commands (optional)
MAP DISPLAY OFF

Rem Greeting (optional)	
WRITE "Good %GREETING_TIME, %FULL_NAME" ⟵──────	Use of capital letters for login variables required when within quotations
PAUSE	

Rem Display login messages (Optional)

Rem Required Search drive mappings	
MAP INS S1:=SYS:PUBLIC ⟵────────	INS option preserves existing DOS path on workstation
MAP INS S2:=SYS:PUBLIC\%MACHINE\%OS\%OS_VERSION ⟵───	Requires directory structure shown in Figure 12-3

Rem COMSPEC	
COMSPEC=S2:COMMAND.COM ⟵────────	S2: will be replaced by DOS path; *do not* place a backslash before COMMAND.COM in path

Rem Common Application search drive mappings
MAP INS S3:=SYS:SOFTWARE.CTS\WP
MAP INS S4:=SYS:SOFTWARE.CTS\DB
MAP INS S5:=SYS:SOFTWARE.CTS\SP

Rem Common Regular drive mappings
MAP F:=SYS:
MAP G:=DATA:
MAP ROOT M:=DATA:MENUS

Rem DOS Prompt setting
SET PROMPT = "PG"

FIGURE 12-6: Leslie's workgroup LOGIN script planning worksheet

---

Rem Mapping for Business workgroup

IF MEMBER OF "BUSINESS" THEN BEGIN

  MAP ROOT H:=DATA:BUSINESS\USERS\%LOGIN_NAME

  MAP ROOT L:=DATA:BUSINESS

  #CAPTURE Q=BUSACC-R1-Q1 TI=5 NB NT ◄——————— The # is necessary to run the CAPTURE command

END

Rem Mapping for Sales workgroup

IF MEMBER OF "SALES" THEN BEGIN

  MAP ROOT L:=DATA:SALES

  MAP ROOT H:=L:%LOGIN_NAME ◄——————— This mapping uses existing L: drive path

  #CAPTURE Q=SAL-LASER-R2-Q1 NT NB TI=10

  MAP ROOT O:=L:\ORDERS

  IF DAY_OF_WEEK = "Wednesday" AND HOUR24 < "09" THEN BEGIN

    WRITE "Remember training at 8:30 a.m." ——— Nested IF

    PAUSE

  END

END

Rem Mapping for Help Desk workgroup

IF MEMBER OF "HELPDESK" THEN BEGIN

  MAP ROOT L:=DATA:HELPDESK

  MAP ROOT H:=L:%LOGIN_NAME

  #CAPTURE Q=HLP-R5-Q1 NB NT TI=5

END

Rem End of LOGIN Script commands

DRIVE M: ◄——————— Changes default drive to the MENUS system

MAP DISPLAY ON

- The Help Desk users will need a default capture command to direct output to the HLP-R5-Q1 print queue.

- Because Mary Read has special requirements, Leslie decided to handle her needs through a user LOGIN script. Since Mary will be helping out Nancy on the PC Help Desk, Leslie decided to map Mary's local drive to the HELPDESK directory at this time. This mapping will be in her personal LOGIN script, so Mary will be able to change it in the future.

    Now that Leslie has defined the known requirements for the workgroups, she can complete the system LOGIN script by filling out the system LOGIN script worksheets, shown in Figures 12-5 and 12-6.

ENTERING THE SYSTEM LOGIN SCRIPT

Let's follow the steps Leslie took as she used the SYSCON program to enter the system LOGIN script for PC Solutions.

1. First Leslie logged in as SUPERVISOR and started the SYSCON utility.

2. To create and maintain the system LOGIN script, Leslie highlighted the Supervisor option and pressed [Enter]. SYSCON's Supervisor Options menu was displayed.

3. To work with the system LOGIN script, Leslie next highlighted the System Login script option and pressed [Enter]. A window showing any existing system LOGIN script commands was displayed.

4. She then proceeded to enter all the system LOGIN script commands from her LOGIN scripts worksheets, shown in Figures 12-5 and 12-6.

5. To save the system LOGIN script, Leslie pressed [Esc] and then responded to the "Save changes" message by pressing [Enter], as shown in Figure 12-7.

Figure 12-7: Leslie's SYSCON screen showing her system LOGIN script

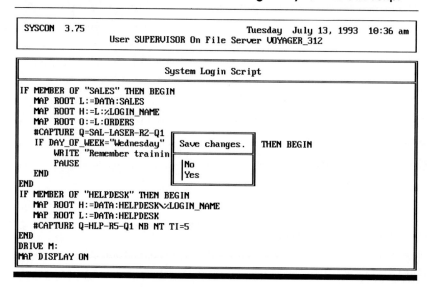

The system LOGIN script file will now be used whenever any user logs in to the file server. In her NetWare class, Leslie learned it is possible to lock up the system by making a serious mistake in the system LOGIN script. To get around a problem of this sort, Leslie's NetWare instructor recommended keeping a copy of the ATTACH command on a local disk drive. The ATTACH command can then be run to connect to a server without executing any LOGIN script statements. For example, the ATTACH VOYAGER_311\SUPERVISOR command would attach Leslie to the VOYAGER_311 file server as SUPERVISOR after supplying the correct password. She could then use the CD SYS:PUBLIC command to change to the PUBLIC directory and run the SYSCON utility to correct the faulty LOGIN script statements.

DEFINING THE USER LOGIN SCRIPTS

In her NetWare class, Leslie learned that it is best to keep as few commands as possible in the user LOGIN scripts. Ron, a network administrator for Automated Diagnostic Instruments, told her that he did not use user LOGIN scripts at all. He placed all commands in the system LOGIN script and used IF statements when necessary to separate special statements by groupname or username. By placing an EXIT statement in the system LOGIN script he stops the LOGIN script processor; no more system or user LOGIN script statements are executed after the EXIT statement. This prevents users from modifying their LOGIN script commands and from creating a LOGIN file in another user's mail subdirectory.

In her system Leslie has decided to use the user LOGIN scripts for special users such as Mary Read, Ann Bonny, and herself. For most users, the user LOGIN script will provide a means of linking the correct menu to the user. Figure 12-8 shows completed user LOGIN script forms for Mary Read, Ann Bonny, and Edward Low. Notice the use of the EXIT "MENU *menu-name*" command at the end of each user LOGIN script. This command will link the LOGIN script to the menu program displaying the specified menu for that user. The DRIVE M: command at the end of the system LOGIN script, as shown in Figure 12-6, will change the workstation's default drive to M:. Because M: is mapped to the DATA:MENUS directory, the DRIVE M: statement allows the workstation to execute the menu program using the correct menu for that user's workgroup.

FIGURE 12-8: Leslie's user LOGIN script worksheet

Basic User LOGIN Script for 99MARREA

MAP ROOT H:=DATA:SUPPORT\99MARREA

MAP ROOT L:=DATA:HELPDESK

MAP ROOT O:=DATA:SALES\ORDERS

EXIT "MENU SUPPORT"

Basic User LOGIN Script for 99ANNBON

EXIT "MENU ANN"

Basic User LOGIN Script for 99EDWLOW

MAP ROOT 0:=DATA:SALES\ORDERS

EXIT "MENU BUSINESS"

ENTERING USER LOGIN SCRIPTS Let's follow the steps Leslie took as she used SYSCON to enter the user LOGIN scripts for Mary Read.

1. First Leslie logged in as SUPERVISOR (she could have logged in as any user who is defined as a user account manager of Mary Read's account) and ran the SYSCON utility.

2. To access Mary Read's user LOGIN script, Leslie highlighted the User Information option and pressed [Enter]. A window showing all usernames was displayed.

3. Next she highlighted Mary Read's username, 99MARREA, and pressed [Enter]. The User Information menu shown in Figure 12-9 appeared.

Figure 12-9: Leslie's SYSCON User Information menu for 99MARREA

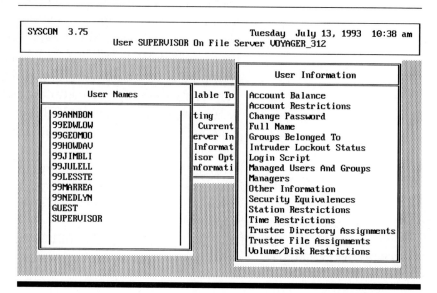

```
SYSCON  3.75                              Tuesday  July 13, 1993  10:38 am
                    User SUPERVISOR On File Server VOYAGER_312

                                                    User Information

              User Names            lable To    Account Balance
                                                 Account Restrictions
         99ANNBON                   ting        Change Password
         99EDWLOW                    Current    Full Name
         99GEOMOO                   erver In    Groups Belonged To
         99HOWDAV                   Informat    Intruder Lockout Status
         99JIMBLI                   isor Opt    Login Script
         99JULELL                   nformati    Managed Users And Groups
         99LESSTE                               Managers
         99MARREA                               Other Information
         99NEDLYN                               Security Equivalences
         GUEST                                  Station Restrictions
         SUPERVISOR                             Time Restrictions
                                                Trustee Directory Assignments
                                                Trustee File Assignments
                                                Volume/Disk Restrictions
```

4. To enter a user LOGIN script for Mary, Leslie highlighted the Login Script option and pressed [Enter]. Because Mary Read does not currently have a user LOGIN script, SYSCON asked where to copy the LOGIN script from, as shown in Figure 12-10. Leslie responded by pressing [Enter] to accept the default name, 99MARREA. A blank user LOGIN script window was then displayed.

FIGURE 12-10: Leslie's SYSCON screen as she created a user LOGIN script for 99MARREA

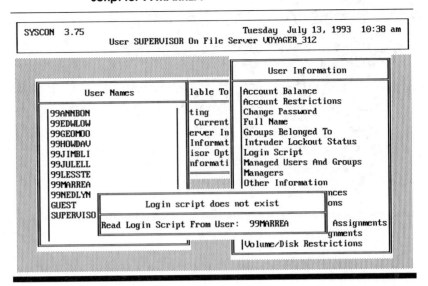

5. Leslie then entered the user LOGIN script statements from her user LOGIN script worksheet, shown in Figure 12-8. To delete an incorrect entry, Leslie pressed the F5 key and then used the arrow keys to highlight the text to be removed. She then pressed the Delete key to remove the highlighted information.

6. When all user LOGIN script statements were entered, Leslie pressed the Esc key and then pressed [Enter] to confirm saving Mary's user LOGIN script.

7. After saving the user LOGIN script, Leslie wanted to document the user ID for this user. To do so she selected the Other Information option. SYSCON displayed the eight-digit user ID shown at the bottom of Figure 12-11.

Figure 12-11: Leslie's SYSCON screen showing 99MARREA's user ID

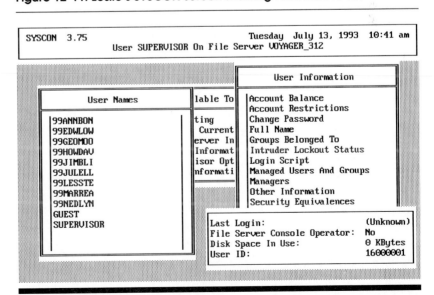

8. Leslie then used the Esc key to return to the username window.

Figure 12-12: Leslie's screen after she logged in as 99EDWLOW

```
F:\>LOGIN 99EDWLOW
Enter your password:
Drive  M: = VOYAGER_311\DATA:MENUS  \
Good morning, 99EDWLOW.

Drive  A:    maps to a local disk.
Drive  B:    maps to a local disk.
Drive  C:    maps to a local disk.
Drive  D:    maps to a local disk.
Drive  E:    maps to a local disk.
Drive  F: = VOYAGER_311\SYS:    \
Drive  M: = VOYAGER_311\DATA:MENUS  \

SEARCH1:  = X:. [VOYAGER_311\SYS:  \PUBLIC]
SEARCH2:  = W:. [VOYAGER_311\SYS:  \PUBLIC\IBM_PC\MSDOS\V5.00]
SEARCH3:  = Z:. [VOYAGER_311\SYS:  \PUBLIC]
SEARCH4:  = Y:. [VOYAGER_311\SYS:  \PUBLIC\IBM_PC\MSDOS\V5.00]

M:\>
```

FIGURE 12-13: Leslie's SYSCON screen showing the EXIT command for 99EDLOW

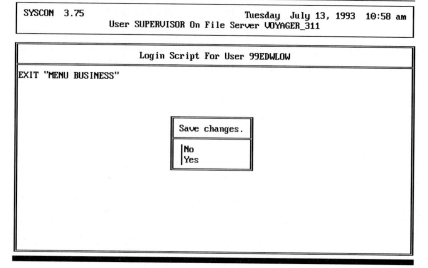

```
SYSCON  3.75                          Tuesday  July 13, 1993  10:58 am
                User SUPERVISOR On File Server VOYAGER_311

                      Login Script For User 99EDWLOW
EXIT "MENU BUSINESS"

                          Save changes.
                          No
                          Yes
```

She then repeated steps 3 through 7 to enter a user LOGIN script and document the user ID for each of her users.

TESTING USER ENVIRONMENTS

To test the environment, Leslie logged in as each user and tested each menu option. After trying each option, she used the Esc key to exit the menu and then typed "WHOAMI /A > PRN" to display all user information. After this she used the LISTDIR g:*.* /E /S > PRN command to display the effective rights in all directories of the DATA volume. After logging in as Ed Low, Leslie noticed that Ed had two search drives mapped to the SYS: PUBLIC and DOS directories, as shown in Figure 12-12. She immediately realized that this occurred because Ed has no user LOGIN script. To prevent this from happening in the future, Leslie created a LOGIN script for Ed containing just the EXIT command, as shown in Figure 12-13.

 # [path] filename [parameters] The pound sign (#) allows you to execute other programs or batch files from a LOGIN script. You must precede commands such as CAPTURE with the # symbol. If a search drive has not been mapped to the directory containing the program or command you wish to run, the path to the command must be given. For example, you would need to use #SYS:PUBLIC\CAPTURE Q=BUSACC_R0 T=5 NB NT to run the CAPTURE command before mapping any search drives. This command can be used to clear the screen by entering the command #COMMAND.COM /C CLS after mapping a search drive to DOS.

ATTACH [fileserver\ [username]] The ATTACH command can be used in a LOGIN script to attach to as many as seven additional file servers. If fileserver or username is not specified, the user will be prompted to enter it when he or she logs in.

COMSPEC = [path]\ COMMAND.COM The COMSPEC command is used to cause the workstation to retrieve the COMMAND.COM program from the specified directory after an application that removes it from memory is run. This command should be included if any workstation boots from a diskette or if you have diskless workstations on your network.

DISPLAY [path] filename The DISPLAY command can be used to display the contents of an ASCII text file on the screen. You could use this command to display a message for each day of the week. For example, if you had a MESSAGE directory containing text files named MONDAY, TUESDAY, WEDNESDAY, and so on, you could use the command DISPLAY SYS:MESSAGE\%DAY_OF_WEEK.

[DOS] SET name = "value" The SET command will store the value contained within quotation marks in name variable of the DOS environment space. You can use this to set the DOS prompt by entering the command SET PROMPT="pg". This command can also be used to store the values in LOGIN script variables for later use in DOS batch files and menus.

DRIVE d: The DRIVE command is used to change the workstation's default drive to the specified drive letter. This drive letter must have been previously mapped to a valid directory in which the user has at least Read and File Scan rights. The DRIVE command was used in this chapter to change the default drive to the MENUS directory before exiting the system LOGIN script.

EXIT [*"filename parameters"*] The EXIT command ends ALL LOGIN script processing and either returns to the default DOS drive or passes control to the filename enclosed in quotation marks. The maximum length of the *"filename parameters"* entry is 14 characters.

FDISPLAY [*path*] *filename* This command is the same as the DISPLAY command except that it will filter and format the file so that only the text itself is displayed. FDISPLAY will not display tab codes.

FIRE PHASERS *n* TIMES Replace *n* with the number of times (up to nine) that you want the "phaser" sound to be made on the computer speaker.

GOTO *label* The GOTO command will transfer control to the label statement and then continue LOGIN script execution. For example, the following command would skip to the label CONTINUE if a user is a member of the Sales workgroup.

IF MEMBER OF "SALES" GOTO CONTINUE
MAP M:=DATA:FORMS
FIRE PHASERS 5 TIMES
DISPLAY DATA:MESSAGES\ %DAY_OF_WEEK
CONTINUE:
WRITE "Good %GREETING_TIME, %LOGIN_NAME"

IF *conditional* [AND/OR/NOR *conditional*] THEN *command* ELSE *command* END The IF statement works the same as IF statements in other programming languages and can be nested in as many as 10 levels. Use AND, OR, or NOR to embed two or more conditionals in an IF statement. Conditionals can include LOGIN script variables, command line parameters, or DOS environment variables. Command line parameters are number (1-9), preceded by a percent sign (%), and contain values specified after the LOGIN command is typed. For example, in the command LOGIN 99MARSTE the command variable %1 contains the value 99MARREA. Command line parameters must be enclosed in quotation marks. The following is an example of a nested IF statement containing LOGIN script variables and command line parameters.

IF "%1" = "SUPERVISOR" THEN GOTO STOP
IF MEMBER OF "SALES" THEN
  MAP ROOT H:=DATA:SALES\ %LOGIN_NAME
    IF GREETING_TIME = "Morning" AND DAY_OF_WEEK="Monday" THEN
      WRITE "Remember sales meeting at 1:00 p.m."
      PAUSE
    ELSE
      WRITE "Good %GREETING_TIME, %LOGIN_NAME"
      PAUSE
    END
END

INCLUDE *[path]filename* — The INCLUDE statement passes control to the specified filename. Replace *[path]* with the directory path to the specified file. The file must contain valid LOGIN script commands in ASCII text format. After the last statement in the subscript file is executed, control will return to the statement following the INCLUDE statement. INCLUDE nesting is limited only by memory, allowing one subscript file to INCLUDE another, and so on.

MAP *[drive:=[path]* — The MAP LOGIN script command works basically the same as the MAP command in Chapter 4. MAP NEXT is not supported. You may use *1 to represent the first network drive (normally F:), *2 for the second network drive, and so on.

MAP DISPLAY OFF/ON — This command turns on or off the echoing of MAP commands.

MAP ERRORS ON/OFF — This command turns on or off the display of error messages when MAP commands cannot be completed.

PAUSE or WAIT — These commands are used to stop LOGIN script execution and display the message "Strike a key when ready."

REM[ARK] *[text]* — This command is used to insert explanatory text into the LOGIN script. In addition to REMARK you may also use REM, *, or ; to precede remark statements.

WRITE *"text"* — Each message may contain text and LOGIN script variables enclosed in quotation marks. When enclosed in quotation marks, LOGIN script variables must be capitalized and preceded by a percent sign (%). Each message appears on a separate line unless a semicolon is placed at the end of the command string. Text strings can also contain the following "supercharacters":

    \r for a carriage return
    \n for a new line
    \" for an embedded quotation mark
    \7 to sound a beep on the speaker

1. LOGIN script commands are executed by the _____ program.

2. The system LOGIN script is stored in a file named _____ within the _____ directory.

3. What causes the default LOGIN script commands to be executed?

4. The _____ utility is used to maintain system and user LOGIN script files.

5. List the options of the utility described in Question 4 you would use to change the system LOGIN script.

6. List the options of the utility described in Question 4 you would use to change 99MARREA's user LOGIN script.

7. List the options of the utility described in Question 4 you would use to find the user ID for 99MARREA.

8. IF the userid for 99MARREA is AA000001, write the path and filename of the user LOGIN script for 99MARREA.

9. If the user 99NEDLYN logs in and you notice that he has two search drives mapped to the SYS:PUBLIC directory, what is most likely the problem?

10. Write a LOGIN script command to map H: as a root drive to each user's home subdirectory located in the DATA:USERS directory.

11. Assume home directories for the Sales Department are stored in the DATA:SALES\USERS directory, and home directories for the Accounting Department are stored in the DATA:ACCTING directory. Write an IF statement that will root map drive H: to the correct home directory path for the sales users.

12. Write two essential system LOGIN script commands.

13. The _____ command can be used to access a file server if the system LOGIN script or SUPERVISOR's user LOGIN script has become corrupted.

14. *True or false:* The EXIT command placed in the system LOGIN script will stop the system from executing LOGIN script commands in either the user or default LOGIN scripts.

15. The EXIT *"command string"* command can be used to link the LOGIN script to another program or batch file. When using the *"command string"* option, _____ is the maximum length of the command string.

16. The _____ LOGIN script command will change the default drive.

17. The _____ LOGIN script command can be used to type the contents of a text file on the screen.

18. The _____ LOGIN script command is used to access LOGIN script statements in another file.

19. Write a LOGIN script command to capture the output from LPT1 port to the print queue BUSACC-R0-Q1 with a timeout of five seconds, no banner, and no tabs.

20. Identify and correct all errors in the following LOGIN script commands.

    TURN MAP DISPLAY OFF

    MAP S1=SYS:PUBLIC

    MAP S2:=SYS:PUBLIC\%MACHINENAME\%OS\OS_VERSION

    MAP ROOT H:=SYS:USERS\LOGIN_NAME

    CAPTURE Q=SUP-PSCRIPT-L1-Q1 TI=5 NB NT

    WRITE "Good %greeting_time, %login_name"

SUPERIOR TECHNICAL COLLEGE

PROJECT 12

In this project you will design, enter, and test LOGIN script files for Superior Technical College. Your user environment should provide for the following:

- Essential NetWare mappings for the SYS:PUBLIC and DOS directories
- Search drive mappings to each software subdirectory in the SYS: SOFTWARE directory
- Search drive mappings for Virg Kent and Rita Dunn to run the graphics software package you installed in Chapter 6
- A root home directory mapping for each user based on his or her workgroup
- A root local drive mapping to the user's workgroup
- A drive mapped to the POLICY work area you created for Virg Kent in Chapter 9
- A CAPTURE command to each workgroup's default print queue as shown below:

Student Services	STUD-DOTM
Instructional Services	INST-LASER
Business	BUS-DOTM
Support	SUP-PSCRIPT

- Necessary drive mappings to run the Menu system
- A reminder to all Instructional Services staff on Mondays that there is a meeting at 10:00 a.m.
- "Phasers that fire" when users log in after 9:00 p.m. to remind them that the system will be down at 11:00 p.m. for the nightly backup

Assignment 12-1: **Design the System LOGIN Script**

❶ Update the network drive pointers chart on Student Answer Sheet 12 to show all drive pointers from Superior Technical College Project 4, plus any additional drive pointers necessary to run the menus or applications.

❷ Fill out the workgroup default printers chart on Student Answer Sheet 12 to reflect the default print environment for each user or workgroup.

❸ Fill in the LOGIN script worksheet on Student Answer Sheet 12.

Assignment 12-2: **Document the Existing System LOGIN Script**
To allow you to have your own "system" LOGIN script file for your Superior Technical College users, the real system LOGIN file contained

in the NET$LOG.DAT file contains special commands to check for your group ##EVERYONE and then execute your system LOGIN script commands from the ##LOGIN file stored in your SCRIPTS directory. To obtain a copy of the existing system LOGIN script commands, do the following:

❶ Log in to your assigned server using your ##ADMIN username. Change to the SYS:PUBLIC directory. Use the TYPE NET$LOG.DAT > PRN command to print the contents of the system LOGIN script. Highlight the commands that will execute your system LOGIN script. Attach your printout to Student Answer Sheet 12.

Assignment 12-3: **Enter Your System LOGIN Script**

❶ Before entering your system LOGIN script you need to create the SCRIPTS directory as required by the existing system LOGIN script. Create a SCRIPTS directory in your Superior Technical College directory as shown below:

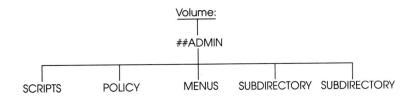

Grant all your users Read and File Scan rights to the SCRIPTS directory. Record the GRANT command you use on Student Answer Sheet 12.

❷ Change to the SCRIPTS directory and type **EDIT ##LOGIN** to use the DOS EDIT program to create your ##LOGIN file. (Replace the ## with your assigned student number.) Use the EDIT program to enter the system LOGIN script commands you recorded on the LOGIN script worksheets in Assignment 12-1. Use the TYPE ##LOGIN > PRN command to obtain a printout of your system LOGIN script commands. Attach your printout to Student Answer Sheet 12.

❸ Test the system LOGIN script by logging in as a user from each workgroup.

Assignment 12-4: **Define the User LOGIN Scripts**

❶ Fill in the user LOGIN script forms provided on Student Answer Sheet 12 for each of your users. At a minimum, your user LOGIN script should use the EXIT "MENU *menu-name*" command to run the correct menu for each user.

Assignment 12-5: Enter User LOGIN Scripts

❶ Use the SYSCON utility to enter each user's personal LOGIN script file. Use the Other Information option to obtain the user ID for each user. Record each user's username and user ID on Student Answer Sheet 12.

Assignment 12-6: Test User Environments

❶ Log in using the username you created for yourself. Select the menu option to direct output to the local printer. Select the Utilities option. Run the Document User option. Attach your resulting printout to Student Answer Sheet 12.

❷ Log in as Virg Kent. Select the menu option to direct output to the local printer. Select the Graphics software option. Use the Change Directory option to change to the directory containing the school catalog. Use the Open option and enter **CATALOG.94** for the filename. Print the screen. Attach your printout to Student Answer Sheet 12.

❸ Exit the menu system. Use the WHOAMI /A > PRN command to document Virg's setup. Then, use the LISTDIR /S /E > PRN command to document Virg's effective rights to your Superior Technical College data directories. Attach your printouits to Student Answer Sheet 12.

❹ Log in as Susan Taylor. Select the menu option to direct output to the local printer. Select the Testing application. Take the test for Chapter 12. Print the screen showing your results. Attach the printout to Student Answer Sheet 12.

❺ Log in as Ode Wiggerts. Select the printer submenu option to direct output to the local printer. Select the Graduate system option. Use the graduate system to add the following student:

Rosemarie Yankovic
1949 Rocky Ridge Drive
Horseman, WI 54868
Major: ADM ASST
Placement status: YES
Graduate Date: 5/15/92

Use the print option to print the report to the printer. Attach the printout to Student Answer Sheet 12

❻ Use the Archive option to archive the report to the REPORTS directory. Exit the menu system. Change to the REPORTS directory. Use the NDIR > PRN command to document all archived reports. Attach the printout to Student Answer Sheet 12.

Turn in Materials

Attach all printouts to Student Answer Sheet 12. If requested, turn in your materials to your instructor on or before the scheduled due date.

Student Name: _____ Date: _____

Assignment 12-1: **Design the System LOGIN Script**

❶ Update the network drive pointers chart below.

Drive	Path	Workgroup/User

❷ Complete the workgroup default printers chart below.

Workgroup	Print Job	Print Queue

❸ Complete the LOGIN scripts worksheet below.

LOGIN Scripts Worksheet for _____
Rem Preliminary commands (optional)
Rem Greeting (optional)
Rem Display login messages (Optional)
Rem Required Search drive mappings
Rem COMSPEC
Rem Common Application search drive mappings
Rem Common Regular drive mappings
Rem DOS Prompt setting
Rem Mapping for _____ IF MEMBER OF "_____" THEN BEGIN   END
Rem Mapping for _____ IF MEMBER OF "_____" THEN BEGIN   END
Rem Mapping for _____ IF MEMBER OF "_____" THEN BEGIN   END
Rem Mapping for _____ IF MEMBER OF "_____" THEN BEGIN   END
Rem End of System LOGIN script commands END:

Assignment 12-2: **Document the Existing LOGIN Script**

❶ Attach your system LOGIN script printout containing highlighted commands.

Assignment 12-3: **Enter Your System LOGIN Script**

❶ Record the GRANT command you used.

❷ Attach your printout from the TYPE ##LOGIN > PRN command.

Assignment 12-4: **Define the User LOGIN Scripts**

❶ Complete the user LOGIN script forms below.

Basic User LOGIN Script for
Basic User LOGIN Script for
Basic User LOGIN Script for
Basic User LOGIN Script for

Assignment 12-5: **Enter User LOGIN Scripts**

❶ Record each user's name and user ID below.

User LOGIN Name	User ID

Assignment 12-6:   **Test User Environments**

❶   Attach the printout for your username.

❷   Attach the printout from running Graphics using Virg Kent's username.

❸   Attach the printouts resulting from the WHOAMI /A > PRN and LISTDIR /S /E > PRN commands.

❹   Attach the printout showing your test results after logging in as Susan Taylor.

❺   Attach your printout from the Graduate system.

❻   Attach your NDIR > PRN printout showing the REPORTS subdirectory.

USING NETWARE 3.12

NetWare 3.12 includes enhancements in the network environment, file server operating system, and client workstation. The enhancements in the network environment increase efficiency and security of data packets transferred over the network. Your instructor can provide you with more information on the network environment changes and enhancements.

Because most NetWare utilities and commands are unchanged by the upgrade to NetWare 3.12, only Chapters 3, 9, and 11 of this text will require modifications.

CHAPTER 3: CREATING THE DIRECTORY STRUCTURE

NetWare 3.12 Concepts

NetWare 3.12 uses ODI drivers to connect client workstations to the network. In addition, the DOS shell program, NETX.EXE or NETX.COM, has been replaced by DOS Requester software. The NETX shell program worked as a front end to DOS, intercepting all requests and directing them to either the file server or the local workstation's DOS. The DOS Requester program with NetWare 3.12 works with DOS, allowing DOS to make requests to the shell for file and print services. The Requester and DOS also share table information, reducing memory use and providing better compatibility. The ODI drivers must be loaded before loading the DOS Requester VLM.EXE. The NetWare Requester consists of a manager, VLM.EXE, and Virtual Loadable Modules. Each VLM supplies a specific function. (Your instructor can provide you with more details on VLMs.) Multiplexer VLMs are used to direct requests between other VLMs, called child VLMs. You can specify which VLMs to load in the NET.CFG file.

Instead of the WSGEN program, NetWare 3.12 includes a client installation program called INSTALL. The DOS INSTALL program allows the installer to select the location to place the NetWare client files, make modifications to the AUTOEXEC.BAT and CONFIG.SYS files, install support for Windows, and select from a wide range of ODI network card drivers that are included with the installation utility. The NET.CFG file contains configuration information for the card drivers and VLM Requester.

The contents of the NET.CFG file for a sample installation are shown in Figure A-1. The FIRST NETWORK DRIVE = F specifies the drive letter to use when logging in to the file server. If the FIRST NETWORK DRIVE parameter is omitted, the Requester will use the drive letter after the last physical drive, which would be D: on a workstation with a single hard disk. Now that DOS and the Requester share the same drive table, the CONFIG.SYS file should contain the statement LASTDRIVE=Z to allow all drive letters A-Z to be available for use by NetWare. The NET.CFG file supplies the drive letter used by the network. This is a major change from the older DOS shell, which used the first drive letter after the DOS drives for the network drive pointer.

Figure A-1: Contents of the C:\NWCLIENT\NET.CFG file

```
C:\NWCLIENT>TYPE NET.CFG

Link Driver SMC8000
        FRAME Ethernet_802.2
        INT 10
        PORT 300
        MEM d0000
NetWare DOS Requester
        FIRST NETWORK DRIVE = F
        USE DEFAULTS = OFF
        VLM = CONN.VLM
        VLM = IPXNCP.VLM
        VLM = TRAN.VLM
        VLM = SECURITY.VLM
    ;   VLM = NDS.VLM
        VLM = BIND.VLM
        VLM = NWP.VLM
        VLM = FIO.VLM
        VLM = GENERAL.VLM
        VLM = REDIR.VLM
        VLM = PRINT.VLM
        VLM = NETX.VLM


C:\NWCLIENT>
```

The STARTNET.BAT file is created by the INSTALL program and contains the commands needed to attach the workstation to the network and load the DOS Requester. The contents of the START-NET.BAT file for the sample installation are shown in Figure A-2.

Figure A-2: Contents of the C:\NWCLIENT\STARTNET.BAT file

```
C:\NWCLIENT>TYPE STARTNET.BAT
CLIENT
SET NWLANGUAGE=ENGLISH
LSL
SMC8000.COM
IPXODI
VLM
CD \

C:\NWCLIENT>
```

NetWare 3.12 Command Differences

■ **NBACKUP:** This utility has been replaced by the SBACKUP NetWare Loadable Module that runs on the server and can be used to backup client workstation files as well as NetWare directories. Refer to the NetWare 3.12 documentation for information on running the SBACKUP utility.

Superior Technical College Project Changes for NetWare 3.12

Assignment 9-8:

Back Up Files with NBACKUP

The NBACKUP program has been replaced in NetWare 3.12 by SBACKUP.NLM. Because the SBACKUP programs runs on the file server, your instructor will demonstrate using the SBACKUP program to back up NetWare and DOS directories. Skip this assignment unless otherwise instructed.

Assignment 9-9:

Restore a Directory Structure

❶ Use FILER to delete your POLICY directory structure.

❷ Use the LISTDIR /S > PRN command to document that the directory structure is no longer there. Write "POLICY structure deleted" on the printout and attach it to Student Answer Sheet 9.

❸ Recreate the POLICY directory structure using DOS MD commands or FILER.

❹ Use the SALVAGE utility to restore the deleted POLICY files into their appropriate directories.

❺ Change to the POLICY directory and use the NDIR /SUB > PRN command to document that the directory structure and files have been restored. Write "POLICY directory salvaged" on the printout and attach it to Student Answer Sheet 9.

CHAPTER 11:
NETWARE MENUS

Netware 3.12 Concepts

The NetWare 3.12 menu system is a streamlined version of the Saber menu system. The concepts of menu planning, menu directory location, and trustee rights necessary to run the menu system discussed in Chapter 11 apply to the 3.12 menu system. The major change in the new menu system is in the command syntax and processing. An advantage of the new menu system is that it makes it possible to prevent a user from exiting to the DOS prompt by simply pressing the Esc key. Exiting to the DOS prompt must now be done by creating a menu option that may be assigned a password.

The new menu system consists of NMENU.BAT, MENUCNVT.EXE, and MENUMAKE.EXE. All these file are in the SYS:PUBLIC directory and are accessible to all users. NMENU.BAT is the command file used to run menus once they have been created.

The MENUCNVT.EXE program may be used to convert existing .MNU menu files to the 3.12 source menu format. For example, to convert the BUSINESS.MNU file to a 3.12 menu, type the command MENUCNVT BUSINESS.MNU. This command reformats the menu command to include the new key words such as MENU, ITEM, or SHOW.

The MENUMAKE.EXE program is used to compile .SRC source menu files into executable menu files that have an extension of .DAT. In addition to allowing the menu program to run faster and be more memory efficient, having executable menu files in binary format allows you to keep your source files in a separate directory where they cannot be changed or viewed by users. After compiling a source menu file, the executable menu file can be copied into the MENUS directory for user access. A BUSINESS executable menu file may be run using the command NMENU BUSINESS.

Commands within the menu script file can be divided into two classifications: organizational commands and control commands. **Organizational commands** consist of the keywords MENU and ITEM. The MENU keyword gives each menu a number and title using the MENU syntax

menu_number,menu_title

The ITEM keyword defines menu options. The syntax of the ITEM command is

ITEM *Option_description {option}*

To save memory, the option {BATCH} can be placed after the menu item to remove the program from memory during the execution of the option. The option {PAUSE} can be used to cause the menu option to pause and display the message "Press any key to continue." To force a specific letter to be assigned to an option, precede the option with a carat [^] followed by the desired letter.

Control commands consist of EXEC, SHOW, LOAD, and GETO. The EXEC filename key word is used to execute a program or internal DOS command. The SHOW*menunumber* command may be used to link to another menu number. The LOAD *menuname* command will pass control to another compiled menu file. The GETO, GETR, and GETP commands allow the user to input an entry, as shown in the DOS Functions submenu of the BUSINESS menu. With the GETO (GET Optional) command, the user can leave the entry blank. With the GETR (GET Required) command, the user is required to make a valid entry. The GETP (GET Parameter) may be used to assign the input to a variable. The syntax and options for the GETx commands are given in Figure A-3 on the following page.

Figure A-3: Syntax and options for use with the GET commands

```
GETO Instruction {Prepend}Length,Prefill,SECURE{Append}
GETR Instruction {Prepend}Length,Prefill,SECURE{Append}
GETP Instruction {Prepend}Length,Prefill,SECURE{Append}
```

Instruction	Replaced by the message you want displayed.
Prepend	Data placed inside { } will be attached before the entry made by the user. Brackets must be used even if no data is to be prepended.
Length	The maximum number of characters for the user input.
Prefill	Data placed here provides a default response.
SECURE	Used to hide the operator's keystrokes so they do not appear on the screen when typed.
Append	Specifies data that will always be appended to the end of the entry. If no data, braces are still required.

Superior Technical College Project Changes for NetWare 3.12

Use the MENUMAKE command to convert your source menu files to executable. Use the NMENU filename command in place of the MENU filename commands used in the assignments.

INDEX

Thinnet, 10
TLIST, 15, 17, 171, 190–191
Trustee rights, 15, 173
  assigning, 132–134, 156–161, 189–190
  removing, 192
TSR, *see* Terminate and Stay Resident

U

Uninterruptible power source (UPS), 14
UPS, *see* Uninterruptible power source
USERDEF utility, 122, 135–139, 142
USERLIST, 16, 18
Users
  access rights, 112
  account balances, 139–140
  account managers, 96, 140–142
  adding to group, 131–132
  creating, 129–131, 138–139
  needs, 33–35

V

VOLINFO, 55, 61
Volumes, 31, 37–38
  DATA, 37–38
  obtaining information, 55–56
  SYS, 37–38

W

WHOAMI, 172, 174, 192
Workgroup, 31
Workgroup manager, 96, 129, 134–135
Workgroup-oriented structure, 38
WSGEN, 50–51, 60

X

XMSNETX, 53